An Introduction to Feminist Philosophy

An Introduction to Feminist Philosophy

ALISON STONE

polity

First published in 2007 by Polity Press

Polity Press
65 Bridge Street
Cambridge CB2 1UR, UK

Polity Press
350 Main Street
Malden, MA 02148, USA

ISBN-13: 978-07456-3882-9
ISBN-13: 978-07456-3883-6 (pb)

A catalogue record for this book is available from the British Library.

Typeset in 11 on 13 pt Scala
by Servis Filmsetting Ltd, Manchester
Printed and bound in Great Britain by
MPG Books Ltd, Bodmin, Cornwall

For further information on Polity, visit our website: www.polity.co.uk

Contents

Acknowledgements

My sincere thanks to all those who have helped me to write this book. My colleagues in the Department of Philosophy (formerly the Institute for Philosophy and Public Policy) at Lancaster University have discussed several chapters of the book at work-in-progress sessions. Dave Archard, Rachel Cooper, Sarah Cooper, Mari Mikkola, Catherine Mills and John O'Neill made very helpful comments on drafts of chapters. Veronika Koller and Garrath Williams made useful suggestions. I am especially grateful to Stella Sandford, whose careful and detailed comments on the whole first draft enabled me to make many improvements. John Varty read each chapter and helped me to clarify many points. I have also benefited greatly from the suggestions made by the anonymous reviewers of the book proposal and by the manuscript reviewers, Alessandra Tanesini and Mary K. Bloodsworth-Lugo; my thanks to them all.

Parts of chapter 1 were presented at the 2006 conference of the UK Society for Women in Philosophy at Birkbeck College, University of London; at the 'Politics of Living' conference at Birkbeck College Law School in 2006; and at the Human Sciences seminar at Manchester Metropolitan University in 2006. I thank the audiences on those occasions for their helpful responses. Chapter 5 draws on my article 'Essentialism and Anti-Essentialism in Feminist Philosophy' in *Journal of Moral Philosophy* 1: 2 (2004), pp. 135–53.

I particularly want to acknowledge John Varty, for his love and support, and Elinor Varty Stone, whose imminent arrival spurred me on to complete this manuscript.

How to Use This Book

Since this book is intended for use by students as well as specialists, here are some suggestions about how to use this book most effectively.

Definitions of technical terms   This book introduces, defines and discusses a number of technical terms – e.g. 'essentialism', 'performativity', 'symbolic order' – used by feminist philosophers. On each occasion when a technical term is first defined, the term is highlighted in bold type: this indicates a definition. If you come across the same technical term later and cannot remember what it means, then looking that term up in the index will show in bold type the page where the initial definition occurred, which you can turn back to. Sometimes an initial definition is refined or revised later in the book. In these cases the revised definitions are also highlighted in bold and, again, these revised definitions have bold index entries for ease of reference.

Further reading   Each chapter ends with a list of recommended further readings. Sometimes these are texts that have been discussed in the chapter, sometimes they are classic feminist works in the field under discussion, and sometimes they are additional secondary texts which introduce or clarify the concepts and debates which the chapter has discussed.

Arguments   Generally, I try not only to expound various feminist theories but also to analyse and assess the arguments for and against them. I do not intend my assessments to be taken as definitive. Rather, I hope by providing these assessments to encourage students to think for themselves about the merits of the various feminist arguments which I introduce.

Introduction: What Is Feminist Philosophy?

1. Defining feminist philosophy

Feminist philosophy arose in the early 1970s and has developed most strongly in Western Europe, North America and Australasia. In these regions, feminist philosophy has become a major subdiscipline within philosophy. There are three main aspects of feminist philosophy.

(1) It investigates how biases against women are embodied in past and present philosophy. Specifically, feminist philosophers study and criticize biases against women within:

i   writings from the history of philosophy, especially writings by canonical authors – Plato, Descartes and others;
ii   areas of contemporary philosophy such as epistemology (the theory of knowledge) and ethics;
iii   patterns of imagery and symbolism that can be found in writings from both past and current philosophy (e.g. the image of woman as irrational).

Having criticized the male biases they have found in past and present philosophy, feminist philosophers have developed new theories – for instance, new moral theories or new theories of knowledge – which are intended to improve on the older, biased, theories. Thus, feminist philosophy both criticizes male biases and develops new theories and concepts to correct these biases.[1]

For example, some feminist moral philosophers – following Carol Gilligan (1982) – have argued that philosophical theories of ethics have traditionally focused on justice and on finding impartial rules for guiding action. Gilligan suggested that only men's reasoning about moral problems is typically based on this sort of concern to be just and impartial. In contrast, when women engage in moral reasoning, they try to see how, in some specific situation, the needs of particular individuals can be met and their relationships maintained. To respect women's experience and ways of thinking, Gilligan thinks, philosophical ethics must recognize and say more about this 'care perspective' as well as about the male 'justice perspective'. Still, not all feminist philosophers accept Gilligan's view. Feminist philosophers disagree with one another on where the biases are to be found within past and present philosophy, and on the content of the new theories that are needed as correctives. A range of diverse, often conflicting, opinions exists in feminist philosophy, as in any other field of philosophy.

(2) The second main aspect of feminist philosophy is that it draws on philosophical concepts and theories to articulate different feminist claims and political positions, and it uses philosophical arguments to establish which of those claims and positions are strongest. For example, some feminist activists have claimed that pornography harms women – that 'pornography is the theory, rape is the practice'. Some feminist philosophers (such as Langton 1993) have tried to articulate these anti-pornography claims philosophically and to assess how coherent they are.

(3) Thirdly, feminist philosophy has introduced into philosophy a range of new concepts that no other fields of philosophy address. Some of the most prominent of these new concepts are the following:

i   sex and ii gender. Central to much feminist thought is the distinction between biological sex – male or female – and social gender – social expectations about what counts as appropriate behaviour for men and women. Many feminists argue that it is social expectations, not biology, which are biased against and disadvantage women and that these expectations – unlike biology – can be changed.

iii   sexuality. Feminists distinguish between a person's sex, gender, and sexuality, and they argue that the fact that someone is male (or female) does not mean that that person must act in a masculine (or feminine) way or that they must be sexually attracted towards women (or men).

iv   sexual difference. Some feminist philosophers have introduced this concept to capture (what they see as) the fact that, for human beings, being male or female always acquires symbolic meanings,

meanings which are conveyed via language and which deeply shape how we experience our own bodies.

v   **essentialism**. In feminist contexts, the problem of essentialism is the problem of whether there is anything that all women (or all men) have in common and, if women are too diverse to have anything in common, what makes them all members of the kind or group 'women'.

vi   **birth**. Compared to death, philosophers have neglected birth. Feminists ask how women experience pregnancy and birth and what the fact that we are all born reveals about the nature of the self and of human life.[2]

Each of these concepts raises particular questions. How should sex and gender be understood? Should gender exist at all? That is, is there any good reason to have systematically different expectations about what men should be like and what women should be like? What are sexual feelings? Could male biases have crept into how we usually think about what sexual feelings are? What makes all women women? These and other related questions are unique to feminist philosophy.

To be sure, feminist philosophical concepts and questions often overlap with questions that arise elsewhere in philosophy. For example, philosophers of sex also ask what sexual acts are; and metaphysicians also ask what makes different things members of the same kind – e.g. what makes different blue patches all instances of the colour blue. But feminist philosophers work with distinctive understandings of the concepts that organize their debates. Within feminist philosophy, the 'essentialism' debates concern whether *women*, in particular, have anything in common that makes them all women. And feminist philosophers take sexuality to be linked to *power* relations and to forms of social organization that benefit men. So the key feminist philosophical concepts are either unexplored by non-feminist philosophers (e.g. sex, gender) or are understood by feminist philosophers in distinctive ways (sexuality, essentialism). As a result, feminist philosophical debates have developed in unique directions and have produced unique arguments not found elsewhere in philosophy.

This book will focus on some of the main concepts and questions – concerning sex, gender, sexuality, sexual difference, essentialism and birth – that are unique to feminist philosophy and that mark it out as a distinctive area within philosophy. In contrast, most other books on feminist philosophy either focus on

i   feminist criticisms and reconstructions of male-biased philosophy (Jaggar and Young 1998) – including feminist criticisms and reconstructions of specific areas of philosophy such as epistemology, ethics, aesthetics, etc. (Fricker and Hornsby 2000, Garry and Pearsall 1996); or on
ii giving a philosophical articulation of different currents in feminist politics (Jaggar 1983a).

I aim instead to position feminist philosophy as a distinctive field of philosophy, alongside ethics, philosophy of mind, etc., defined by its own problems and questions. As I see it, it is in asking these new questions (What is gender? What makes women women?) that feminist philosophy has been most original and creative and has most expanded the scope of philosophy as a whole.

2. Philosophy, feminism and reason

Unlike most other fields within philosophy, feminist philosophy remains controversial amongst philosophers. Some philosophers are suspicious of it or reject it altogether. Herta Nagl-Docekal (2004: xiv) suggests that some philosophers reject feminist philosophy because they reject feminism – that is, they oppose or see no need for a political movement for women's equality. Yet philosophers might be – and sometimes are – sceptical about feminist philosophy without having to reject feminism as a political project. What they are sceptical about is whether feminist philosophy is *philosophy*.

Of course, it is very hard to give a satisfactory definition of what philosophy is. Still, many philosophers would agree that philosophical thinking is open-ended and involves following the logic of arguments wherever they lead. If one assumes, in advance of argument, that one particular conclusion is right and that one's arguments must lead to this specific conclusion, then one is just not proceeding philosophically (on this view). Consider how in many Platonic dialogues, Socrates starts by showing his interlocutors that there are problems with their long-held convictions. Socrates believes that once these convictions have been shaken up, his interlocutors will then be able to start to think philosophically, i.e. open-mindedly.

This does not mean that philosophical thinking requires one to have no initial convictions at all. When thinking one cannot avoid beginning with certain convictions, but one must be aware that these convictions can be questioned and need to be defended with argument. One must also be aware that one's attempts to defend these convictions may fail, so that one may have to abandon or revise one's convictions. Thinking in an open-ended way does not mean starting from nowhere, but it does mean being able to arrive wherever thought and argument lead.

Yet feminist philosophy, as Alison Jaggar and Iris Marion Young say, 'presupposes a substantive ethical or political commitment to opposing women's social subordination' (Jaggar and Young 1998: 2). What worries some people here is that feminist philosophy *presupposes* this commitment to feminism instead of arguing that women's subordination exists and should be opposed. The activity of making arguments for particular political positions such as liberalism or feminism is generally recognized to be a legitimate part of philosophy – namely, political philosophy. In line with this, philosophers often think that feminist philosophy is legitimate if it is a branch of political philosophy that defends feminism. However, as we saw in section 1, feminist philosophy not only articulates feminist politics but also explores its own original concepts such as sex and gender, as well as criticizing male biases in epistemology, ethics, etc. At this point some people worry that feminist philosophy has begun to assume, rather than question and argue for, the truth of feminist politics. Of course, nobody can question all their beliefs at once, and plausibly feminist philosophers cannot question male bias in the tradition and question their own feminism at exactly the same time. But the worry that some people have is that feminist philosophers have ceased ever to question or argue for feminism at all.

Readers who are already familiar with feminist philosophy may be shaking their heads in dismay. Is it not already clear from the abundance of good work in this area (these readers might say) that feminist philosophy is perfectly good philosophy? Those who doubt this fact (the same readers might add) usually know little about feminist philosophy, and since their doubts about feminist philosophy stem merely from ignorance of the area, I am wasting time by taking these doubts seriously. I believe, though, that these doubts about feminist philosophy raise important issues about the nature of philosophical thought, the nature of (feminist) politics, and the relation between the two. So I think it worth devoting some time to these doubts and to the issues that they raise.

Against these doubts, many feminist philosophers have argued that philosophical thinking can never really *be* open-ended. Rational arguments, they point out, must always be constructed according to accepted standards for what counts as a valid argument. And different standards for what counts as valid reasoning or argument have existed at different times. Here some feminist philosophers have been influenced by the early work of the French philosopher Michel Foucault. Foucault (1966) suggests that in different historical periods there are different 'rules of formation' or *epistemes* which specify what kind of claims count as knowledge in those periods, and what kinds of thinking count as rational or logically valid. Some feminist philosophers such as Genevieve Lloyd (1984) have added that these changing conceptions of reason, or standards of what counts as reason, all incorporate associations between reason and being male. According to Lloyd, philosophers from Plato to Sartre all – in varied ways – understand reasoning to require standing above, or 'transcending', one's emotions and one's body. These same philosophers also associate reason with maleness, believing that maleness is something that one must achieve by overcoming one's 'female' – emotional, embodied – dimension. Arguably, then, ideas of reason have a history of being linked to ideals of maleness that degrade women.

If ideas of reason have a history, then what of the worry that feminist philosophy is not genuinely philosophical because it cannot allow open-ended reasoning? The fact that ideas of reason have a history suggests that reason and argument never really *are* open-ended, because any particular style of reasoning or argument presupposes a specific set of assumptions about what reason and argument consist in and – at the same time – about what it is to be a man or a woman. Consider the 'adversary paradigm' that reigns in much contemporary philosophy (on which, see Moulton 1983). Under this paradigm, it is assumed that the philosopher's job is to find faults in and counterexamples to other the philosopher's arguments, and to argue for claims by trying to defend them against the strongest objections that can be imagined. This 'adversary paradigm' assumes that reasoning must be adversarial, and it associates adversarial reasoning with being male, assuming that males are aggressive.

It seems, then, that reason and argument have long been understood in ways that link them to maleness. Very few feminist philosophers conclude that reason and argument should be rejected outright. Many feminist philosophers try instead to argue for claims in ways that assume different conceptions of reason, according to which reason includes qualities that have traditionally been thought to be 'female'. For instance, one might try to build constructively on sound parts of the work of other scholars, rather than setting out to expose the flaws in their arguments. In this case one is reasoning in a way that includes 'female' qualities of sympathy and openness to others.

Those who believe that philosophical thought must be open-ended might reply that these feminist criticisms and rethinkings of standards of rationality are worthwhile because, actually, they are *models* of open-ended philosophical thought. They break out of entrenched (male-biased) horizons and question standards that are often taken for granted. So, it might be argued, feminist philosophical arguments against open-endedness actually still presuppose that philosophical thought should be open-ended. But then the problem remains of how this open-endedness is compatible with feminist politics. At this point, we need to ask exactly what feminists, including feminist philosophers, are committed to politically.

3. Feminism and post-feminism

It is often assumed that feminism is the belief that women are equal to men and should be – but currently are not – treated accordingly. But this definition of feminism is far from adequate. Some feminists argue that what women really need is not equality with men, but to be recognized and valued in their difference(s) from men. Other feminists believe that women need neither equal treatment nor respect for their difference, but liberation from oppression. Still others deny that feminism aims to improve the lot of women at all. They think that what it *is* to be a woman is to have been made into an oppressed being, into someone who is inferior and secondary to men. The aim of feminism, then, must be to abolish womanhood. On this view, feminism seeks to improve the lot of those people who have been made into women, but it cannot rightly be said that feminism seeks to improve the condition of women – that would be an impossible, self-contradictory mission.

This brief survey hardly touches the huge variety of feminist views, but we can already see that there is considerable disagreement among feminists over what the goal of feminism is. As Rosalind Delmar says, 'it makes more sense to speak of a plurality of feminisms than a single one' (1986: 9). Yet one might think that there must be some underlying commitment which all feminist positions share, and which makes them all *feminist*. Valerie Bryson suggests that all feminists share 'the belief that women are disadvantaged in comparison with men, and that this disadvantage is not a natural and inevitable result of biological difference but something that can and should be challenged and changed' (Bryson 1993: 192). But some feminists would reject even this, perhaps on the grounds that women's biology *does* disadvantage them but that recent technologies such as the contraceptive pill allow women to overcome their biological limitations (Firestone 1970).

Alison Jaggar offers a more inclusive definition of feminism. For her, 'feminism' 'refer[s] to all those who seek, no matter on what grounds, to end women's subordination' (Jaggar 1983a: 5). What is '**subordination**'? According to the *Concise Oxford Dictionary*, a person or group is subordinated if they are made to be of inferior importance or rank, or are made secondary, or are placed in a subservient relation, to another person or group. So to say that women are 'subordinated' is to say that women are seen as secondary to, less important than, or subservient to men. This does not have to imply that men do the subordinating. But the claim that women are subordinated does imply that women are *made*, not born, subordinate and that this situation can and should be changed.

Different feminists interpret women's subordinated condition in different ways. Some understand this condition as one where women are not treated equally. Others think that women are subordinated in that their distinctive traits are not valued. For others, women are subordinated just by being made into women in the first place. But all feminists agree that women are, in some sense, subordinated and that this should be changed.

The idea that women are subordinated may be vague and admit of many different interpretations, but it is not so vague that absolutely everyone accepts it. Many people – perhaps some readers of this book – are not convinced that women, or at least women in western industrial societies, can rightly be described as subordinated. Most people accept that western women were subordinated in the past – when they could not vote or own property, and when it was not a crime for a husband to rape or batter his wife. (Although we should recall that marital rape was recognized as a crime only very recently – in 1991 in the UK, and in 1993 in the US.) Still, many people not unreasonably believe that women's position has now improved significantly. Those who believe this are sometimes called **post-feminists**: they accept that women should not be subordinated, but they think this goal has basically been achieved, so that no special feminist campaign against subordination is needed any more.

Firstly, here, it is helpful to remember some ways in which women's situation still leaves much to be desired. In the UK in 2005, full-time women workers still only earned 82 per cent of what full-time male workers earned, and only 20 per cent of MPs and 14 per cent of professors were women. In these (and other) respects, women have still not achieved equality with men. It could be replied, though, that the *basic* battles for women's equality have been won. After all, equal rights and anti-discrimination laws have been passed in the UK and many other countries. One might think that over time the effects of this legislation will inevitably trickle through society and change people's attitudes and expectations. We just have to let this process work itself out.

Yet even if women did gain equality with men in pay, politics and professional standing, this would leave untouched many other things that are wrong with women's position in western (as well as non-western) societies. Consider that women are vulnerable to rape, sexual assault and domestic violence which, in the vast majority of cases, are inflicted by men.[3] Consider too that much of contemporary culture depicts women as sex objects. Most of us find ourselves endlessly surrounded by images of alluring, more or less naked, women – from paintings of female nudes in galleries to pop videos to tabloid newspapers. And consider, too, that in most households women still do the bulk of housework and childcare (between 66 and 80 per cent of it on recent estimates; Saul 2003: 8).

One might think that I am painting an overly pessimistic picture and casting women as helpless victims. Certainly, on almost all fronts women's position has improved over the past forty years, and women themselves have fought for many of these improvements (for instance, campaigning for marital rape to be recognized as a crime). Moreover, not all the aspects of women's situation considered above are *wholly* negative. For instance, having the main responsibility for childcare is not merely a burden. It usually results in deeply reward-ing and valuable relationships with one's children.

Being a woman, then, has positive as well as negative aspects. So, after all, is nothing ultimately wrong with women's social position because its positive features balance out its negative ones? Generally, feminists view the negative features as more fundamental and as con-nected together to constitute the basic context in which women (and men) live. On this view, the positive aspects of being a woman arise from (1) women's (and sometimes men's) resistance to this negative context and from (2) women's efforts to lead worthwhile lives despite the constraints imposed by this context.

These claims might still sound implausibly pessimistic. But femin-ists have arguments for *why* the negative features of women's situa-tion should be considered basic. They argue that these features are basic because almost all societies are organized or structured in ways that continually produce and reproduce these negative features. The negative features are therefore *systematic*: societies' basic institu-tions, legal arrangements, and cultures continually produce them. And therefore these societies can be said to *subordinate* women: they subject women to harms and disadvantages (e.g. sexual objectifica-tion) to which these societies do not subject men, at least not to the same extent. As such, women are effectively treated as less important than, or as secondary to, men.

In saying this, though, we must bear in mind that the same soci-eties do inflict many harms on men. For example, historically, in most European societies men have been more at risk than women of being injured or killed during wars or in industrial accidents. But generally men have suffered these harms because they have been encouraged into social roles (e.g. as army combatants) that privilege them over women or, at least, over specific groups of women (e.g. manual workers versus their wives at home). So the fact that societies cause men, *as* men, to suffer many harms is consistent with those same societies systematically subordinating women to men.[4]

Taking it, then, that (almost all) societies systematically subordinate women, how exactly do societies do this? Different feminist positions answer this question differently. Each gives a different account of the basic character of society, the kind of systematic wrongs it inflicts on women and the kind of social changes that are required to end these wrongs. So we now need to get an initial understanding of some of the main feminist political views. This will also reveal how feminist political views begin to introduce the concepts such as sex, gender and sexuality which are unique to feminist philosophy.

4. Feminist political positions

Liberal feminism arose in Europe in the seventeenth and eighteenth centuries when feminist thinkers such as Mary Astell and Mary Wollstonecraft, accepting the Enlightenment belief in innate human reason, argued that women are equally as capable of reason as men. They argued that women therefore deserve an equal education and, for Wollstonecraft (1792), equal rights to own property, be economically independent and have careers. Wollstonecraft admitted that many women in her day were irrational, frivolous and helpless. But she argued that this was due to their upbringing and circumstances, not their nature. Here Wollstonecraft's argument anticipates the sex/gender distinction, since she is saying that women's helplessness is not caused by their female biology but is something into which they have been socialized – that is, it is a matter of gender not sex.

Campaigns for women's equal rights gathered pace throughout the nineteenth century in most industrializing countries and culminated in the struggle for the vote. Women gained equal voting rights in, for example, New Zealand in 1894, in the US in 1920, in the UK in 1928 and in France in 1944. After the suffrage campaigns liberal feminist struggles abated somewhat, but they were rekindled in the 1960s. This rebirth of liberal feminism was driven by the recognition that, alongside formally equal rights, there persisted (1) inequalities in pay and (2) informal barriers and prejudices which were blocking women's access to the public sphere and forcing women to pass unfulfilled lives confined to the home. Partly in response to liberal feminism, equal pay and anti-discrimination laws were passed in countries such as the US and UK in the 1960s and 1970s. Yet real inequalities persist, partly because of the widespread assumption that women must take the main responsibility for childcare. This responsibility restricts many women to part-time work, which tends to be poorly paid. Many liberal feminists have inferred that far-reaching changes – such as a restructuring of work patterns and large-scale provision of funded childcare – are necessary conditions of genuine equality.

The basic liberal feminist idea, then, is that women are naturally equal to men in reason, and therefore deserve equal access to education and to the public sphere – but that entrenched barriers, formal or informal, block this access. Here liberal feminists seem to assume that a fulfilling life requires both the exercise of one's reason and participation in the public sphere. But other kinds of feminist (e.g. Pateman 1988) have objected that reason and the public sphere have a history of being interpreted and organized in ways that exclude and devalue whatever is seen as female. (We saw this earlier in the case of conceptions of reason.) Thus, liberal feminism seems to take for granted the superior value of just those features of human and social life that have been identified as male.

Radical feminism arose in the late 1960s and 1970s, most prominently in North America. Its central claim is that the domination of women is the most fundamental and widespread of all forms of domination. Unlike liberal feminists, radical feminists stress that women, as a group, are dominated by *men* as a group. Individual men may live up more or less well to the role of dominator that they are expected, as men, to perform.

A classic radical feminist statement is the Redstockings Manifesto:

> Women are an oppressed class. Our oppression is total, affecting every facet of our lives. . . . We identify the agents of our oppression as men. Male supremacy is the oldest, most basic form of domination. . . . All other forms of exploitation and oppression . . . are extensions of male supremacy. . . . Men have controlled all political, economic and cultural institutions. . . . *All men* receive economic, sexual, and psychological benefits from male supremacy. *All men* have oppressed women. (Redstockings in Morgan 1970: 533–4)

Many radical feminists call male domination **patriarchy** – to mean rule by males (not rule by fathers as the term might suggest). Because radical feminists think that men dominate women as a group, they argue that women have a shared interest in opposing patriarchy and that women need an independent, women-led and perhaps women-only, feminist movement.

According to radical feminism, patriarchy pervades all aspects of life. In particular, patriarchy pervades sexuality – women's sexuality has been controlled and channelled in directions that serve men. So for radical feminists, sexuality is not merely natural and innate but is something that is shaped by power relations and is currently defined in male-centred ways. Radical feminists hold, too, that men have seized control of culture, religion, belief systems and even language. Consider how the word 'man' refers to both males and humanity as a whole, and how in monotheistic religious cultures gods and religious leaders are almost all male.

Why have men dominated? Some radical feminists believe that male biology compels men to dominate. But, more often, radical feminists see male dominance as the effect of a patriarchal social system – a set of linked institutions, beliefs and expectations – which educates men to behave in dominating ways while it trains women to be subservient. This system persists because it schools all of us to act in ways that keep it going. Again, then, these radical feminists distinguish between sex and gender and they see patriarchy as a result not of biology but of social expectations about how men and women should act.

Radical feminists have disagreements about femininity. Some think that femininity should be rejected because it has tended to be defined in ways that serve men. (For instance, many people think that it is 'feminine' to be polite, helpful and somewhat deferential towards others.) But other radical feminists (e.g. Griffin 1984) think that female biology gives women nurturing, cooperative qualities which are a valuable contrast to the patriarchal focus on power over others. On this latter view, these feminine qualities should become the basis of a new female culture. Some radical feminists (e.g. Daly 1978) therefore advocate **separatism**: creating women-only spaces and institutions in which female/feminine culture can germinate.

Radical feminists have been criticized for their view that all men as men are in a position of dominance. Arguably, race and class inequalities give some women more power than some men – for instance, women managers have power over their male employees. The problem with radical feminism here is that it is *essentialist*. That is, radical feminists claim that all women have something in common – they all suffer domination by men as a group. But this claim seems to be implausibly simplified, as some women actually have power over some men.

Socialist feminism arose in the late 1960s and 1970s. It tries to combine insights from radical feminism and from **Marxism**. According to Marx, the most basic human activity is the activity of producing things to satisfy our needs. The social relationships within which people carry out this activity make up the 'economic structure' or 'economic base' of a society, from which other institutions – such as law and the state – arise. Throughout most of history, these 'social relations of production' have been class relations in which some people control and exploit the productive activity of others. In capitalist societies, those who own the 'means of production' – machinery, buildings, materials and assets – exploit the work of those who are forced to sell their labour to make a living. Based on this Marxist framework, some 1960s and 1970s feminists argued that capitalism requires male supremacy in the home, because capitalism requires women to perform the 'reproductive' labour of generating, maintaining and tending the workforce. Women are thus exploited by having to perform unpaid 'domestic labour' in the home.

Socialist feminists (such as Barrett 1988) criticized this argument, arguing that the reason why *women* in particular are expected to do this 'domestic labour' is not simply because of capitalism. Rather it is because of (1) pre-capitalist ideas about women's proper role and (2) men's struggles to keep women in the home, especially working-class men's struggle in the early nineteenth century for a 'family wage'. Men's aim in this – largely successful – struggle was to be recognized as breadwinners and paid accordingly. Men wanted this outcome, according to socialist feminists, not only for financial reasons but also because it benefited them to have power over their financially dependent wives.

Some socialist feminists (e.g. Hartmann 1979) concluded from historical analyses of this kind that patriarchy and capitalism are two distinct social systems that have become intertwined. Others (e.g. Young 1981) argued that capitalism is a unified system which has patriarchal aspects built into it. According to Young, capitalism has developed so that it segregates men and women into different jobs and activities – doctors versus nurses and midwives, plumbers versus secretaries – where men's activities are almost always rated as more highly skilled and are better paid. Young calls this system 'gender-divided capitalism' (1981: 61, 63).

A problem with socialist feminism is that, following Marx, it focuses on productive activities. Hence socialist feminists treat child-bearing and child-rearing as specific forms of productive activity. But since production has traditionally been seen as a quintessentially 'male' activity, socialist feminists seem to be approaching birth and childcare through a male-biased framework. Perhaps feminists need instead to rediscover how women themselves experience birth and to develop new categories that reflect women's experience – something that existing, male-biased, frameworks of thought arguably cannot do.

Socialist feminists try to conceive male domination and class exploitation as equally basic dimensions of society. But they have tended to give less centrality to racial inequality. For this, socialist feminists – along with radical and liberal feminists – have been criticized by **black feminists**. Black feminism has developed most fully from the 1970s onwards, although it dates back at least to nineteenth-century anti-slavery campaigns. Describing black feminism is complicated by the fact that the meaning of 'black' is 'radically unstable', as Katiadu Kanneh puts it (1998: 86). 'Black' has different meanings in different social contexts, and these meanings have changed over time and are argued over. In the US, 'black' usually refers to African Americans while Latinos, Native Americans and Asian Americans are defined as 'people of colour'. However, sometimes 'people of colour' is used to include African Americans too. In the UK, 'black' has sometimes served as a common label for people from various ethnic groups all of whom have been taken to deviate from the white norm (Mirza 1997: 3). Claiming the common title 'black' allowed people from these groups to stress their shared experience of being treated as deviant and to form political alliances to oppose it.

Setting these definitional questions aside, much 1970s and 1980s writing by black women and women of colour criticized radical, liberal and socialist feminism. Radical feminists, especially, were criticized for their essentialist claim that all women are in the same social position (the position of being dominated by men). This claim overlooks differences of power between women, especially the greater power and confidence of white women.

More generally, black feminists argue that modern societies are not simply patriarchal or patriarchal-capitalist, but rest on *several* 'major systems of oppression', including racial oppression (Combahee River Collective 1979: 362). These systems reinforce and shape one another to form a 'matrix of domination' (Hill Collins 1990: 225). While black women are oppressed under several systems simultaneously, white women are oppressed in terms of gender but benefit from the racial system. Black feminists stress that feminists must recognize the equal importance of all these systems, and must understand how they interrelate.

When black feminists speak of a system of racial domination, they see this system as social. The vast majority of scientists and scholars now agree that there is no biological basis for racial classifications. Traditionally, the belief in race was the belief that there are a few distinct human types (black, white, Asian, Native American) each with a unique set of inherited physical traits – a certain skin colour, hair texture, facial structure, etc. In fact, there is a whole continuum of human skin colours, hair textures, etc., and decisions about where one 'type' begins and another ends are arbitrary. (For further problems with the belief in race, see Taylor 2004: 49–52.)

Racial categories may have no biological basis, but they have been and remain very important in shaping society. Individuals are treated very differently depending on what racial category they are assigned to (on the basis of visible features such as skin colour). Because people are treated differently – and unequally – depending on their supposed race, racial classifications shape people's lives and experiences and so people do identify with, and understand themselves by means of, racial categories. Because racial categories shape our experience, the experience of being a woman is always related to and affected by the lived experience of being of a particular 'race'. This is just as true for white as it is for black women – but white women (and men) are less likely to notice how their 'race' impacts on their experience. This is partly because their classification as white tends to benefit rather than disadvantage these women, and partly because they are likely to live in cultures that treat being white as the norm. Black feminists have stressed, though, that feminists must pay attention to the 'racialized' aspects of *all* women's lived experience.

We have now reviewed some of the main positions in feminist politics. These positions have begun to open up some of the problems that are unique to feminist philosophy – problems about the nature of sex, gender, sexuality, birth and essentialism. However, we should note that many individual feminist thinkers combine elements of several different positions – few thinkers endorse any single feminist position in its pure form. Moreover, our review of feminist political views has been far from exhaustive. For one thing, the views we have looked at have been developed very largely within western countries, so there is debate about how far their claims apply to non-western societies. (On this debate, see chapter 7.)

Each position gives an account of what the basic social institutions and arrangements are like such that women's condition is one of subordination. According to liberal feminists, most societies build in either legal inequalities or informal prejudices and barriers which tend to confine women to the home or to poorly paid work, and which generally prevent women from enjoying lives as fulfilling as those of men. For radical feminists, almost all societies are patriarchal. Their cultures, belief systems, institutions and norms push men to pursue dominance and push women towards submission. For socialist feminists, the economic structure of modern societies is capitalist. But capitalism has interacted with earlier patriarchal ideas to become 'gender-biased': its institutions push women and men into different kinds of work and reward men's work more highly. For black feminists, the basic arrangements of modern societies realize a web of systems of oppression within which all women are 'penalized by their gender but [some] are privileged by their race' (Hill Collins 1990: 225).

All this confirms that feminists share a commitment to the general view that women are subordinated and that this can and should be changed. But feminists never hold this view in its general form. Each feminist holds a specific *interpretation* of what women's subordination consists in, and so of what kind of change is needed. For liberal feminists, women are subordinated in that they are treated unequally; equal treatment is needed. For some feminists influenced by Marx, women are subordinated in that their domestic work is exploited; a fair distribution of productive activity is required. For radical feminists, women are subordinated in that men dominate them; women need to achieve autonomy. That is, women need to be able to create and live by their own values and goals. For socialist feminists, women are subordinated in that they are streamed into undervalued kinds of work and activity. The solution is what Nancy Fraser calls a 'deep restructuring [both] of the relations of production' and of cultural assumptions about women's inferiority (Fraser 1997: 27). Black feminists agree, but argue that a deep restructuring of racial assumptions is needed too.

Feminist claims about women's subordination, then, are always interpretive: they figure in overall theories of the nature of society.

As such, feminists can rarely avoid – and, if they are philosophers, certainly cannot avoid – being aware of these different and conflicting interpretations. As a feminist philosopher, one cannot inflexibly hold a particular form of feminism. One must honestly consider the merits of the form of feminism to which one inclines, and must listen as open-mindedly as possible to the arguments others make on behalf of other feminisms.

So holding the feminist conviction that women are subordinated is compatible with engaging in open-ended – philosophical – argument about what this subordination consists in and about what kind of social change is possible and desirable. Sceptics might still say that feminist philosophers cannot open-endedly debate whether women are subordinated *at all*. It is true that one cannot deny that women are subordinated if one is to be a feminist philosopher. But this does not prevent feminist philosophers from arguing open-endedly about the merits of different interpretations of what women's subordination is.

Moreover, feminist philosophers not only argue about the merits of pre-existing forms of feminism. In articulating these forms of feminism and in drawing out the concepts that they invoke such as gender and sexuality, feminist philosophers define these concepts in varying ways. Other feminist philosophers then identify problems with these definitions and propose alternative definitions. For example, suppose we unpack the radical feminist claim that men dominate women sexually by saying that men use heterosexual intercourse to dominate women. If men do indeed do this, then, in the resulting social climate, the prevailing view of sexual activity will probably be that it consists in acts of male-dominated heterosexual intercourse. And if so, then perhaps feminists need to give an alternative definition of sexuality – for instance, by defining loving, intimate feelings and relationships as 'sexual'. This new definition may be too broad. But as feminist philosophers argue about how best to define sexuality, their different conclusions will lead them to different views of how exactly sexuality is connected to power relations. In this way, articulations of and arguments about concepts such as sexuality or gender give rise to *philosophical* forms of feminism which differ from any pre-existing feminist political views. These philosophical forms of feminism, structured by particular interpretations of the concepts unique to feminist philosophy, are the focus of this book.

5. Male bias and its criticism

Feminist thinking about sex, gender and other new concepts has emerged not only out of articulations of feminist political views but also out of feminist criticisms of male bias in philosophy. These criticisms did not result from the mechanical application to philosophy of any pre-existing forms of feminist political analysis. Rather, some women philosophers who became involved in feminist politics became sensitized to occurrences of male bias, which they then began to notice in philosophy.

Political philosophy was the first area of philosophy in which feminist philosophers noticed male bias. This bias was manifest in that contemporary political philosophers focused on the state, the law and distributive justice (i.e. how economic resources should be distributed). These political philosophers were almost wholly silent about the family and sexual relationships, which they did not see as part of the subject matter of political philosophy at all. It seemed that contemporary political philosophers were uncritically accepting the division that exists in modern societies between the 'public' sphere – politics, economic life, and work – and the 'private' sphere – the family. And these philosophers seemed to take for granted that the public sphere is more important or more truly human. In contrast, political philosophers from the past, such as Locke, Rousseau and Hegel, had dealt with the family. But, as feminists soon found, their views on the family usually involved the claim that wives should be confined to the domestic realm and should be governed by their husbands. John Locke, for example, claimed that there is a 'foundation in nature' for wives being 'subject' to their husbands (Locke 1698: 174).

These initial feminist engagements with political philosophy raised issues that pointed beyond political philosophy as such.

1   Had the focus of philosophers on the public sphere skewed the whole way in which core values of moral and political philosophy had been conceived?
2   Might the sexist views on women and the family which traditional philosophers held bear on their philosophies more broadly? Could these sexist views reflect more general male biases which are also manifested, in less explicit ways, in other areas of philosophers' thought?

3   What, anyway, is the relationship between bias and knowledge? Does bias necessarily obstruct knowledge, or can it sometimes be enabling?

Questions 1, 2 and 3 respectively set the agendas for feminist ethics, feminist history of philosophy, and feminist epistemology, all of which flourished in the 1980s.

(1) *Feminist ethics* emerged out of a recognition that women tend to have different experiences from men because, historically, women's lives have centred on the 'private' realm of the family. Feminists usually deny that biology is what makes (most) women family-focused and makes (most) men work-focused. Rather, women and men have these different orientations because social expectations have channelled them into the private and public spheres respectively. But, feminist ethicists argued, women's family-focused experiences have been neglected in (pre-feminist) moral theory, and new moral theories are needed which 'take adequate account of the experience of women' (Held 1993: 89).

Probably the single most important text for feminist ethics is Carol Gilligan's *In a Different Voice* (1982), mentioned earlier. Gilligan argues that moral philosophy has focused on justice, rights, impartiality and moral rules, but that this focus really reflects only men's experience. Because women have a special responsibility to care for their family members (Gilligan 1982: 7), women have different values and a different 'moral voice' from men. Women approach moral problems (e.g. whether to steal an unaffordable drug if one's spouse is ill) from the perspective of an **ethic of care**. Women ask how the unique needs of the particular individuals who are involved in a problem-situation can be met. Women also ask how the networks of relationships in which each of these individuals is involved can best be maintained. The care perspective is thus (i) focused on particular situations and is (ii) concerned with meeting the needs and (iii) maintaining the relationships of (iv) the particular individuals involved. Moreover, the care perspective (v) takes emotions to be very important in moral thinking. The judgement that a certain person is in need can never be dispassionate. It is always embodied in a certain kind of emotional response towards that person – a feeling of care.

Gilligan aims to correct the bias of traditional ethics towards male experience by producing a theory that reflects female experience. But other feminist philosophers have found a number of problems in her theory, including these:

i   The 'ethic of care' reinforces the traditional view that women should care for their children, husbands and relatives even at the expense of their own needs. Diemut Bubeck (1995) argues that women who are the main carers in families suffer injustice because these women give others more care than they receive themselves. Their caring responsibilities in turn disadvantage these women in respect of work by obliging them to work part-time for less pay. Yet if these women adopt the ethic of care (as their caring role inclines them to), then this ethic directs them to attend *only* to considerations of care – how to meet others' needs and protect others from harm. The care perspective thus leads these women to neglect considerations of justice, including the injustice they are suffering. This suggests that the ethic of care should not replace but must be combined with an ethic of justice which calls for a fairer distribution of caring work.

ii   Not all women's lives are focused on the private realm – many women have always had to work outside the home for a living. Although Gilligan aims to correct the male bias of traditional ethics, her own theory seems biased too – biased towards the experience of white middle-class women, whose economic circumstances have not obliged them to work outside the home. This is the problem of essentialism again – the problem of whether women really do have a shared focus on family-focused caring as Gilligan suggests they do.

iii   Rosemarie Tong (2003) asks whether approaches like Gilligan's are feminist. Certainly such approaches are femin*ine* – they express women's experience. But if these approaches reinforce rather than challenge women's subservient role in the family, then how can they be called femin*ist*? My answer is this. We have defined 'feminist' as one who thinks that women are subordinated and that this can and should be changed. Gilligan fits in with this: she believes that women's distinctive perspective and virtues are persistently misrecognized and undervalued, and that women are constantly judged by male standards and found wanting. This is her interpretation of *how* women are subordinated. Gilligan wants women's voice to be heard and respected, and her work aims to help bring about this change.

Turning to (2) *feminist history of philosophy*, this has

i   criticized how women philosophers have been left out of the canon – so much so that people sometimes think there have never been any women philosophers. Some women philosophers have been almost entirely forgotten, like the metaphysicians Margaret Cavendish (1624–74) and Anne Conway (1631–79). Others have been wrongly classified not as philosophers but as 'mere' writers, like Simone de Beauvoir, or 'merely' political thinkers, like Hannah Arendt.

ii   As well as rediscovering the ideas of these neglected women, feminist historians of philosophy have also rediscovered the sexist statements made by many canonical philosophers. Kant remarked that 'the scholarly woman . . . uses her *books* in the same way as her *watch* . . . so that people will see that she has one, though it is usually not running' (Kant 1798: 171). Still, it might be thought that such statements are marginal to philosophers' main theories and can be ignored. But feminist historians of philosophy have denied that these sexist statements are merely marginal. They believe that these statements manifest deeper-lying *masculinist* biases which run through the philosophical theories in question. In order to identify these masculinist biases that they sensed to be present, feminist philosophers have come up with some innovative methods of interpreting historical texts.

(a)   A first method argues that conceptual frameworks are masculinist if they reflect, express or articulate patterns of thought and evaluation which men typically hold. But what thought-patterns *are* typical of men? The influential psychoanalytic feminist Nancy Chodorow (1978) answers that, almost everywhere, women do childcare at home while men go out to work, which causes mothers to treat their male and female children differently. According to Chodorow, mothers encourage boys to become properly masculine by breaking away from their mothers and from the early infantile world of dependency and of strong bodily sensations and emotions. Boys' and men's personalities and ways of thinking become structured around oppositions between mind and body, reason and emotion, self and relationships with others.

Based on these claims by Chodorow, Jane Flax (1984) argues that many major philosophical theories are structured in the same way as masculine personalities. These theories, too, are organized around hierarchical oppositions between mind and body, reason and emotion, self and relationship. Flax concludes that the philosophical tradition has arisen as an expression of men's experience, which is why this tradition involves a series of hierarchical oppositions. Others have made similar points without relying on Chodorow. Nancy Hartsock argues that men tend not to be responsible for the concrete work of caring for other people's subsistence needs. As a result men come to see 'masculinity [as] an abstract ideal to be achieved over the opposition of daily life' (Hartsock 1983: 241). Again, the claim is that men's experience becomes structured around oppositions, and that these oppositions find expression in philosophy.

(b) A second method of identifying masculinist bias argues that philosophical concepts and theories are masculinist if they are understood in terms of symbolism (or metaphor) which favours the male over the female. We saw earlier how Genevieve Lloyd – who adopts this second approach – argues that throughout western philosophy reason has been symbolized as male. Reason has been thought to require the overcoming of the passions and embodiment, which are symbolized as female. Lloyd denies that these patterns of symbolism could be removed from our ideas of reason (Lloyd 1993: 82). The metaphors go deep: they shape how philosophers describe and understand reason in the first place. We could not have the concepts of reason we do without the attached imagery.

iii Recently, feminist historians of philosophy have moved beyond simply criticizing the tradition. They have started to look for elements in traditional texts which avoid or challenge masculinism (and on which feminists can build). For instance, earlier feminist philosophers (e.g. Bordo 1987) often saw Descartes as masculinist because he opposes mind and body, arguing that they are separate substances. But recently there has been more recognition that Descartes also studied how the mind and body interact and that he believed that many mental states, including perception and emotion, involve an indissoluble mixture of mind and body.

The works of individual philosophers, and the history of philosophy as a whole, are more complex and contain more ambiguities than earlier pictures of an unbroken history of sexism had suggested (Lloyd 2000).

Feminist criticisms of male bias or masculinism suggested that less biased theories are needed. Yet it also seemed that one must hold feminist views before one could begin to detect these long unnoticed biases. It seemed, then, that some biases – feminist biases – advance rather than retard knowledge. (3) Some *feminist epistemologists* tackled this 'paradox of bias' by developing the concept of 'standpoints'. Hartsock (1983), for example, argues that because men and women occupy different social locations they tend to develop different ways of seeing the world. Women tend to do concrete, physical work meeting subsistence needs and so they tend to see material, life-preserving work as the most basic social activity. Men tend not to be responsible for this work and so they tend to develop the – distorted – view that 'transcending' the body is what is really human. Usually, though, women are unable to articulate their standpoint fully because, as men have more power, their standpoint prevails and women internalize it. Women only really achieve their own standpoint if they struggle against the male-dominated character of society. The femin*ine* standpoint can only be realized in the form of a femin*ist* standpoint. So political interests – interests in removing male domination – enable women (and men, if they join feminist campaigns and learn from women) to increase their knowledge by attaining an undistorted standpoint. In general, the standpoint feminist idea is that those whom a society oppresses have more potential to see the real – oppressive – nature of that society than those whom it favours.

A problem with these **feminist standpoint epistemologies** is that they suggest that those people who are most oppressed, or who bear the greatest burden of subsistence work, must – potentially at least – have the least distorted standpoint. But, it could be argued, the vast majority of us act oppressively in some ways while being oppressed in others. Once again here, we encounter the question of 'essentialism': of whether all women really do share a common position of oppression and a common standpoint.

Postmodern feminist epistemologists, such as Donna Haraway, hold that there are indeed many overlapping forms of oppression and so, too, there are many 'partial perspectives'. Each is insightful with respect to some dimensions of reality but distorted with respect to others. Haraway's metaphor for this is that each of us has eyes crafted from the blood of others (Haraway 1991: 192). The ability to see some features of the world always depends on being privileged over certain others in ways of which one is unaware.

Other feminist epistemologists have returned to the initial puzzle about how some biases can be enabling and others unhelpful. **Feminist empiricists** argue – with particular reference to science – that biases are bad if they lead would-be knowers to neglect relevant evidence, to draw invalid inferences from the evidence they have, or to explain or describe their findings in question-begging ways while ignoring alternative explanations and descriptions. Many scientific studies of reproductive biology commit several of these errors: they describe sperm as active and ova as passively waiting to receive them, despite evidence that ova actively select and clasp particular sperm (Biology and Gender Study Group 1988: 177). (This raises a question about whether our standard views of male and female biology are themselves male-biased. Perhaps feminist philosophers need to rethink the nature of biological sex and cannot simply rely on standard scientific views.)

Biases, then, can – but do not always – lead to errors; when they do, biases are a problem. In other cases biases may be revealing. Thus, engaging in inquiry, including scientific inquiry, *as* a feminist is not as such a problem. Helen Longino (1990) proposes that science should be organized democratically so that no one set of biases becomes dominant and unquestioned. For Longino, researchers with different biases must all have voices within science so that they can critically examine one another's biases and root out the ones that cause errors.[5]

This brief survey has not covered the whole range of approaches that feminist philosophers have developed in political philosophy, ethics, history of philosophy or epistemology. Nor has it covered the approaches feminist philosophers have developed in other major areas of the discipline: philosophy of mind, language, religion, aesthetics, etc. (For good reviews of feminist work in these areas, see the 'Feminism' entries in the *Stanford Encyclopaedia of Philosophy*.)

One thing we have seen is that feminist criticisms and reconstructions of male-biased philosophy regularly circle back to the concepts that are distinctive of feminist philosophy. For example, the ethic of care and standpoint epistemology both have problems with essentialism, while the work of feminist epistemologists raises questions about how reliable our scientific knowledge about biological sex is.

It also emerges from our brief review that much feminist philosophical work is interdisciplinary. This work is often informed by social-scientific studies of women's (and men's) position in society, as well as by literary and cultural studies of the definitions that exist in various cultures of what it means to be a woman (or a man). Many of the questions that feminist philosophers explore have been prompted by research carried out within other disciplines. For example, Gilligan's work is in part empirical psychology involving interviews with individual men and women. The interdisciplinarity of feminist philosophy does not damage its status as philosophy. On the contrary, often it is *because* feminist philosophers cross disciplinary boundaries that they can challenge existing horizons of thought and so can think in a truly philosophical way. Moreover, much of the social-scientific and humanities research from which feminist philosophers learn is itself philosophical to varying degrees: often it challenges familiar horizons of thought and is informed by and engages with philosophy. So when I have argued that feminist philosophy is philosophical, I have not meant to imply that it cannot or should not be interdisciplinary. Rather, it may be that genuinely philosophical thought *requires* interdisciplinarity.[6]

6. Review and conclusion

Near the start of this introduction we saw that some people think that feminist philosophy cannot be philosophical because it presumes a political commitment to feminism. Yet it proved hard to identify a single political commitment which all feminists, as feminists, share: there are many different versions of feminism. Even the very general conviction that women are subordinated is one that feminists only ever hold under particular interpretations. So although feminist philosophers do (as feminists) have political commitments, there is no single commitment that all feminist philosophers must share, and thus the particular commitments that they have are always open to (philosophical) debate. Moreover, philosophical considerations often lead feminist philosophers to rethink these political commitments and to introduce new forms of feminism.

These philosophical considerations are of two kinds. Firstly, philosophical thinking and rethinking of new concepts such as sex, gender and sexual difference can lead feminist philosophers to produce new forms of feminism. For instance, the French philosopher Luce Irigaray looks at the history of philosophy and concludes, like Lloyd, that it contains entrenched patterns of imagery and symbolism concerning maleness and femaleness. Irigaray also argues that this imagery shapes how we experience our bodies, in a deep way that the sex/gender distinction fails to capture. Irigaray infers that liberal feminist attempts to open social institutions up to women are superficial. These attempts leave in place the patterns of imagery that affect us so deeply. So she proposes that feminists should aim, instead, to change our patterns of cultural symbolism. In this way Irigaray produces a new version of feminism – known as 'sexual difference feminism' – based on her philosophical thought about sex, gender and sexual difference.

Secondly, feminist criticisms of male bias often imply that feminist political views need to be rethought. For instance, recall that radical feminists think that male domination prevents women from living autonomously, that is, from living by values that women have chosen or created for themselves. But now suppose that traditional notions of autonomy have proved to be masculinist because they imagine the self to be separate from others. Suppose also that a non-masculinist view of autonomy must see it as consistent with dependence on others. In that case the radical feminist picture of autonomy needs to be rethought.[7] This will lead to a revised understanding of the nature of women's subordination – of what it means for women's autonomy to be blocked – and of how this subordination should be ended.

So feminist philosophers do not unquestioningly assume the truth of (some versions of) feminism when they examine the philosophical tradition. Rather, feminist philosophers constantly re-examine their feminist politics and their approaches to the tradition in relation to one another. As such, the fact that feminist philosophers have political commitments is consistent with them engaging in genuinely philosophical thought. Feminist philosophers also constantly re-examine their politics in relation to their thinking about new concepts such as sex and gender. These concepts have arisen out of the various forms of feminist politics, but this does not prevent feminist philosophers from articulating, redefining and arguing over these concepts in an open-ended way. The relation between politics and philosophy has not prevented feminist philosophers from doing philosophy, but has enabled them to carve out a distinctive area *of* philosophy defined by a unique range of problems.

Each of the next six chapters of this book focuses on one of the concepts that, I have suggested, are original to feminist philosophy: sex, gender, sexuality, sexual difference, essentialism and birth. Chapter 7 returns to the question of what feminism is. This introduction has provisionally argued that all feminists believe that women are subordinated and that this can and should be changed. But we will need to ask whether this answer still stands up after we have examined some of the new, philosophical forms of feminism that feminist philosophers have developed. This confirms yet again that feminist philosophy is philosophical: rather than taking feminism for granted, it inquires into what feminism itself is.

Notes

1 Feminist philosophers understand what a 'male bias' is in varying ways. I will take a **bias** to be a background belief or assumption which some person or group of people holds, often without realizing it, and which organizes and pervades how that person or group thinks about a whole range of topics. A **male bias** is a background belief of this kind according to which men, or whatever is associated with men or maleness, have more worth or importance than women, or than whatever is associated with women or femaleness.

2 Arguably other concepts too are unique to feminist philosophy, for instance care. My list is indicative, not exhaustive.

3 As Jackman (1999) notes, it is hard to measure levels of domestic violence, rape and sexual assault accurately. But consider this revealing example: a 1992 survey found that 22 per cent of US women had suffered forced sex at least once (virtually always inflicted by men), whereas only 4 per cent of men had ever suffered it (and half their assailants were men). See Jackman (1999).

4 There is now a good deal of sociological work on masculinity. Following this work, chapters 2, 3 and 5 will argue that

   1 societies tend to expect different forms of masculinity from different groups of men (e.g. from working- and middle-class men)

   2 some forms of masculinity are privileged, giving those men power over other men (e.g. middle- over working-class men)

3   each form of masculinity gives the relevant group of men power over a particular group of women (e.g. working-class men over working-class women).

5   The distinction between standpoint, postmodern and empiricist feminist epistemologies comes from Harding (1986).

6   Here I disagree with Judith Butler when she argues (2004: ch. 11) that worrying about whether feminist philosophy is 'really philosophy' merely reinforces an artificial boundary between professional philosophy and the theoretical work that is done in other areas of the humanities.

7   One radical feminist who rethinks autonomy as autonomy-in-community is Hoagland (1988: 12, 237–41).

Further Reading

The 'maleness' of reason   Lloyd 1984 (pp. 38–50, on Descartes, has been especially influential). Grimshaw 1986: ch. 2 is a useful critical account.

Feminism, its diversity and its definition   Haslanger and Tuana 2006.

Feminist political theories   Bryson 1992; Jaggar 1983a.

Feminist ethics   Tong 2003 succinctly introduces this huge area.

Feminist history of philosophy   Lloyd 2000; Nye 2003 looks in detail at feminism and modern philosophy from Descartes to Kant.

Feminist epistemology   Harding 1986: ch. 6 is now quite old but remains hugely influential; Tanesini 1999 is a good book-length introduction to the area.

1 Sex

1. The sex/gender distinction and feminist thought

The distinction between sex and gender has been fundamental to the development of feminist thought, including feminist philosophy, since the late 1960s. According to the distinction, sex is biological and most people are biologically male or female. **Gender** is social and consists of:

1   social expectations and assumptions about what behaviours and traits are appropriate for male and female individuals. For example, it is commonly expected that males will relish confrontation while females will try to avoid it.
2   the psychological traits, and the understandings of themselves, that individuals tend to develop under the influence of these social expectations. For instance, males often do come to relish confrontation more than females.

If one satisfies social expectations about what is appropriate for female (or male) individuals, then one is feminine (or masculine). So we can also say that gender consists of social ideas and expectations about what femininity and masculinity consist in, or about what traits someone must display in order to count as feminine and masculine. These ideas about femininity and masculinity are organized by a higher-level expectation that feminine and masculine behaviours and traits are appropriate, respectively, for members of the female and male sex. There is a higher-level expectation that females should be feminine, males masculine.

This distinction between sex and gender first emerged in the 1960s in writing by psychologists such as Robert Stoller (1968). Prior to this, 'gender' referred solely to grammatical gender, that is, the classification of words as masculine or feminine, as in the French *le* and *la*, or Spanish *el* and *la*. The sex/gender distinction was seized on by key feminist thinkers of the late 1960s and early 1970s such as Kate Millett (1971) and Ann Oakley (1972). They valued the distinction because it implied that gender expectations and ideas are products of culture and society, and so can be changed. This challenged the view, widely held at that time, that women's and men's biology causes them to have the social positions and statuses that they do. But (on this view) female and male biology cannot be changed, therefore women's and men's social positions cannot be changed either. (For example, according to this view, women rarely have senior, highly responsible, jobs because their biology – e.g. their proneness to pre-menstrual tension – makes them unable to do these jobs well. But women will always have this biology, so it would be futile to try to change the situation.) This view is sometimes called **biological determinism**, because it states that biology determines what shape social arrangements take.

In contrast, feminist theorists used the sex/gender distinction to argue that women and men occupy the social positions they do because of social expectations about what is appropriate for them. These expectations, feminists added, do not themselves result from biology. In making this argument, feminists drew on anthropological evidence of huge variation in gender expectations across different cultures. The feminist sociologist Ann Oakley stressed that every society has rules about what behaviour is appropriate for each sex, but that what these rules specify varies from one society to another (Oakley 1972: 128). For example, she reports that in some traditional African communities, women work at heavy agricultural labour and femininity is associated with strength. Meanwhile men do minor cleaning tasks and craft activities. These gender rules are clearly different from those of modern western societies. This variation could not exist if biology determined what gender rules a society adopts, for then, since biology does not vary, all societies would have the same gender rules.

Against Oakley, one might argue that all societies *do* agree that men are superior to women and that men should occupy a privileged position. That is, one might argue that all societies are patriarchal. John Dupré (1993: 78) points out, though, that even if this is true – and most known societies have been patriarchal – it does not refute the claim that gender rules vary across cultures. The concrete forms that

patriarchal ideas take and the concrete ways in which societies imple-
ment patriarchal expectations vary. Again, these variations would be
impossible if the ideas and activities in question were determined by
biology.

In Stoller's psychological research feminists found another piece of
evidence to support the claim that sex does not determine gender.
Stoller had written about male transsexuals – people who identified
themselves as feminine, and consistently acted in typically feminine
ways, despite being biologically male. Conflicts between gender and
sex of this kind would hardly be possible if one's gender were determined by one's sex. Kate Millett concluded that the sex/gender distinction enabled feminists to recognize 'the overwhelmingly *cultural*
character of gender' (Millett 1971: 29). For example, she argued, the
distinction enables us to recognize that boys tend to be more aggressive than girls not because they have a biological tendency to aggression but because society encourages boys to express their aggressive
impulses. Meanwhile society encourages girls to stifle their aggression or to direct it inward and to harm themselves rather than others.
Although social expectations such as these are harmful to women,
these expectations are effects of society and not biology, and as such
can be changed.[1] Hence it is not inevitable that women should always
be disadvantaged in society.

Since the sex/gender distinction was introduced and developed by
feminist thinkers, use of the term 'gender' has become widespread. But
at the same time 'gender' has come to be used differently to how 1970s
feminists used it. Take the following statement from the Wikipedia
(2006a) website: 'The word gender describes the state of being male,
female, or neither.' Here 'gender' – as is now very common – is simply
used to mean biological sex. The main reason why 'gender' has come
to be (mis)used in this way is that it enables people to avoid mention-
ing 'sex', which suggests sexual activity.

But the use of 'gender' to mean sex need not be merely an effect of
modesty or confusion. Many feminist philosophers have argued that
the sex/gender distinction has conceptual and political problems and
is inadequate for understanding many features of the social relations
between women and men. Some feminist philosophers have concluded that the distinction needs to be redefined and made more complicated. Others have concluded that the distinction must be rejected
altogether and replaced by different concepts (such as the concepts of

'sexual difference' or the 'lived body', at which we will look later in this book). The result of all these arguments is that current feminist thinkers work with varying understandings of sex and gender, which makes it unsurprising that popular uses of 'gender' and 'sex' are similarly varied.

The whole of current feminist thought about gender and the body is informed by these criticisms and reassessments of the sex/gender distinction. Some of these criticisms and reassessments have been directed more towards the 'sex' pole of the distinction, and others more towards the 'gender' pole. Chapter 2 turns to those criticisms that address the 'gender' pole. The rest of this chapter looks at some important feminist discussions of biological sex.

2. Biological sex

We need a working definition of what **sex** – the condition of being bio-logically male or female – consists in. Any standard account of sex such as that of Archer and Lloyd (2002: 40–3) tells us roughly the fol-lowing. In most mammals, including human beings, a foetus, from the moment of conception, has among its chromosomes a pair of chromosomes which either look like XX or like XY. If the foetus has XY chromosomes, then its gonads (sex glands) will eventually develop into testes, which produce sperm cells. Otherwise, its gonads will develop into ovaries, which produce egg cells. Testes and ovaries also secrete hormones, which fall into three main groups: androgens (including testosterone), oestrogen and progesterone. Testes produce more androgens than oestrogen and progesterone; ovaries produce more oestrogen and progesterone than androgens. (Androgens are often called 'male' hormones, oestrogen and progesterone 'female'. This simplification can be misleading, since both testes and ovaries produce all three hormones – just in different proportions.) The higher quantity of androgens secreted by an XY foetus causes it to develop 'male' genitalia, that is, internal structures such as a prostate gland and urethra, and external structures such as a penis, scrotum and testicles. These androgens also prevent the foetus from develop-ing female genitalia. In contrast, an XX foetus develops 'female' genital anatomy, both internally (uterus, vagina) and externally (labia, clitoris). At puberty, hormonal secretions again cause the develop-ment of 'secondary' sex characteristics: deepened voice and body hair in males; breasts, fat redistribution and menstruation in females.[2] To sum up:

- A human being is biologically male if they have XY chromosomes, testes, 'male' internal and external genitalia, a relatively high proportion of androgens, and 'male' secondary sex characteristics.
- A human being is biologically female if they have XX chromosomes, ovaries, 'female' internal and external genitalia, relatively high proportions of oestrogen and progesterone, and 'female' secondary sex characteristics.

One might accuse these definitions of being circular, since they say that part of what defines being male (or female) is having 'male' (or 'female') genitalia and secondary characteristics. However, 'male' (and 'female') here are only being used as shorthand for, and could be replaced by, a list of the relevant genital parts – e.g. penis, prostate, etc. – and characteristics – e.g. deep voice, narrow hips, etc. This would remove the circularity.

Earlier, we saw how feminist thinkers in the late 1960s seized on the sex/gender distinction because it implied that gender is not determined by sex. We can now be more precise about what it means to say that sex does not determine gender. Namely, when people form particular ideas about gender, or behave in typically masculine or feminine ways, or understand themselves as masculine or feminine, none of these activities is caused by features of those individuals' biology such as their hormone levels. Yet it seems unlikely that these biological features do not influence our social activities at all. Since our levels of hormones affect our moods, must they not over time influence what psychological traits we have? Sociobiologists claim that the difference between whether one produces sperm or egg cells may indeed have consequences for men's and women's behaviour. According to sociobiologists, we all seek to maximize the chance of our genes surviving. Because males each produce around a million sperm cells, their best bet is to fertilize as many eggs as possible, i.e. to be promiscuous. Females produce far fewer eggs, so their best bet is to nurture those that become fertilized, i.e. to focus on tending offspring.

Feminists (see, among others, Bleier 1984; Kaplan and Rogers 1990) have criticized these sociobiological arguments. One feminist counterargument is that hormones, differences in cell size, etc., may indeed influence our behaviour, but that these influences take different forms, or manifest themselves differently, in different cultural contexts. This argument concedes that our behaviour (and so, too, what we expect of one another) is influenced by our biological features. Yet if we also assume that these biological features are unchangeable, then it seems that biology must always press social arrangements to go in one particular direction, even if different sets of social arrangements negotiate this pressure differently. Moreover, since most known societies have been patriarchal, it begins to look as if biology exerts a pressure towards patriarchy. But then it might, after all, be impossible to change society to make women and men fully equal.

Feminist philosophers have been reluctant to accept that conclusion, and have therefore tried to find problems with the reasoning that has made it seem plausible. Alison Jaggar, in her article 'Human Biology in Feminist Theory' (1983b), accepts that it is implausible to say that biology has no influence on social arrangements. Rather, Jaggar claims, society 'responds to' biology and biology is 'relevant to' the form of social organization.

However, Jaggar rejects the assumption that biological sex cannot be changed. She defends what she calls a 'dialectical' theory of human biology, according to which social arrangements affect and alter human biology over time. She gives the following examples. Many societies give women less chance to exercise, and this causes them to become weaker than men over time. Women's diets are often inferior, which causes them to become smaller than men. In some societies, though, there is very little dimorphism between men and women: women have very small breasts, men have very little body hair. To Jaggar this suggests that the relatively exaggerated dimorphism found in western industrial societies is an effect of social forces. It is the effect of men having chosen, over generations, to have sex and reproduce with women who conform to exaggerated ideals of femininity (Jaggar 1983b: 85). Thus, Jaggar concludes that although our biology influences how we live and how we organize our societies, some of our biological features – including our hormone levels and secondary sex characteristics – can themselves be changed.

Jaggar says that she rejects the sex/gender distinction on the grounds that 'there is no line between nature [sex] and culture [gender]' (1983b: 85). Here she overstates her distance from the sex/gender distinction. Her position is that some of our biological features as males and females can be, and are, altered by gendered behaviour and expectations, which, in turn, are influenced by biological sex. Thus, although (on Jaggar's model) sex and gender interact, they remain analytically distinct. So we should conclude from Jaggar not that the sex/gender distinction should be rejected but that it should be revised to say that sex and gender influence and alter one another. But there are other problems with the sex/gender distinction. A second problem concerns the status of the science that professes to tell us about the nature of biological sex.

3. Sex, science and gender

Feminist philosophers have pointed out that if one uses the sex/gender distinction then one risks uncritically accepting current scientific views about what biological sex consists in. Yet feminist philosophers have argued that scientific views about sex tend to reflect, and reinforce, prevailing social assumptions about gender. We can see this by looking at some of the historical changes that have taken place in scientific views about sex.

Thomas Laqueur (1990) and Londa Schiebinger (1989) have shown that there was a transformation in scientific views of sex difference in the late eighteenth century. Until then, the same basic view of sex difference had persisted ever since the ancient Greeks. On this view, which Laqueur calls the 'one-sex' model, female genitals are essentially the same as male ones, but are on the inside of the body. The vagina was seen as an internal penis, the uterus as an internal scrotum. Supposedly, women had these internal male organs because women's bodies had less heat with which to expel the organs outwards. In the late eighteenth century, a 'two-sex' model displaced this 'one-sex' model. Scientists began to think that the female body was radically different from the male body, and that every aspect of female anatomy manifested this difference. Female anatomical structures were given their own names, and the first anatomical drawings of the female skeleton were made.

What does this tell us? (1) It shows that we need to be cautious about assuming that we know – or that science tells us about – biological sex as it really is. How scientists think about and study biological sex is informed by conceptual models such as the 'one-sex' and 'two-sex' models. Arguably, the two-sex model is still influential today, leading scientists to look for evidence of difference between the sexes (e.g. to search for differences between 'male' and 'female' brains) and discouraging research into similarities. The popularity of the two-sex model also means that findings concerning differences tend to be more widely reported in the media than findings concerning similarities.

(2) The research of historians such as Laqueur and Schiebinger shows that the one-sex and two-sex models reflect expectations about gender. Before the late eighteenth century with its dramatic upheavals such as the French revolution, it was widely believed that society had a stable hierarchical order in which, among other things, women are subordinate to men. This social hierarchy was thought to reflect a hierarchical metaphysical order, descending from God through angels to men, women, non-human animals and lastly inanimate objects. Women's biological features, it was assumed, expressed their status as inferior versions of men. Interestingly, then, it was assumed that biological sex reflects and expresses gender, the social position of women and men (Schiebinger 1989: 161).

During the French revolution, Schiebinger argues, public spaces emerged in which people could engage in political debate and criticism. In this context the old assumptions about social hierarchy could no longer be taken for granted, so men needed to find new justifications for maintaining their privileged position. They therefore sought to show that the female body's radical difference equipped women poorly for public life. For example, the (male) scientists who drew female skeletons often chose as their models skeletons with large pelvises. As a result, their drawings suggested that women were specially suited for giving birth and staying in the home to rear children (Schiebinger 1989: 203). Rather than thinking that sex expresses gender, these scientists now took it that gender derives from sex. They assumed that women's and men's biological features dictated which social positions they could occupy. Yet these scientists intended their claims about biology to affect people's beliefs about what behaviours were realistically possible for men and women. In particular, scientists intended to strengthen the belief that women should be excluded from the public sphere. Since scientists carried out their research with this intention, their claims about biological sex reflected prior assumptions about women's and men's appropriate social positions, even though they claimed merely to describe sex as it really is.

So particular scientific views about sex tend to be influenced by, and to support, particular expectations about gender. But now these views about sex threaten to become part *of* gender. Views of sex, it seems, are part of the network of ideas which specifies appropriate behaviour and traits for males and females. However, we can still distinguish between (i) ideas about what traits and behaviour are appropriate for people who have male or female bodies and (ii) ideas about what those bodies themselves consist in at a biological level – that is, ideas about what biological maleness and femaleness consist in. Ideas about gender and sex remain conceptually distinct even if in practice they always influence and support one another.

So far, we have looked at two feminist criticisms of the sex/gender distinction, and, specifically, of the concept of sex which is at work in this distinction. The first criticism was that sex is not unchanging, but is affected, at least in part, by gender. The second criticism was that scientific views of what biological sex consists in are not unchanging but are influenced by changes in society, including changes in gender expectations. I have suggested that neither criticism should lead us to reject the sex/gender distinction as such. Rather, we can retain the distinction while recognizing that gender interacts with both (i) sex and (ii) scientific views about sex. But since scientific views are always likely to be influenced by gender assumptions, we need to be cautious about accepting any particular scientific account of biological sex. We should be careful to ask what assumptions may be present within particular scientific accounts. And we should bear in mind that scientific accounts are never infallible but are always subject to ongoing revision and correction.

4. Sex and intersex

Now let us look at a third line of feminist philosophical criticism of the concept of sex. According to this, the very idea that there *are* two sexes is an effect of the assumption that gendered behaviour must fall into two opposed patterns, feminine and masculine. Gender assumptions, it is argued, affect not only how we understand the natures of the sexes, but also – more basically – whether we think there are two sexes at all. But this belief in two sexes is not actually warranted by biology, it is argued. Those making these arguments draw support from the fact that not all individuals are biologically either male or female. A minority of people are born with bodies that are **intersexed**, i.e. ambiguous with respect to standard criteria for being male or female.

Because intersex has become important to recent feminist debates about sex, we need to spend some time considering intersex and its philosophical implications.

Estimates of the number of intersexed people vary. Alice Dreger (1998: 42) suggests that one person in 2000 is born with visibly ambiguous genitals. However, Anne Fausto-Sterling includes people whose ambiguities become visible only later in life and so suggests that around 1.7 people in every 100 are intersexed (2000: 51–4). Carrie Hull (2005: 66–9) gives a more cautious estimate of 0.373 intersexed people per 100.

Various physical conditions can make people intersexed. The following are some of the most common conditions. Some people have XXY chromosomes and consequently are born with male genitals but develop female secondary characteristics, such as breasts, at puberty. Others have XX chromosomes but, due to exposure to excess androgens in the womb, their female internal genitalia are accompanied by ambiguous or male external genitalia. Other individuals with XY chromosomes have androgen insensitivity syndrome (AIS). They have male internal genitals but their bodies do not respond to the androgens that their testes produce and so they develop more-or-less female external genitals and body shape.

Some cultures have accepted the intersexed – many Native American cultures recognized them as a third sex – but modern western societies have been among the less accommodating. For much of the twentieth century, it has been standard for the medical profession to use surgery and artificial hormones so as to make intersexed individuals look as unambiguously male or female as possible. Sometimes, doctors have done this against the will of the individuals affected – or without their knowledge, with infants being operated on shortly after birth and raised in ignorance of the fact. Doctors have adopted these policies for largely humanitarian reasons. They have assumed that, in a society that presumes that everyone is either male or female, one cannot live happily unless one belongs to one sex or the other. But, well-intentioned as doctors may have been, their policies have had the effect of reproducing the assumption that everyone is either male or female, and so helping to maintain a set-up in which it is hard for the intersexed to live happily.

In recent decades intersexed people have begun to organize politically to challenge these medical practices. They have affirmed their right to lead lives free from unwanted surgery and medication, and free from the shame and secrecy that have long surrounded intersex. The Intersex Society of North America, founded by Cheryl Chase in 1993, is a leading organization that campaigns for 'systematic reform in the social and medical treatment of people with intersex conditions' (see www.isna.org).

The fact that a minority of people are intersexed challenges the standard way in which we tend to think about biological sex. The definitions of biological maleness and femaleness which I gave above reflect this standard view. According to these definitions, one is biologically male if one has all of the following set of properties: XY chromosomes, testes, relatively high secretions of androgens, male genitalia and male secondary sex characteristics. And one is female if one has all of the following: XX chromosomes, ovaries, relatively high levels of oestrogen, female genitalia and female secondary characteristics. These definitions embody an assumption that all the properties in each set must go together. (If one has testes, then one will have higher levels of androgens, etc.)

But the fact that there are intersexed people shows that these properties need not go together in sets. Fausto-Sterling (2000: 1–3) tells the story of the athlete Maria Patiño, who had AIS. She was barred from competing in sports as a woman when she was found to have XY chromosomes. She mounted a legal challenge and was reinstated as female on the grounds of her external form. Considered in terms of external anatomy and form, Patiño counted as female, but in terms of chromosomes she did not. Thus, conventional sex categories, which presume that XX chromosomes must go with female anatomy, ran into problems when applied to Patiño's case.

Perhaps, among the various properties that are relevant to maleness and femaleness, there is one key biological feature (XY chromosomes, perhaps) that is necessary and sufficient for maleness and another (XX chromosomes, perhaps) that is necessary and sufficient for femaleness. The idea here is that this feature must be present and that it, alone, is enough to make someone male (or female). But this would be an arbitrary and unconvincing stipulation, since people are not currently classified on the basis of any such single feature. Doctors often appeal to chromosomes – for example they class as female XX people who have developed external male genitals because of exposure to excess androgens. Yet as Patiño's case shows, at other times sex is decided based not on chromosomes but external form. As Georgia Warnke says: 'If we . . . call some . . . individuals "men" on the basis of their chromosomes, and if we answer the question of external form versus chromosomes in conflicting ways', then our categories of sex are in a 'muddle' (Warnke 2001: 128).

What conclusions should we draw from all this? Before we can answer this question, we need to consider two other phenomena – transsex and transgender – which also expose the muddle within conventional categories of sex.

5. Sex, transsex and transgender

In addition to the intersexed, two other groups who have become increasingly politically organized in recent decades are transsexual and transgendered people. Now, one might assume that there is a firm distinction between being transsexual and being transgendered. **Transsexuals**, one might think, are those who change their sex, or seek to change or are in the process of changing it, through surgery and synthetic hormones. This is because they feel that their sex does not agree with their gender (stereotypically, they might feel like 'a man trapped in a female body').

On the other hand, one might think, a person is **transgendered** if they have an ambiguous gender identity and way of behaving. This ambiguity can take several forms. One's identity and behaviour may include elements of both feminine and masculine genders. Or one's identity and behaviour may not fit in with either gender. Or one might have a gender identity and way of behaving which conflict with what other people expect based on one's biological sex. For example, one might be a female who acts in a masculine way, jarring with most people's expectations that females should act feminine. In short, transgendered people are 'transgressively gendered' (Bornstein 1994: 134–5). Note, then, that being transgendered need not involve changing from one gender to the other, as one might assume by analogy with transsexualism. So transsex and transgender look clearly distinct: the former, it seems, involves changing sex; and the latter, it seems, involves having an ambiguous or transgressive gender. But actually the boundaries between transsex and transgender are fuzzy.

A novel that shows how transsex and transgender blur into one another is Leslie Feinberg's *Stone Butch Blues* (1993). The central character, Jess Goldberg, is born female in 1950s America. In early childhood, she develops an ambiguous gender identity, prompting other people constantly to ask whether she – or 'it' – is a boy or a girl. The novel implies that the ambiguity arises because Jess often acts in ways that are perceived as masculine and as incongruous given her female sex. The adult Jess finds a way to make sense of her ambiguous identity by becoming a butch lesbian. By her twenties, Jess can no longer endure the violence she suffers from the police and other hostile individuals. She has a mastectomy and takes testosterone so she can pass as male. She becomes a bearded, muscular man – but at much personal cost, including losing a sense of connection to her life before her sex-change. So eventually Jess stops taking hormones. As a result his/her biological sex ends up being indeterminate. In the closing chapters, Jess comes to understand and accept him/herself as someone who confounds and keeps moving between gender categories. S/he also becomes more accepting that his/her body is now indeterminate as to sex.

As Jess's story shows, many transgendered people change, or wish to change, their anatomy. They sometimes wish to make their anatomy more ambiguous, so that it is consistent with their sense of self. Other transgendered people identify with the gender opposed to their sex, but they do not set out to completely change their sex so that it agrees with their gender. Instead they take hormones to change their bodies partially, enough to support their gender identity. Thus, many transgendered people do change their sex to some extent. Moreover, some transsexual people who complete a sex-change feel that because they have undergone this transition they can never unequivocally belong to either sex. They come to see themselves *as* transsexed (Stone 1991) and hence as necessarily ambiguous in gender as well.[3] There is, then, extensive overlap between transsex and transgender rather than a clear dividing line between them.

What do transsex and transgender imply for the concept of sex? Like intersexed people, transsexed and transgendered people resist straightforward classification in terms of sex categories. Even people who undergo a complete sex-change retain their original chromosomes. So, although a post-operative male-to-female transsexual counts as female (in most contexts) because of her genitals and secondary characteristics, she stills lack the XX chromosomes that are often thought necessary for being female. Those who undergo only partial surgery, or only take hormones, or deliberately try to craft an ambiguous body, will have an even more mixed set of characteristics. Again, this shows that the various properties that are relevant to maleness and femaleness need not go together in sets. The case of sex-changed people also suggests that one can be male or female without having to have the whole set of properties that are relevant to a given sex.

6. Male and female as cluster concepts

Intersex, transsex and transgender show that our usual categories of sex are muddled. It is routinely assumed that someone must have the whole set of 'male' properties to count as male, yet people may be classed as male when they do not have – and are known not to have – all these properties. Nor is there any single property that we can non-arbitrarily take to be necessary and sufficient for giving someone a particular sex. So are standard sex categories hopelessly muddled?

In this section I will suggest that there is a sound element within conventional understandings of sex onto which we can hold. This element is the idea that there are *clusters* of properties which are relevant to being male or female. When a human individual has enough of the properties in one of these clusters, that individual is male or female.

In philosophy of biology, Richard Boyd (1988: 196–9) has developed a useful account of how having enough of a set of clustered properties makes something a member of a particular species. According to Boyd:

1   Certain properties form clusters, i.e. they often occur together.
2   This is no accident. It happens either because the presence of some of these properties tends to encourage that of the others, or because some underlying mechanisms or processes tend to support the presence of all these properties, or both.
3   The clustering together of the properties has important causal effects.
4   Things in which the clustering of most of these properties occurs form a kind.
5   A thing may display some, but not all, of these properties (and some, but not all, of the relevant underlying mechanisms).
6   Consequently, it may in some cases be impossible to resolve conclusively whether a thing belongs to a particular kind.

Boyd's account can be applied to sex. (For simplicity I will focus on the female sex.) Certain properties – having XX chromosomes, ovaries, vagina, breasts, etc. – often occur together, and so they form a cluster. This is not accidental. These properties often co-occur because having XX chromosomes encourages the formation of ovaries, which, in turn, tend to secrete relatively high quantities of female hormones. This, in turn, encourages the growth of female genitals, and so on. That is, the presence of each of these properties favours that of the others. The clustering of these properties – the ovaries, hormones, genitals, etc. – also has an important causal effect. It gives many of the bodies that have enough of these clustered properties the ability to make a distinctive contribution to reproduction – i.e. to gestate, give birth to and breast-feed babies. Still, although all these properties tend to encourage one another's presence, they need not always occur together. Various factors such as AIS can intervene to stop them from co-occurring. But if enough of these properties do occur together, then the body to which they belong is female.

If, then, someone is female or male when they have a sufficient number of the relevant properties, being female or male is a matter of degree. By 'a matter of degree', I mean that one can be female in virtue of having all of the relevant properties, or only most of them (e.g. a woman who has had a mastectomy or a post-operative male-to-female transsexual). In the case of an intersexed person, or of a transsexual or transgendered person who has only changed their sex partially, one might have only some of the relevant properties. In such cases there is no determinate answer to the question of whether one is female or male. But the fact that intersexed people and some transsexual and transgendered people are indeterminate as to sex does not make them radically different from everyone else. Rather, they are towards the centre of a spectrum on which everyone else is also located. No rigid dividing line separates the intersexed from the sexed, the transsexed from the sexed.

Moreover, in the case of many of these properties that are relevant to sex, having them is itself a matter of degree. Both men and women have different degrees of secondary characteristics, like body hair, depending on different levels of hormones. Women's breasts vary greatly in size; and as for the genitals: 'Clitorises and penises . . . come in a wide range of shapes and sizes' with some relatively large clitorises and some relatively small penises (Dreger 1998: 4). So, one can be female or male in virtue of possessing enough of the properties in the relevant cluster to a high degree or just to varying lesser degrees.

Taking it that concepts of 'male' and 'female' are cluster concepts, what does biological **sex** consist in?

- To be female is to have enough of a cluster of properties (ovaries, breasts, vagina, etc.), which cluster because they encourage one another's presence.
- To be male is to have enough of a cluster of properties (testes, penis, scrotum, etc.), which cluster because they encourage one another's presence.

These revised definitions of what it is to be female or male face at least two problems. (1) Some intersexed people have a condition known as 'true hermaphrodism'. They have one ovary and one testis (or, sometimes, a fused ovo-testis). Often they produce both egg and sperm cells, androgen and oestrogen, and develop internal and external genitals which have a mixture of male and female attributes. Given my definitions, these people are both female and male. Strictly speaking, then, I should say that someone is female if she has enough of the properties in the female cluster and, in addition, has either none of the properties in the male cluster or, at least, not enough of them to make her a hermaphrodite. The situation for males is reversed.

(2) The definition of femaleness which I have proposed might be thought to imply that what it is to be female is to be able to give birth. But women are not able to give birth throughout their whole lives. Are girls prior to menarche, and women after the menopause, not female? What about infertile women – are they not female? And, if being female means being able to give birth, then does this not imply that all women ought to have children, because it is only by so doing that they can realize their female nature?

Actually I have not claimed that being female consists in being able to give birth. Rather, I suggested that being female consists in having enough of the relevant cluster of properties, where

i   one can have enough of these properties to be female but not enough (or, perhaps, not in the right combination) to be able to reproduce. For example, a post-operative male-to-female transsexual may have enough properties to be female but will be unable to conceive as long as she lacks ovaries.

ii   Moreover, even if in principle one has all the properties necessary for reproduction, this is not sufficient to ensure that one will be able to conceive and give birth. Further conditions must also be met: one must be of suitable age and no causes of infertility may be present.

In at least these two ways, it is possible for someone to have enough properties to be female but still to be unable to conceive or bear children. In sum: having enough of the relevant cluster of properties is what makes someone female, not having the reproductive ability that often follows if one has enough of these properties. Since, then, femaleness is not the same as being able to give birth, there is no implication that all women need to realize their nature by having babies.

7. The influence of gender expectations on sex classifications

I have argued that concepts of maleness and femaleness are best understood as cluster concepts. If this is right, then we need to revise our definitions of sex (1) to acknowledge that sometimes there is no definite answer as to what sex one is, or what sex someone else is; and (2) to acknowledge that one's sex, and the sex of others, is always a matter of degree.

But some other feminist philosophers who have thought about intersex have concluded that we need to change our ways of classifying one another more radically. Judith Butler (1987), Anne Fausto-Sterling (2000), Suzanne Kessler (1998), Georgia Warnke (2001) and Monique Wittig (1992) have all argued – in different ways – that we only believe that there are two biological sexes because we are committed, socially, to the existence of two and only two genders. On this argument, the belief in two sexes is an element *within* our social assumptions about gender. Warnke's version of this argument is particularly clear, so we can usefully focus on it. She starts her argument by referring to the medical profession's treatment of intersexed people.

As Kessler (1998: 19, 25) has shown, when doctors operate on intersexed infants, they have generally obeyed the following principles. If an infant is XY and has what doctors see as a viable or potentially viable penis, then doctors classify the infant as male (and then use whatever surgery and hormones are necessary to sustain this). If an XY infant has a penis that seems unviable – that is, too small to penetrate a vagina – then the infant is classed as female. XX infants are generally classed as female and have their clitorises reduced if they are deemed too big. Their vaginas are enlarged if they are judged too small for penetration by a penis. Basically, doctors assume that a male body is one capable of penetrating a female and that a female body is one capable of being penetrated by a male.

Warnke argues – as do Dreger (1998: 8) and Fausto-Sterling (2000: 45–8) – that this not only reveals the basis on which doctors assign intersexed people to male or female categories. It also reveals the underlying basis on which we *all* tend to classify one another by sex. Typically, we assign someone to the male or female sex based on whether or not we take that person to be physically capable of fulfilling the relevant set of *gender* expectations. For instance, if we deem someone to be physically capable of fulfilling the social expectation that men should have penetrative intercourse with women, then we will classify that person as male.

Butler (1990a) would add that four higher-level social expectations are at work here. These expectations are that: (1) everyone must be either masculine or feminine; (2) masculine and feminine traits should be sharply opposed; (3) everyone should be heterosexual; and (4) – from (2) plus (3) – masculine and feminine individuals should play opposed roles in (heterosexual) sex. It is against the background of these expectations that we insist that everyone must be either male or female – that is, that everyone must be physically capable of playing either a masculine or a feminine role. No indeterminacy or exceptions are allowed, hence the perceived need to surgically reconstruct intersexed people. Warnke concludes:

[I]f assumptions about gender drive the distinction of sexes, sex is less inborn than interpretive. Assumptions and expectations about proper and distinct gender activities erect the interpretive frameworks through which certain features and combinations of features appear to be fundamental to bodies and to comprise their sex. . . . The idea that some of these features [of bodies] cluster together to indicate a 'sex' sorts bodies according to a particular model. The idea that we just are essentially male or female is thus less an idea about nature than it is an interpretation of natural properties, one that begins with the activities and presumptions of gender and works backward, as it were, toward the body. (Warnke 2001: 130)

As a whole, Warnke's argument is this. Because we perceive and categorize bodies with respect to their capacity to satisfy gender expectations, we are led to categorize bodies on the basis of that sub-set of their properties which enables them to satisfy these expectations. These are the properties which enable bodies to engage in heterosexual sex and reproduction – i.e., the internal and external genitals (and the chromosomal and hormonal properties that cause those genitals to develop). Warnke concludes that, if we did not seek to categorize bodies in relation to gender expectations, then we would not see the properties that enable bodies to meet those expectations as clustered.

But does this conclusion – which challenges my cluster-based reconstruction of sex categories – follow? Let us analyse Warnke's argument more closely. (1) Her own argument implies that there are some bodily properties that really are necessary for genital sexual activity, including kinds of genital sexual activity which can result in reproduction if the people involved have the right chromosomes, gonads and hormones. It is only because certain properties *really are* necessary for heterosexual, reproductive sex (among other kinds of sex) that these properties become the focus of people's attention given a social norm stipulating that men and women must have reproductive sex. So Warnke's argument implies that when these properties – the genitals, chromosomes, gonads and hormones – occur together they have this important causal effect of enabling reproduction.

Moreover, (2) unless a fairly large number of people were able – given the right circumstances – to reproduce, a social norm prescribing reproduction could not obtain as Warnke thinks it does. But for all these people to be able to reproduce, the properties that jointly support this ability must occur together fairly regularly – regularly enough that this co-occurrence cannot be accidental but must be caused by the properties encouraging one another's presence. So Warnke's claim that there is a social norm prescribing reproduction, together with her implicit view that some bodily properties do jointly enable reproduction, already imply that these properties are clustered – that they non-accidentally tend to co-occur and that this has important causal effects. Contrary to what she claims, Warnke's own argument implies that the gonads, genitals, hormones (etc.) are clustered independently of how we perceive them in light of assumptions about gender.

However, Warnke makes a further argument that even if biological properties *do* cluster so that there is a natural sex difference, we need not classify people on the basis of this natural difference. She proposes that, just as we do not currently categorize people by eye colour or shape of nose, we could cease to categorize people by sex. The only reason why we do currently use sex to classify people, Warnke argues, is because our society stipulates that reproduction (and therefore heterosexual sex) is all-important, necessary for a complete human life. This is a legacy of the Biblical command to 'be fruitful and multiply'. If reproduction were given less importance, Warnke thinks, then there would be no need to categorize people in terms of those of their properties which support reproductive ability.

Here it might help to distinguish two questions. (1) Must sex be *the* central and basic principle of human classification? Certainly sex is so used at the moment, and this is reflected in how sex classifications are written into grammar – 'he' or 'she', 'his' or 'her', etc. Plausibly, this use of sex as the basic principle of classification does reflect an assumption that reproduction is the central goal of human life. Because of that assumption, the sex differences which are necessary for reproduction come to count as *the* decisive differences between human beings. But this could be changed. One can at least imagine a world like that described in Marge Piercy's science fiction novel *Woman on the Edge of Time*, where the words 'person' and 'per' have replaced 'he', 'she', 'his' and 'her'. Thus, when one of the characters in the novel is dying, it is said that 'Sappho is dying . . . person is very old. It's time for per to die' (Piercy 1978: 150).

But (2) could we stop classifying one by another by sex altogether? If there are natural clusters of properties that are relevant to sex, then it is unlikely that we could ever completely abandon sex classifications, even if we gave up the Christian preoccupation with reproduction. Many of the properties that are relevant to sex are noticeable – e.g. breasts, levels of body hair – and create visible differences between different kinds of people. Moreover, our sex-properties are bound to influence our behaviour in some way, even if these influences are mediated by society. As we saw earlier, the view that biological properties have no effect at all on human thought and behaviour is not plausible. If sex-properties affect behaviour then this, again, means that in any society people will inevitably notice one another's sex and classify one another by sex. It does seem, though, that in a different kind of society we might be able to treat sex as just one basis of classification amongst others. (By **sex-properties** I mean the various biological properties that feature in either the male or the female clusters.)

Warnke is right, though, that in present-day society classifications of people by sex are never simply that. Given a society which prescribes sharply opposed genders, what we look for when we try to classify people is whether they are able to realize norms of masculinity or norms of femininity. (By **norms of masculinity/femininity** I mean a society's standards for what behaviour and traits count as appropriately masculine/feminine.) In a two-gender society, we categorize people never simply on the basis of their sex-properties, but on the basis of their sex-properties *interpreted as*, specifically, what enables people to realize one or other set of gender expectations. Thus, we categorize people not simply in terms of their reproductive function – e.g. the ability to give birth – but in terms of their reproductive function interpreted as what makes them able to live up to a given set of gender expectations – e.g. to be a properly motherly woman.

If there are indeed natural clusters of properties that are relevant to sex, then in itself categorizing someone as male or female need not be interpretive. In principle, these categorizations could simply be based on observing and judging that someone has enough properties to belong to a given sex. In society as currently organized, though, categorizations of sex are generally entangled with judgements about gender. This, in turn, encourages us to misunderstand the nature of maleness and femaleness as properties. Because we interpret maleness as what sustains masculinity, and we assume that masculinity is sharply opposed to femininity, we are led to interpret maleness as sharply opposed to femaleness. This way of thinking supports the conventional view that one must have all of the properties relevant to maleness in order to be male. It thus impedes us from recognizing that maleness and femaleness are matters of degree (such that one may be female/male by having enough but not all of the relevant properties and while perhaps having some of the properties of the other sex as well). Thus, given a society that prescribes opposed genders, whenever we categorize people as male or female we tend, simultaneously, to do two further things. (1) We interpret these people in terms of whether they can display suitably masculine or feminine behaviours. And (2) we see their maleness or femaleness as absolute, opposed, qualities.

8. Review and conclusion

This chapter has looked at three feminist criticisms of the biological concept of sex. The first criticism was that – contrary to what the original sex/gender distinction suggested – sex affects gender, while gendered habits and institutions can and do alter at least some elements of sex. The second criticism was that understandings of biological sex cannot be taken for granted, but undergo constant change influenced by social assumptions about gender. The third criticism of the concept of sex was that the very idea that there are two sexes is merely an effect of gender.

In each case I have argued that the concept of sex, and the sex/ gender distinction of which it is part, may be retained. I have suggested the following:

1   Although in reality sex and gender always shape one another and alter one another over time, we can draw a conceptual distinction between them for the purposes of theoretical analysis.
2   Ideas about gender also tend to influence scientific ideas about what biological sex consists in, but we can still distinguish between these two groups of ideas. The former group of ideas concerns what behaviour and traits are appropriate for people of a given sex. The latter group of ideas concerns the nature of people's biological sex itself.
3   Ideas about gender are also entangled with the ways in which we classify people by sex. But we can still distinguish in principle between classifying someone by sex – in terms of the number of relevant properties that they have – and classifying someone as masculine/feminine.

Thus, I think it is worth retaining three distinctions –(1) between sex and gender, (2) between scientific ideas about sex and ideas about gender, and (3) between classifications by sex and classifications in terms of gender. It is worth retaining these distinctions because doing so gives us a wider range of concepts with which to analyse the social relations between men and women.[4] The more concepts we have at our disposal, the more precisely we can pick apart the different processes and factors that contribute to particular social phenomena and to particular instances of male domination within society.

There is a fourth feminist criticism of the concept of sex, not considered in this chapter, according to which sex in human beings can never be a matter of bare biological facts. Human beings are a uniquely meaning-making species. In the course of everyday life, each of us constantly invests our circumstances and our bodies with significance, and this significance builds up over time. So for me, my body can never be a mere collection of biological processes. Neither do other people ever see my body as a mere biological thing. Other people attribute meanings to my body and these inform the meanings that I myself give to my body. For example, I never simply experience myself as having the biological property of being five feet tall. What I experience is that other people perceive me as short; I may fear that they are 'looking down' on me; and these experiences form part of what it is to be me. In lived experience, no distinction can be drawn between biological properties and their meanings; the two are totally interwoven.

Again, though, I would argue that we can distinguish analytically between biological properties and the meanings that we give to them in lived experience. To be sure, no such distinction ever appears within lived experience itself. But, I suggest, one task of feminist philosophers is to stand back from lived experience and explain why women and men have the particular lived experiences that they do. This requires distinguishing the factors that affect people's lived experiences, factors that include biological facts about those people's bodies. I may never experience myself simply as being five feet tall, but the biological fact that I am five feet tall is one fact that contributes to bringing about my lived experience of being short. So I will assume for now that the fact that human bodies are always-meaningful or 'lived' bodies need not invalidate the concept of sex. (Chapters 2, 6 and 7 will explain and assess this idea of the 'lived' body more fully.)

Some feminist philosophers might have additional worries about my account of sex. I have argued that, because sex-properties visibly differentiate people, we could never dispense altogether with the practice of classifying one another by sex. But if we must invariably classify one another by sex, then doesn't it follow that people will invariably – in any possible society – devise different norms about what behaviour and traits are appropriate for males and females? After all, if sex observably differentiates people then (as Delphy 1993 argues) it will probably always serve as a readily available basis for assigning different social roles, and different types of work and activity, to different types of people.

The worry, then, is that if two sexes exist – even on the basis of clustered properties – then there must be two social genders as well. Moreover, this means that in practice sex classifications will *always* be surrounded and informed by gender judgements. It will never be possible to classify people by sex without referring to gender as well. But is it necessarily a problem to have two genders? Feminist thinkers such as Delphy, Kessler and Warnke think this *is* a problem. So they want to show that sex is not a biological reality precisely because they worry that having two biological sexes – undesirably – makes two genders inevitable as well. To see why the institution of having two genders might be undesirable in itself, we will need to look more at what gender is and at some major feminist criticisms of gender. Chapter 2 will do this.

So far, though, looking at feminist criticisms of the concept of sex has led us into a range of questions and issues which mark out the field of feminist philosophy of sex. Feminist philosophy of sex overlaps with, and contributes to, a number of existing areas of philosophical debate. For example, it bears on:

1   Discussions in metaphysics about what natural kinds are, and what sorts of properties things must share in order to belong to the same kind.
2   Philosophical thinking about the body, since sex is a central feature of the human body. Historically, the body has received far less attention from philosophers than the mind, but major philosophers in the continental European tradition, such as Friedrich Nietzsche and Maurice Merleau-Ponty, have written about the human body. Their work is now becoming increasingly influential in Anglo-American philosophy (see Proudfoot 2003).
3   Feminist research into changing scientific understandings of sex bears on questions in the philosophy of science. What role do conceptual models play in science? Have male biases damaged scientific research, especially research into sex? Even if they have, must biases always be bad for scientific research, or can they sometimes be enabling?

Feminist philosophy of sex is important not only for how it bears on pre-existing philosophical inquiries into natural kinds, the body, and science. It is also important in its own right, because it explores a new range of questions. What is biological sex? What is it to be male or female? Does biological sex exist at all independently of our beliefs about sex and/or gender? How do norms of masculinity and femininity affect scientific understandings of sex? What can intersex, transsex and transgender teach us about the nature of sex? Could and should we abandon the practice of classifying one another by sex? These questions mark out a new area of philosophical inquiry: inquiry into the nature of biological sex.

Notes

1 Later feminists have objected that it can be easier to change one's biology than to change society.
2 Some feminists object that the phrase 'secondary sex characteristics' implies that the primary or most important sex characteristics are those that directly relate to reproduction. This suggests that being sexed is all about reproducing and that being female is all about having babies. I sympathize with this criticism and will argue in this chapter that 'primary' and 'secondary' characteristics are all equally relevant to sex. I will continue to use the word 'secondary' merely as a convenient shorthand.
3 But see Prosser (1998) who defends a more traditional account of transsexualism as involving the wish to pass from one sex to the other and to find a secure 'home' in one's new sex.
4 Plumwood (1989) likewise defends the sex/gender distinction on the grounds that it enables us to make finer conceptual distinctions and so to analyse society more precisely.

Further Reading

Jaggar's dialectical theory of human biology   Jaggar 1983b.
Gender and the history of science   Martin 1987: ch. 3; Schiebinger 1989: 160–88.
Intersex and its philosophical implications   Dreger 1998: ch. 1; Fausto-Sterling 2000: esp. ch. 3; Warnke 2001.

2 Gender

1. Gender and power

Like the concept of sex, the concept of gender has been the subject of intense debate within feminist philosophy and theory of the past thirty-five years. To follow these debates, we must first deepen our grasp of the initial definition of gender which psychologists and sociologists produced in the 1960s and which feminists took up.

As psychologists and sociologists initially defined gender, it consists of: (1) social expectations about what behaviours and activities are appropriate for male and female individuals; (2) the mental traits and self-understandings that individuals tend to develop under the influence of these expectations. To expand:

- Social expectations, or norms, are conveyed to individuals by other people and by being embodied in cultural artefacts, such as films and novels, and in institutions. (**Institutions** are humanly created organizations that shape social life, such as the state, law, the family, the health service and the media.) These expectations or norms specify which behaviours are masculine and which feminine. People and institutions enforce expectations by applying rewards and punishments. For example, if girls are expected to be deferential, then they will be punished or receive negative responses when they behave assertively.
- Masculinity and femininity are social positions or roles. According to sociologists, a **role** is a position within society (e.g. the position of teacher, the position of parent). Each role is defined by a set of norms about how those occupying this role should behave. Each role is defined in relation to other roles: what is expected of teachers depends on what is expected of pupils and vice versa.

- Different societies have different norms of masculinity and femininity (e.g. whether it is masculine to wear tights as in the Renaissance, or trousers as today). But almost all societies share a higher-level expectation that males should be masculine and females feminine.
- Individuals are not only expected to perform the actions appropriate to their gender; they are also expected to identify, or understand, themselves as members of that gender. Robert Stoller (1968: 29–30) argued that most people form a 'core' sense of gender identity by age 2–3.

Feminists found this complex concept of gender useful for two main reasons. Firstly, it gave them a language with which to describe (what they saw as) the way in which societies render women subordinate to men through norms of femininity and masculinity. For instance, if women are expected to act deferentially and men to act assertively, women will become subordinate to men in various ways. Women will tend to give way if competing against men; to stop speaking if men interrupt them; and to insist on their own needs less than men insist on theirs. (This is not to deny that men, too, can be harmed in many ways by the very gender norms that privilege them – for instance by norms that encourage them to hide and repress their emotions in the name of being 'strong' and protective.)

Secondly, feminists found the concept of gender helpful because it entailed that masculine and feminine roles are defined by society, not biology. This implied that these roles could be changed. Femininity could be redefined so that it ceases to require deferential behaviour. Or, rather than redefining what masculinity and femininity are, we could get rid of gender roles altogether and cease to distribute people into masculine or feminine positions. To change the content of gender roles would be to 'restructure' gender; to abolish gender roles would be to **degender** society.

But the concept of gender roles had problems from a feminist perspective. This concept did not in itself explain *why* gender norms tend to subordinate women to men. That is, the concept of gender roles does not explain why it is that in almost all societies these roles have a patriarchal content. Feminists therefore felt a need to combine the concept of gender roles with theories that explained (what they saw as) the pervasiveness of feminine subordination.

The radical feminist explanation is that women's subordination is the result of men dominating women. On this view men use violence, threats, and economic and cultural mechanisms to keep women in a state of servitude. For Catherine MacKinnon rape, sexual harassment, domestic violence and prostitution are key practices through which men maintain dominance over women. She sums up: 'The social relation between the sexes is organized so that men may dominate and women must submit' (1987: 3). Adrienne Rich (1980: 638–40) lists the following features of male domination: men denying women their own sexuality; men forcing their sexuality upon women; men confining women physically; men commanding and exploiting women's labour; men cramping women's creativity and withholding from them large areas of society's knowledge and culture.

In claiming that men 'dominate' women, these radical feminists are claiming that men exercise (i) *power* over women in a way that (ii) *harms* women by preventing them from choosing how to live for themselves. But this radical feminist view of men's power has difficulties. It takes insufficient account of the other kinds of power relations that exist in society, notably class and race. The effect of these other power relations is that, contrary to the radical feminist view, some women have power over some men – e.g. female company directors over their male employees. And sometimes radical feminists come close to depicting women simply as victims of male power – never as benefiting from male power or acting in ways that affect and alter how male power is exercised. (On these criticisms, see Allen 1999: 11–18.)

These problems with radical feminist views of male power prompted a number of feminist thinkers to conclude that, rather than trying to find one single cause of women's subordination (such as men's urge to dominate women), it might well be more fruitful to look at the different factors that have caused this subordination to evolve into different forms within different societies. Feminists have been most interested in how gender subordination has evolved in modern societies. To understand this evolution, many feminists writing in the later 1980s and early 1990s (e.g. Bartky 1990: ch. 5; Diamond and Quinby 1988; Sawicki 1991) found it helpful to draw on the theory of power developed by Michel Foucault. Some feminists (e.g. Hartsock 1990) have criticized Foucault, but many have found his theory of power useful. So we should introduce Foucault's theory and then see how it has helped feminists to understand how women's subordination has evolved and persisted in modern times.

2. Foucault and feminism

Foucault (1976b) set out to grasp what is novel about power relations within modern societies. He argued that in these societies, power no longer belongs to the monarch but is spread, less visibly, across a whole range of institutions: prisons, schools, hospitals, asylums, factories. In these institutions, specific strategies of power are developed and exercised for specific local purposes, such as making pupils more docile. These strategies are then copied across from one institution to another and become applied in other areas of social life.

Foucault (1975: 170–94) found three main strategies to be at work in prisons and similar institutions.

1   'Hierarchical observation': buildings and spaces are arranged so that inmates can be continuously observed. Knowing that they may always be under observation, the inmates start to monitor themselves. The prisoner becomes his or her own jailer.
2   'Normalizing judgement': prisoners (or schoolchildren, factory workers, etc.) are incessantly measured against norms of good behaviour, and are punished if they deviate from these norms.
3   Examinations: these are used to rank individuals against one another and to assemble a body of documentation about each individual over time. Examinations are used not only in schools, to rank pupils, but in other institutions too, e.g. medical examinations, military reviews, job interviews.

The kind of power that is exercised through these three strategies is **disciplinary power**. Disciplinary power trains prisoners or pupils to regulate, observe, and take responsibility for themselves as individuals. Once these strategies of power have taken hold at the level of society as a whole, government institutions start to draw on them (e.g. when governments school people who are receiving unemployment benefits to be responsible 'job-seekers').

From his account of power in modern institutions, Foucault extracts a more general 'analytics' of the nature of modern (disciplinary) power (1976a: 94–6). According to this:

- Power is at work throughout all social relationships and is exercised in diverse forms. Power is built into doctor/patient, teacher/pupil and gaoler/prisoner relationships (amongst others), but works in slightly different ways in each case.
- Power comes from 'below', from the multiplicity of social institutions and relationships, rather than being imposed from 'above', by the state.
- Power gives rise to knowledge – as in the case of examinations, the exercise of power over individuals generates knowledge about them. This knowledge could not exist without these power relationships that give rise to it and give it its meaning.
- Power is relational. An individual only ever holds power because of the position he or she occupies within a set of relationships (e.g. the position of jailer). But relationships like that of jailer/prisoner only survive as long as prisoners and gaolers act in ways that maintain these relationships. Hence, those who are subjugated (the prisoners) cannot wholly lack power but must have at least enough power to play a part in maintaining the overall gaoler/prisoner relationship.
- Power always provokes resistance. Since those who are subjugated are never wholly without power, they are always potentially able to resist the power relationships in which they are located. So diverse 'local' forms of resistance are continually arising within specific relationships and institutions.
- Contrary to radical feminist views, power is positive and productive rather than negative and limiting. Foucault means that (modern) power never simply prevents people from acting or making choices. In modern societies, power relations always do cut off some options, but at the same time these relations make other options available. Moreover, modern power actually gives people the ability to choose responsibly between options. The exercise of discipline over people makes them able to regulate themselves and to think responsibly about how to act – and, potentially, to use these abilities to act in ways that resist power.

By using Foucault's conception of power to study how gender relations have evolved in modern societies, feminist theorists concluded that:

1   Men have various different forms of power over women, each the effect of specific sets of gender norms that have arisen within different social institutions. For instance, male doctors have a certain form of power over female patients, different from the form of power they have over their wives or, again, over female nurses. So there is no single reason why women in modern (as in other) societies tend to be subordinate. There are different reasons why different forms of masculine power have arisen within specific institutional settings.

2   Once they have begun to arise, the various forms of masculine power strengthen and influence one another, so that they often become similar or develop common features. This mutual influence produces an overall social pattern of masculine power.

3   Often, institutions keep women subjugated with little need for men to exert any direct control or authority over women. Sandra Bartky (1990: ch. 5) discusses how the images used in beauty and cosmetics advertising establish norms for what counts as an attractive feminine appearance. Women can hardly avoid measuring and regulating themselves against these norms. Thus, these images exercise disciplinary power: they produce self-regulating, self-punishing, feminine individuals. This trend reinforces masculine power, by leading women, for instance, to develop more constricted postures and ways of moving than men, or to limit and watch their eating more than men do.

4   Masculine power can only persist as long as women participate in reproducing it. For example, women (inadvertently) reproduce masculine power when they internalize a concern about their appearance and become preoccupied with looking attractive.

5   Resistance by women is always possible, and can be expected to take the form of various 'local' struggles against specific sites of masculine power. Commonly, feminist movements have taken this kind of form – for example, in 1969 feminists protested against the Miss World contest – rather than aiming for a global transformation in how power is organized.

3. Butler on gender

The idea that femininity and masculinity exist in diverse forms, each bound up with specific social institutions and roles, has been developed

by Judith Butler. Her *Gender Trouble* (1990a) is one of the most important and influential books in contemporary feminist philosophy. It is
also difficult. Butler presumes knowledge of a wide range of theorists,
including Foucault, and she tends to make her claims not directly but
through her interpretations of these other theorists.

Butler is one of several feminist theorists who are often classified
as postmodernists. **Postmodernism** is a broad intellectual movement
in which many recent philosophers – Foucault, for example – can be
included to some extent. Postmodernism centres on the ideas (1) that
there is no progress in history; (2) that each self is fragmented and is
governed by various impulses and influences rather than being coherent and in control of itself; (3) that moral codes and systems of knowledge are always connected to power relations. (Recall Foucault's idea
that examinations produce knowledge about individuals, knowledge
that gives the examining institutions the power to classify and rank
those individuals.) However, some people find the label 'postmodernism' unhelpful because it lumps together philosophers whose
detailed views are very different. I agree. For example, both Butler and
Luce Irigaray can be classed as 'postmodern' feminists yet they hold
opposed views on almost all issues. (On Irigaray, see chapter 4.) So the
notion of postmodernism will play no role in my discussion of Butler.

In *Gender Trouble*, Butler introduces the idea that there are 'regula-
tory practices that govern gender' (1990a: 16). We become gendered as
the result of engaging in certain practices. A **practice** is any social
activity that is done according to a conventional pattern. Games and
sports are obvious examples of practices, but almost any social activity can be regarded as a practice: queuing at bus stops, going shopping, cleaning the house. We engage in particular practices because
'socially instituted and maintained norms' (Butler 1990a: 17) encourage and constrain us to do so. Thus, these practices 'regulate' our
activities in that we are obliged to participate in them.

By using this concept of practices, Butler stresses that we become
gendered by doing particular conventional activities. Moreover, we do
these activities at the level of our bodies and bodily habits, not at
the level of conscious reflective thought. By regularly wearing certain
kinds of clothes, walking in certain conventional ways, growing and
styling one's hair in particular ways, one becomes masculine or feminine. Gender, Butler holds, is something that one *does*, not something
that one is or has. One only remains feminine to the extent that one

keeps engaging in the relevant practices. However, since social norms constrain us to engage in these practices, no one can simply opt out of the conventions and start acting completely differently. The norms that constrain us are conveyed by other people and by being embodied in institutions. For example, when buildings provide separate public toilets for men and women, this conveys an expectation that one must use the 'correct' toilet.

According to Butler, anybody who, over time, repeatedly engages in these 'feminizing' or 'masculinizing' activities will form the belief that they have a persisting feminine or masculine self, or that they are a feminine or masculine person. Butler writes: 'the experience of a gendered psychic disposition or . . . identity is . . . an achievement' (Butler 1990a: 22). It is not that we first identify with a particular gender then follow the corresponding set of social norms. Rather, norms endlessly compel us to participate in the practices corresponding to one gender or the other. Only insofar as we keep up this participation will we tend to understand ourselves as feminine or masculine. These claims underlie Butler's well-known idea that gender is **performative**. 'Gender reality is performative which means, quite simply, that it is real only to the extent that it is performed' (Butler 1990b: 411).

According to Butler, different gender norms exist within different institutions and practices. One of the advantages of recognizing that there are multiple gender norms is that it helps us to see that people are expected to conform to different norms depending on their race or class. Tina Chanter (2006: 62–3) points out, for example, that in Victorian society white middle-class women were expected to be pure, modest and chaste, whereas black women were expected to be 'hypersexualized'.[1]

Butler also argues that the content of each of the various gender norms that exist in any society is constantly changing. Whenever people act out a particular set of norms, inevitably they do so in ways that differ slightly from any previous ways in which others have acted out these norms. This is inevitable because people are unique: people act out norms in the context of their unique life-circumstances and their unique personal histories. But whenever someone acts a norm out in a new way, this changes how other people expect that norm to be carried out. If one girl starts wearing trousers to school, then others may start to think that wearing trousers to school is consistent with dressing feminine. This will alter how these people carry out gender norms themselves – they too may start wearing trousers. As everyone is now acting slightly differently, the norm for feminine schoolwear has changed. Butler sums this up by saying that all norms are constantly undergoing **resignification** – their content is constantly being altered.

For Butler, then, there are many different norms for how to act feminine or masculine and each norm is constantly changing. But this diversity exists against the backdrop of an overarching set of norms which pushes everyone to act *either* masculine *or* feminine. Butler calls this set of norms the **heterosexual matrix** (Butler 1990a: 151).[2] This is a web of very general ideas and assumptions about the nature of sex, gender and sexuality. These ideas seep into all the specific norms about masculine and feminine behaviour which apply in particular settings.

Central to the heterosexual matrix is:

1   The view that gender must 'express' sex – that is, people must behave and understand themselves in ways that correspond to and express their sex. Males, being male, must act in one – masculine – set of ways. Females, being female, must act in a different – feminine – set of ways. Males may not act or understand themselves to be feminine and females may not act or understand themselves to be masculine. An interesting example is that in Germany guidelines on name-giving say that a child must be given a first name that is unambiguously either masculine if the child is male, or feminine if it is female (Wikipedia 2006b).

2   The heterosexual matrix also includes the idea that maleness and femaleness as biological properties are sharply opposed. So masculinity and femininity, too, must consist of sharply opposed sets of characteristics – aggression/nurturance, promiscuity/monogamy, assertiveness/deference.[3]

3   This web of ideas supports the further idea that heterosexuality is natural, because it implies that gendered individuals need to make themselves into complete, 'rounded', people by uniting with someone of the opposite gender. Thus, it is assumed, all those who are feminine – and female – must desire men, and all who are masculine – and male – must desire women. (The character Aristophanes in Plato's *Symposium* invents a myth that reflects

these views. He says that each female or male person was originally both female *and* male – but, having been chopped in half by
the god Zeus, we each want to become whole again by reuniting,
in erotic love, with our lost 'other half'.)

Butler believes that the heterosexual matrix organizes social institutions and expectations so that male and female individuals are
pushed to engage, respectively, in masculine or feminine forms of
behaviour. Although individuals always carry out the expected kinds
of behaviour in unique ways, the resulting diversity of forms of femininity and masculinity remains, for the most part, only diversity
within the prescribed two-gender set-up. The diversity is in people's
ways of acting *either* masculine *or* feminine. It is not a diversity that
goes beyond any masculine/feminine framework.

However, Butler argues, some ways of acting out gender norms
implicitly or explicitly challenge the idea, central to the heterosexual
matrix, that gender expresses sex. She uses drag as an example (Butler
1990a: 136–9). Men getting up in drag, doing the gestures and postures and wearing the clothes which signify femininity, shows that
'being' feminine is just a matter of doing certain activities. Drag shows
that these activities can be done by anyone of any sex and need not be
expressive of the agent's female sex. Drag thus reveals that gender is
'performative' – existing only so far as it is performed.

Another of Butler's examples is butch/femme relationships
between lesbians. In these, the butch adopts conventionally 'masculine' attributes – strength, emotional awkwardness, protectiveness –
while the 'feminine' femme is caring and emotional. This shows that
these masculine and feminine attributes exist only as long as people
perform them, and that females as well as males can perform masculine traits (Butler 1991). Butler considers drag, butch/femme roles, and
any other kinds of activity that similarly expose the performative status
of gender, to be *subversive*. These activities subvert or undermine the
matrix of assumptions that organizes our society. Specifically, these
activities subvert the norm that males must act masculine and females
feminine.

Butler's drag example might seem to suggest that she believes that
anyone can subvert the heterosexual matrix by choosing to engage in
drag and other, related, activities. Yet Butler also denies that anyone
can ever simply opt out of a society's gender arrangements. There is,

as she puts it, no 'doer behind the deed' (1990a: 25). That is, none of us has a core of pure selfhood which is unaffected by social norms and which can choose to throw those norms aside. Norms affect and constrain us all the way down. How then are subversive actions possible?

Butler answers that social norms work by encouraging people to monitor themselves and to check whether they are conforming to social norms. For example, many women constantly monitor their weight to check whether they are conforming to the norm for an attractive feminine figure. But by causing people to regulate themselves, norms are instilling in individuals the more general capacity to reflect critically on their own behaviour, to assess it and modify it. Having acquired this capacity, people can use it to reflect on how their gendered behaviour is linked to an oppressive gender system. This can motivate people to change their behaviour and act subversively.

These claims of Butler's apply Foucault's argument that disciplinary power is always productive. Disciplinary norms not only restrict how individuals can act. These norms also give people capacities for critical thought which can be turned against the very norms that have produced them.

Butler has told us *how* subversive acts are possible. Another question is *why*, in her view, it is desirable to subvert the heterosexual matrix. Why is it a problem if all females are expected to act feminine and all males to act masculine? Part of the answer is that femininity and masculinity are defined hierarchically: generally, becoming feminine means assuming a subordinate position relative to men. For example, learning to act feminine means learning to walk and move in a more constrained and less confident way than men (see Young 1980).

Yet if the problem with gender is only that at present gender is hierarchical, then the solution would be to redefine the genders non-hierarchically. But Butler thinks that having two genders *at all* is a problem. She believes it undesirable for societies to expect males and females to act in systematically different ways. This is undesirable (1) because it means that anyone who does not sufficiently conform to their expected gender will be marginalized and frowned upon – and this is likely to be all of us at some time or other. Moreover, (2) if there are two genders in society, then inevitably they will appear to need one another as complements and so heterosexuality will seem normal and natural. Thus, having two genders means that homo- or bisexual people will be treated as deviant and unnatural.

So Butler objects that gender oppresses women, transgendered people, non-heterosexuals and ultimately all of us – including men – as individuals. Hence Butler believes that it is desirable to try to subvert gender, by acting in ways that show that males can act feminine and females masculine. For if females show that they can act just as masculine as males, then this shows that it is not inevitable that females should have to act in systematically different, distinctively feminine, ways compared to males. And this in effect shows that we could do away with gender.

In an early article, though, Butler says she is in favour not of removing gender but of multiplying the number of genders. She recommends a 'proliferation of genders' (1987: 136). The idea is that, as well as the masculine and feminine genders, there might be others – transgendered and transsexual genders, perhaps, and others besides. But other feminists have argued – convincingly in my view – that multiple genders are impossible. Toril Moi argues that 'the word "gender" refers to the systematic social organization of sexual difference – the imposition of only two general categories of being as normative for all people' (Moi 1999: 28). That is, gender just *is* the norm that males should act masculine and females feminine. So if gender exists, then necessarily there can only be two ways to be gendered: masculine and feminine. Transgendered and transsexed people are not, either actually or potentially, members of a new gender; rather, they cross over (in various ways) the feminine/masculine divide.

But if gender is necessarily two, then when Butler argues that it is undesirable to expect males to act masculine and females feminine, she is arguing that gender should be eradicated, not multiplied. Indeed, in the article in which Butler mentions a 'proliferation of genders', what she actually seems to mean is a proliferation of styles of individual bodily behaviour. She thinks it would be desirable for individuals to develop their own unique styles of bodily activity without being constrained to act either masculine or feminine. She is using the word 'genders' here to mean *genres*, individual styles of bodily action.

To sum up the key points of Butler's approach to gender:

1   Gender only exists insofar as we engage in social practices that are organized by norms about gender. Gender is performative: it only exists as long as it is performed.

2   Different social practices embody different sets of gender norms and the content of each set of norms is constantly changing because individuals always act norms out in slightly different ways. Gender undergoes constant resignification.

3   This diversity of gender norms is limited by a heterosexual matrix of higher-level assumptions that (i) gender must express sex, (ii) femininity and masculinity must be sharply opposed and (iii) heterosexuality is normal because the genders need one another as complements.

4   It is desirable for individuals to subvert this matrix by doing activities that demonstrate that gender is merely a matter of performance. Anyone of any sex can act out any gender; gender need not express sex.

5   Individuals are able to act subversively because social norms make them into responsible, self-critical agents who can reflect on how to act.

6   Ultimately, the aim of subversive activity is to abolish gender: to abolish the idea that males and females must act in systematically different ways.

Based on Butler's claims, we may refine our initial definition of gender. We may now say that **gender** consists of (1) norms of masculine and feminine behaviour which are embodied in social practices, and (2) the habitual ways of acting that people acquire as an effect of those norms.

4. Butler on sex

One of Butler's key ideas is that when we act according to gender norms we do so with our bodies, by acquiring bodily habits. To be feminine is to keep adopting the bodily postures, gestures and movements that a given society takes to be feminine. So we can say that people's engagement in gender practices makes their *bodies* become gendered. Human bodies, after all, are not inert things. Our bodies have – and perhaps largely consist of – habits, and what habits our bodies acquire depends on what activities we have been doing, activities that are constrained by gender norms. So if, following Butler, being masculine consists in having certain habits of behaviour, and if it is our bodies that take on these habits, then being masculine consists in having a certain kind of body. In many contemporary societies bodies of this kind tend to have short hair, to be unsmiling, and to cry rarely.

Moreover, again following Butler, one's sex does not dictate which habitual acts one performs. In principle, if one can avoid the constraints of our sex–gender system, one can be both female and masculine-bodied. This requires not just thinking and acting masculine, but also assuming a masculine sort of body, or a masculine form of embodiment. An example is Brandon Teena, whose life was dramatized in the film *Boys Don't Cry*. Brandon, born Teena Brandon, dressed and acted as a man and for a while succeeded in 'passing' as a man in front of his friends (until these so-called 'friends' find him out and rape and kill him).[4]

For those used to the sex/gender distinction, this talk of *bodies* assuming gender may seem odd. The distinction between biological sex and social gender was initially taken to mean that people's bodies are biologically sexed while their acts and thoughts are gendered. But actually the sex/gender distinction does permit us to speak of gendered bodies. For while the distinction says that people are (usually) biologically male or female, it does not say that bodies are biological or wholly biological entities. The distinction leaves it open that bodies may be just as much cultural as biological entities. That is, bodies may consist to a significant extent of habits and features which result from social practices and norms.

Indeed, Butler suggests that the features of our bodies may be more extensively cultural and less biological than we tend to assume. Once a body has acquired certain characteristics as a result of engaging in practices, it appears as if that body had these characteristics all along. As Butler puts it, 'repeated [bodily] acts . . . congeal over time to produce the appearance of . . . a natural sort of being' (1990a: 33). Gender norms compel bodies to acquire particular masculine or feminine traits which, once acquired, look as if they were innately present all along. Embodied habits come to look like innate features because the history that produced those habits is unknown or forgotten.

Butler not only argues (1) that, having acquired gendered habits, we tend to misperceive these habits (both in ourselves and in others) as innate biological features. She also argues (2) that our claims about the innate, biological features of bodies affect how we act and so what habits we acquire. More specifically, our claims and beliefs about the natures of the two biological sexes encourage us to act in one set of ways if we are male and another if we are female. The result is that human bodies become divided by gender. And, from (1), people's resulting gender-divided traits tend to look innate, reinforcing our belief that the two sexes have different natures.

For example, suppose people believe that part of the innate nature of females is to be weaker – or at least to have less upper-body muscular strength – than males. If so, then females will be discouraged from doing jobs that require this kind of strength such as building work. As a result, females will not learn the right habits for lifting heavy objects etc., and their upper-body muscles will not develop. This reinforces people's initial belief that females are naturally weak. Butler concludes (1993: 30) that whenever we claim to know about the natural features of bodies, our claims have the effect of producing in bodies the very features that we were claiming existed merely naturally.

Here Butler need not be claiming either that we have no biological properties (i.e. that all our bodily properties are produced entirely by culture) or that biological sex does not exist.[5] Her key point is rather that any claims to know about biology have effects on how people act (Butler 1993: 10). For Butler, knowledge-claims about biology and about biological sex are not necessarily false; rather, they are *normative*. They convey or communicate expectations about how people should act.

Yet these arguments have dramatic implications. Earlier, this chapter defined gender as norms about what behaviours are appropriate for males and females, and the masculine and feminine traits which males and females acquire as a result. Yet according to Butler knowledge-claims about sex already contain or convey norms about what behaviours are appropriate for males and females. So she concludes that ' "sex" . . . was always already gender, with the consequence that the distinction between sex and gender turns out to be no distinction at all' (1990a: 7). More precisely, for Butler, *claims* about sex are part of gender. These claims are part of, and do not differ in kind from any other parts of, a society's arsenal of gender norms.

I mentioned in chapter 1 that feminist philosophers have criticized the sex/gender distinction in many ways. We have now encountered another of these criticisms. For Butler, claims about sex are always normative and as such they are no different from gender norms about how men and women should act.

I think we need to qualify Butler's thesis that sex claims are normative and so are part of gender. Claims and beliefs about sex such as 'females are weaker than males' are not *merely* normative. These claims do aim to describe the real biological features of females (e.g. their specific upper-body musculature). But these claims about biology also have normative implications. The belief 'females are weaker than males' implies, given that some jobs require more physical strength than others, that females should avoid – or perhaps be kept out of – those jobs that demand the most strength. So it would be more accurate to say not that claims about sex *are* gender norms but that they *imply* gender norms, i.e. they imply that females/males should act or be treated in certain ways. Meanwhile, gender norms are often justified with reference to the claims about biology which imply them.

Butler also thinks that claims or beliefs about sex *necessarily* are – or, I would say, imply – gender norms. That is, when any claims are made about sex, gender norms always follow from them. If so, then a problem arises. I argued in chapter 1 that there are two biological sexes, that many of people's sex-properties are observable, and that therefore we cannot avoid classifying one another by sex. Now, let us take it that whenever people classify one another by sex, they do so against the background of some general beliefs about what properties female and male individuals have. Following Butler, these beliefs necessarily have normative implications for how females and males should act. It follows that when I classify someone as female or male, my classification implies that this person should act, or can rightly be expected, to act in certain ways. Thus it appears that, if we classify one another by sex, then we will inevitably have two genders as well: we will expect females and males to act in systematically different ways. Yet Butler has plausibly argued that having two genders is undesirable. Does this mean that, after all, we should abandon the practice of classifying one another by sex?

Not necessarily. Suppose that a view of sex like that defended in chapter 1 became generally held – the view that sex is a matter of degree. By this I mean the view that (1) someone can be female or male by having enough but not all of the relevant sex-properties and (2) while having some of the properties of the other sex as well. If we had this view in the background when we classified one another by sex, then our classifications would not imply that all females should act in one set of ways that is systematically different from how all males should act. This implication would not follow, because our classifications would be based on a recognition that females (and males) differ greatly from one another in terms of which sex-properties they have and in the extent to which they have each of these properties. We would also recognize that females and males can be more or less similar to one another physically. So we would have no reason to expect all females to act alike and all males to act alike. In this situation, we *could* classify one another by sex without this leading to an – undesirably – gender-divided society.

Where does this leave Butler's arguments regarding sex? I think Butler is right that bodies become gendered by acting in line with conventional practices and acquiring certain habits as a result. I also think she is right that we are prone to mistake gendered habits for innate features. But when she says that claims about sex are always normative and so always part of gender, it would be more accurate to say that (1) sex claims imply gender norms and (2) that they only do so if we assume that maleness and femaleness are sharply opposed. Presently we *do* tend to assume this, Butler rightly notes. But if instead we believed sex to be a matter of degree, then neither our beliefs about sex nor our acts of sex classification would imply gender norms.

Again, then, I conclude that feminists may affirm that most bodies are biologically sexed. Now if people indeed have biological sex-properties, and if – following Butler – people take on gender at a bodily level, then presumably people's sex-properties must affect the ways in which their bodies can take on gender norms. But exactly what effects do sex-properties have, and how might gendered habits affect these sex-properties in turn?

Before we can answer these questions, we need to deepen our grasp of the process by which bodies take on gender. Butler's view that bodies take on gender presupposes that bodies have a kind of practical intelligence (or are the seat of our practical intelligence) such that they can be informed by and can learn habits from culture. Traditionally, though, philosophers – notably Descartes – believed that only minds can think, understand meanings and affirm beliefs, while bodies are merely 'extended'. On this view, bodies are unintelligent things that occupy and move within regions of space, being moved either by other bodies or – somehow – by the minds 'within' them. Butler rejects this view of mind and body, as have many feminist philosophers. We must see how feminist philosophers have rethought the nature of the body and have, in the process, developed the idea that gender is necessarily taken on at a bodily level.

5. Feminist philosophy of the body

Most recent feminist philosophical work on the body tends in one of two directions. Some work is more empirical. It studies how bodies become feminine in different ways within different cultural contexts where different sets of gender norms apply. (For a survey, see Schiebinger 2000.) Other work is more conceptual, thinking about the general nature of the processes by which bodies become gendered, and about what bodies must be like such that they can assume gender. This empirical/conceptual distinction is not sharp, though. To get some idea of the range of feminist philosophical work on the body, we can look at the ideas of just three of the many authors working in this area: Susan Bordo, Moira Gatens and Shannon Sullivan. (I will spend most time on Gatens, because her work on the body also makes important criticisms of the sex/gender distinction.)

(1) *Susan Bordo's Unbearable Weight* (1993) is partly empirical and partly conceptual. She studies contemporary ideals of feminine slenderness and investigates how women strive to embody these ideals. It is often said that media images of thin women have driven many women and girls to become obsessed with dieting and to develop eating disorders such as anorexia. Bordo argues that this happens because these media images become models by which women measure and discipline themselves. But why, she asks, *are* modern western cultures so full of these images, and how do these images come to exert disciplinary power over women?

Drawing on writings by anorexics, Bordo argues that anorexia expresses three connected views that are deeply ingrained in western culture and that go back to Descartes' time:

i   The body is seen as different from the self, which is equated with the mind.
ii   The body is seen as voracious and unruly, in need of control.
iii The body is seen as female – many of the anorexics Bordo studied associated the body specifically with their mothers, who were often quite traditional and full-figured women.

Bordo concludes that the anorexic woman's body embodies a deep-rooted cultural ideal, the ideal of having mental control over one's 'female' body. In a less extreme form, thin women's bodies embody or 'crystallize' the same ideal. After all, most western women who are thin have to work at it, by exercising self-control – in a cultural context where self-control means the mind controlling the female-associated body.

(2) The Australian feminist *Moira Gatens*'s many writings on the nature of the body emerge out of her article 'A Critique of the Sex/Gender Distinction' (1983). Here Gatens argues against using the sex/gender distinction and proposes an alternative way of thinking about the relation between embodiment and society, centred on the concept of the **imaginary body**. This concept has several elements.

Gatens believes that our most basic form of experience is *perception* (1983: 8) of the world with our senses, and that we cannot perceive without experiencing ourselves to be embodied. She is drawing on arguments made by Merleau-Ponty (1945). Merleau-Ponty argues that perception is our most basic form of experience, and that I cannot perceive unless I see some things as nearer or further away than others, other things as below or above others. In turn, I cannot make sense of anything being near, above, below (etc.) anything else unless I feel able to navigate in space. But I can only feel able to navigate in space if I experience myself to have a body that is located, and can move, within space. So, Merleau-Ponty concludes, those who have experience necessarily experience themselves to be embodied. So all our experience must include a dimension of awareness of our own bodies, even though this awareness is not fully conscious (Merleau-Ponty 1945: 98–102. Taylor 1979 clearly reconstructs Merleau-Ponty's arguments here.)

According to Merleau-Ponty, to be aware of my body in space I must be aware of what actions and movements the parts of my body can do or make in relation to one another and to the surrounding environment. In sum, I must have a **body-image** – an inner (but not fully conscious) map of my body with respect to its possibilities for action within its environment.[6] My body-image guides what actual patterns of behaviour I can engage in. Consider the phenomenon of 'phantom limb'. This occurs when someone who has had a limb amputated feels, and tries to act, as if it is still there. Over time, this person has, as a body, built up an implicit self-image or internal 'map' of their body's possibilities for action which has not yet adapted to the amputation. This person will only adjust their map gradually, without their conscious awareness, as they relearn to move and handle things without the limb.

Gatens concludes that our bodies are always imaginary:

i   in that each of us always operates with a largely unconscious image, or map, of our body – this is our *body-image*.

She then adds three further senses in which our bodies are imaginary:

ii   We begin building up our body-image in infancy, and at that time the image contains a large element of *fantasy*. Infants imagine their bodies to be more self-controlled and competent than they really are. Throughout life, our body-images continue to have a fantasy element: we imagine our bodies to be more coherent and competent than they generally are.[7]

iii   In 'mapping' the different parts of our bodies, we also give them varying levels of *emotional* significance (see Alsop, Fitzsimons and Lennon 2002: ch. 7). For instance, most women probably feel more deeply about their breasts and bellies than their toes or knees.

iv   In forming one's body-image, one cannot avoid drawing on *publicly available ideas* about the biological properties of one's body. For example, when a girl starts menstruating, she needs to adapt her body-image to this fact, which involves drawing on available ideas about menstruation – as embarrassing and dirty, or a welcome sign of fertility. These ideas will affect how she feels about her menstruating body. Our publicly shared ideas about bodies make up what Gatens calls a **social imaginary** – 'a loosely connected set of images embedded in social practices [and] literary and philosophical texts' (Gatens and Lloyd 1998: 151). So our bodies are imaginary in a fourth sense that we construct our 'maps' of our bodies using shared images and ideas.

Gatens accepts that bodies have biological properties independently of culture. But she is reluctant to say that any of these biological properties in themselves make people male or female. She says: 'the biological determination of sex is . . . not clear and we must acknowledge sex as a continuum' (Gatens 1983: 19). However, Gatens argues, our social imaginary assumes that everyone is either male or female. As a result, people build up body-images that give special importance to those biological properties which fit in with social ideas about maleness and femaleness (1983: 9–10). Against this cultural backdrop, for example, menstruation becomes very important within girls' and women's body-images because it seems to give special confirmation that they are female.

By interpreting their biological properties in terms of a cultural imaginary of male/female difference, then, people acquire body-images as male or female. These body-images then guide people to acquire male or female habits and bodily characteristics, e.g. strength or weakness. So for Gatens maleness and femaleness are not biologically given but culturally acquired properties. (Section 6 will argue that she is wrong about this.) But, although maleness and femaleness are culturally acquired, they are properties that we acquire at a bodily and not narrowly mental level.

I set out in this section to see how feminist philosophers have thought about the nature of the body and about the process by which bodies become gendered. But Gatens in fact rejects the concept of gender. She puts forward the concept of the social imaginary as an alternative to it. So, unlike Butler, she does not say that our bodily habits and (many of our) bodily features are shaped by norms of femininity and masculinity. Rather, Gatens says that our bodily habits and bodily features are shaped by social imaginary ideas about the significance of various biological properties. Here I want to turn aside from introducing feminist approaches to the body to argue that Gatens is wrong to reject the concept of gender.

6. Gender and imaginary bodies

I suggest that Gatens is wrong to reject the concept of gender because this concept captures an aspect of social life which the concept of the imaginary does not. The concept of gender captures the fact that we have a set of social norms specifying how people who have certain biological properties (who are male or female) should act (i.e. masculine or feminine, respectively). These norms do not specify what the cultural and emotional significance is of the biological properties of maleness and femaleness in themselves. Rather, gender norms specify how people should act and what roles they should occupy given that they have certain biological properties. Two examples – ideas about menstruation and about genius – will clarify this.

1   Our cultural imaginary gives menstruation a rich range of cultural connotations – connotations of fertility, uncleanliness, and danger amongst others (Grosz 1994: 205). Menstruation therefore takes on a lot of emotional importance within the body-image of many girls and women. On the other hand, most of our social institutions, especially workplaces, embody a norm that menstruating women should keep their periods out of sight and should maintain high levels of personal hygiene (Martin 1987: 93–101; Young 2005: 113–17). In this case gender norms and imaginary ideas about the significance of biology are in tension with one another. Gender norms state that females should keep their periods out of sight, while the imaginary specifies that menstruation is very important and emotionally meaningful. That gender norms and imaginary ideas can clash in this way shows that they are different.

2   Christine Battersby (1989: ch. 1) shows that in the late eighteenth century the Romantics produced a new view of 'genius' as a kind of creativity that emerges out of a person's natural instincts and emotions. The gender norms of the time also specified that acting 'naturally' – from instincts or emotions – was feminine. So in praising genius, the Romantics were placing new value on these 'feminine' traits. Yet the Romantics did not value the female body. They only valued feminine traits when these occurred in male-bodied people – only 'feminine' males like Coleridge or Shelley could be 'geniuses'. Thus, gender norms of femininity changed – so that feminine traits gained in value – but negative images of the female body and its worth remained unchanged. This confirms, again, that gender norms and imaginary ideas differ.

So we can distinguish analytically between gender norms and imaginary ideas around biology. Of course, in practice they shape one another. Gender norms are often justified with reference to imaginary ideas. Often it only makes sense to say that people should act in certain ways given that they have physical properties *because* those properties are presumed to have a certain imaginary significance. For example, expecting males to be more creative or dynamic than females given that males have penises only makes sense if one holds the – imaginary – assumption that penises are the seat of creative vitality. Still, although gender norms and imaginary ideas shape and reinforce one another, we need to distinguish conceptually between them in order to analyse in detail *how* they support one another. So – against Gatens, who wishes to reject the concept of gender – it benefits feminist philosophers to work with both concepts.

7. Feminist philosophy of the body (continued)

We can now return to our review of some feminist philosophical approaches to the body. So far we have looked briefly at (1) *Bordo* and (2) *Gatens*. However, I have only looked at Gatens's earlier work. We should take note, briefly, of how her later work (Gatens 1992, 1996a) revises her account of imaginary bodies.

In this later work, Gatens no longer argues that the cultural imaginary shapes what habits and capacities bodies acquire. Rather, Gatens now says that social institutions, and the power relations they embody, shape what activities bodies do and so what powers and capacities bodies develop. These institutions *correspond* to the cultural imaginary which, Gatens now says, shapes our minds – our thoughts and emotions. So the cultural imaginary shapes minds into 'male' and 'female' minds, while correspondingly institutions shape bodies into two sexes with different sets of powers and capacities – more limited powers in women's case, more extensive powers in men's case. Here Gatens still thinks (as she did in her earlier work) that sex is not a set of biologically given properties but a set of abilities that bodies acquire as an effect of society.

(3) *Shannon Sullivan*, in *Living Across and Through Skins* (2001), denies that minds and bodies are independent items. She holds instead that each body is composed of a particular set of habits. If a body becomes conscious of the meaning of its habits, then it has acquired mind as well as being a body. What habits a body forms depends on the customs and environment shaping its patterns of activity. At the same time these customs only exist insofar as bodies learn to act habitually in ways that maintain those customs.

Sullivan holds that ideals of gender are among the cultural conditions that currently form bodies. Because of these conditions, bodies take on male or female habits, and thereby become male or female. Sullivan is reluctant to think that bodies are born with any properties, such as male or female properties, that could affect how these bodies take on habits. To think that bodies have such properties, Sullivan argues, would entail thinking that bodies have a kernel of inborn properties that the social environment cannot affect. Sullivan, instead, claims that bodies' relation to their environments is 'transactional'. She means that it is an ongoing process in which every aspect of bodies is formed under the influence of their cultural environments (Sullivan 2001: 16, 45).

Sullivan, then, holds that being male or female results from absorbing cultural ideals into one's body. She therefore uses the word 'sex' to mean, roughly, 'gender ideals which have been absorbed into the body' (see Sullivan 2001: 58). Rather like Sullivan, the later Gatens uses 'sex' to mean 'social power relations which have been absorbed into the body'. This shows us that there is a tendency in some recent feminist philosophy to use 'sex' to mean, roughly, 'embodied gender' or 'embodied power relations' – rather than, as it originally meant, the biological properties that make people male or female.

Why has this tendency arisen? Well, we saw earlier that the sex/gender distinction was initially taken to mean that sex is a property of the body while gender is a property of society, minds and human actions. Yet feminist philosophers noticed that social ideals of gender get absorbed into and shape bodies as well as minds. So it can rightly be said that bodies are or become 'gendered'. But then it also becomes intelligible to say that social norms that have been absorbed into a body are its 'sex', since these norms have actually become part of that body's physical character.

The tendency to use 'sex' to mean embodied gender, or embodied power relations, is reinforced by the tendency in some recent feminist work on the body to deny that biological sex exists. This denial comes in stronger and weaker forms. The stronger form (Sullivan) denies that bodies have any inborn biological properties. The weaker form (Gatens, Warnke) accepts that we have biological properties but denies that these properties in themselves make bodies male or female. I argued against this weaker claim in chapter 1. I am also unconvinced by Sullivan's stronger argument, because – contrary to Sullivan – I believe that bodies can be born with biological properties, including biological sex-properties, without those properties having to be unchangeable. I will argue for this belief in the next section. Since I am unconvinced by either the stronger or weaker arguments against biological sex, I think we should continue to believe that there are clusters of biological properties which are relevant to sex.

Yet if biological sex does indeed exist, then it makes sense to use the word 'sex' to refer to it instead of using 'sex' to refer to embodied gender, which is actually best described *as* 'embodied gender'. Moreover, if sex-properties indeed exist then they must exert some influence on gender. Granting Butler's claim that we take on gender by taking part in conventional practices, one's sex must influence one's gender by affecting how one takes on gender practically. Section 8 sketches an account of how sex affects our bodily taking on of gender.

8. Sex, gender and the body

Taking it that each body has biological properties, including sex-properties, these must affect the ways in which that body is able to carry out conventional practices. This, in turn, will affect the particular form of the gendered habits and traits that that body assumes. Consider masculine females: as chapter 1 argued, different females have each of the properties that are relevant to femaleness to a greater or lesser degree. Some females are broad-shouldered, small-breasted, lean and tall. They will be able to carry out masculine practices in different ways to small, narrow-shouldered, larger-breasted females. If females of the latter kind want to act masculine at the level of their bodies, they will probably find themselves enacting some form of masculinity which is not culturally dominant. One can change what kind of masculinity one is biologically able to enact, for instance by taking synthetic hormones to increase one's muscle density.

Now, Gatens has shown that one cannot engage in habitual practices unless one simultaneously builds up a body-image. This is because having (and adjusting) an inner 'map' of one's body is a precondition of being able to move in space and hence to build up patterns of habitual activity. People's body-images draw on the cultural imaginary. But the particular biological nature of an individual's body parts also affects what imaginary significance those body parts can assume. Consider breasts. Our cultural imaginary often links large breasts with intellectual and practical incompetence (Bordo 1993: 178–9). Therefore, a woman with large breasts might experience them as a source of frustration and misrecognition. A different woman might feel that her small breasts make her a competent agent and yet not sufficiently female. So bodies' biological properties, including their sex-properties, affect what imaginary meanings bodies can assume. Because these meanings guide how bodies act, by affecting those meanings biological properties again affect how bodies perform gender practices.

The meanings, habits and characteristics of bodies, then, are affected by both sex and gender. On the one hand, the habits and features of a body result from its taking on of gender. On the other hand, how that body takes on gender is itself affected both by that body's sex-properties and by its imaginary meanings which, again, must take account of – and in that sense are affected by – the body's sex-properties. To say that sex necessarily affects how we assume gender is not to revert to the view that a person's gender must express their sex. As Butler says, whether one is masculine or feminine (or neither) depends on what social practices one engages in. Nonetheless, people carry out gendered practices in different ways depending on what meanings and forms of action are possible given their biological properties, including their sex-properties.

In turn, the specific gendered habits and traits that bodies take on can, and regularly do, alter most of their sex-properties. Diet, stress, and activity levels all alter bodies' levels of hormones and (at least some of) their sex characteristics. For instance, exercise reduces the size of female breasts and hips – think of the physiology of female athletes. The same factors can also affect the gonads: some – controversial – research suggests that British children are starting puberty as early as seven due to higher hormone levels caused by richer diets, while at the other extreme, anorexia can cause menstruation to stop. And one can also alter one's sex-properties chemically or through surgery, for instance by having breast implants or breast reduction surgery. Moreover, a body's imaginary meanings also indirectly alter its sex-properties, by affecting the gender activities that a body can engage in.

However sex-properties get changed as a result of gendered habits, these changed properties in turn affect how the body goes on to enact norms and to assume meanings. This means that the relation between sex and gender is – to use Sullivan's helpful term – 'transactional'. That is, this relation takes the form of an ongoing process by which, over time, many of the body's biological properties are altered to at least some degree. Even if some biological properties (e.g. the chromosomes) are never directly altered, they will still be altered in the indirect sense that they will come to have very different effects on the body at different times, because they can only ever affect the body in concert with other properties which *do* undergo gradual alteration.

9. Review and conclusion

Feminist thought about gender began with the idea that people become gendered masculine or feminine as a result of acting on, and internalizing, social norms that specify what behaviour is appropriate for people of their sex. But feminists needed to combine the concept of gender with a theory of the power relations between men and women. One such theory was the radical feminist view that men dominate women. By the 1980s this had largely given way to the view, informed by Foucault, that in modern societies masculine power takes multiple forms, each embodied in particular institutions. Building on this, Butler argued that gender is performative: it results from individuals carrying out conventional practices and taking on habits at a bodily level.

From Butler, we can conclude that **gender** consists of (1) norms which are embodied in social practices and which regulate masculine and feminine behaviour, (2) the habitual ways of acting that people acquire because of those norms, and (3) the bodily features that people acquire because of these habitual ways of acting. We can also take from Gatens the idea that, in order to acquire bodily habits, we must build up images of our bodies which draw on cultural ideas about male and female biology. Thus, cultural ideas about the meaning of biological sex interact with norms regarding gender.

This chapter has defended the sex/gender distinction from several criticisms:

1   Butler argued that claims about sex are necessarily normative and as such *are* gender norms. Against this I argued that claims about sex imply gender norms, and do so not necessarily but only given the – false – belief that maleness and femaleness are sharply opposed.
2   Gatens proposed to replace the concept of gender with the concept of the social imaginary. I instead argued for a distinction between (i) ideas about the imaginary meanings of biological features and (ii) norms about what actions and social roles are appropriate for people who have certain biological features.
3   Even though gender ideals become absorbed into the physical features and flesh of bodies, I still think these resulting features are best understood *as* 'gendered' and not as 'sex'. The term 'sex' is

best used to refer to biological sex-properties which, I believe, exist, affect, and are affected by how we take on gender.

As a whole, feminist thinking about gender bears on such existing areas of philosophy as:

1   Social philosophy, the branch of philosophy which studies social life and phenomena. Feminist inquiry into gender has produced insights into many components of social life – power, practices, norms, and habits. Feminists have also suggested new frameworks for understanding social life as a whole, e.g. the idea that it is performative or is structured by imaginaries.

2   Philosophical thinking about the self. Is Butler right that one cannot understand oneself to have a 'self' without seeing that self as either masculine or feminine, depending on which practices one has been engaging in? Is Gatens right that our most basic sense of ourselves as individuals is an 'imaginary' sense of our bodies and of their powers and their cultural and emotional significance? As these questions show, feminist writers on the self generally explore 'the social, relational, emotional and bodily dimensions of selfhood' (Mackenzie 1998). These feminist writers are critical of how non-feminist philosophers of mind tend to focus

   i   on the mind and cognition rather than the body and emotion;
   ii   and on abstract metaphysical questions about personal identity, such as what makes someone the same person over time. Feminist writers generally focus on more concrete questions about how one's sense of self is affected by the kind of body one has and by how others perceive that kind of body.

As well as opening up inquiry into these neglected aspects of selfhood, feminist thinking about gender has generated a whole new area of philosophical inquiry: philosophy of gender. This emerging field encompasses the following questions among others: What is gender? Is gender mental or bodily, or is this a false opposition? Does gender exist only to the extent that we perform it? Should the concept of gender be replaced or supplemented by the concept of the imaginary body? And should feminists aim to redefine the genders, to eradicate gender altogether, or to bring about a range of genders beyond the existing two?

Notes

1 As an example of this 'hypersexualization' Chanter mentions Saarjite Baartman, or the 'Hottentot Venus' as she became known. Baartman was an African woman who was publicly exhibited in nineteenth-century England on account of her supposedly oversized buttocks, and whose supposedly enlarged genitals were dissected and studied after her death by scientists researching 'primitive' sexuality. (On Baartman, see http://www.english.emory.edu/Bahri/Exhibition.html.)

2 Butler drops the term 'heterosexual matrix' after *Gender Trouble*. But she continues to believe that there is a ruling set of ideas which specifies that sexuality should express gender and that gender should express sex.

3 Why is it assumed that maleness and femaleness must be opposed? The heterosexual matrix is circular here. It reasons that because the genders must be opposed, and because gender expresses sex, the sexes must be opposed in character as well (Butler 1987).

4 Halberstam (1998) gives many examples of masculine females in literature and film.

5 However, at times Butler seems, like Warnke, to believe that biology in itself does not make us sexed and that the belief in sex is an effect of gender norms.

6 The phrase of Merleau-Ponty's that is translated (in Merleau-Ponty 1945: 98) as 'body-image' is *schema corporel* – 'corporeal schema'. This translation is potentially misleading, because some scholars think that Merleau-Ponty actually distinguishes between a person's corporeal schema – their practical and immediately given awareness of their body and its mobility in space – and their body-image – which results from conscious ideas and thought about one's body. However, other scholars such as Weiss (1999: 2) think that Merleau-Ponty 'uses the words body image and corporeal schema fairly interchangeably'. In any case, feminist philosophers who use the concept of body-images generally do not distinguish these from corporeal schemata. This is because (as we will see with respect to Gatens) these feminist philosophers think that our awareness of our bodies is never really immediate but is always filtered, if not through conscious thought exactly, then at least through shared cultural ideas and thoughts about bodies.

7 Here Gatens is influenced by the psychoanalytic thinker Jacques Lacan, who claims that infants imagine their bodies to be more capable of self-controlled movement than they are biologically. See chapter 4, section 2.

Further Reading

Feminism and Foucault   Bartky 1990: ch. 5 draws on Foucault to study how women are disciplined to regulate their bodies.

Butler on gender   All Butler's writings are difficult, but Butler 1991 is a fairly self-contained introduction to her approach to gender. Butler 2004 is a recent more accessible set of essays. Alsop, Fitzsimons and Lennon 2002: ch. 4 is a clear secondary account.

Feminist philosophy of body   Bordo 1993: 139–64; Gatens 1983 is a difficult but important article. Another major book in this area is Grosz 1994.

3 Sexuality

1. Sexuality and feminist philosophy

An individual's **sexuality** consists of their sexual desires and feelings, and the activities and relationships into which that individual enters because of those desires and feelings. What makes certain desires, feelings and activities sexual? This will be a central question in this chapter, but for now, we may say that sexual desires are desires for bodily pleasures of a particular kind. (Which kind is something this chapter aims to clarify.) Sexual feelings are feelings of, or about, this kind of bodily pleasure. And sexual activities are activities in which one engages with the aim of experiencing bodily pleasures of this kind or giving pleasures of this kind to others. People differ as to what kinds of sexual activities they prefer. People also differ as to whether they typically desire people of the same sex, the opposite sex, or both – in other words, people differ as to whether their sexual orientation is heterosexual, homosexual or bisexual.

This definition of sexuality clarifies that there is an analytical distinction between (1) a person's *sexuality* and (2) their biological *sex* – male or female – and (3) their socially produced *gender* – masculine or feminine. Just as someone can be female without necessarily having to be feminine, so someone can be either female or feminine without necessarily having to desire men.

This distinction between sex, gender and sexuality has not always been upheld. The term 'sexuality' only emerged in the nineteenth century. Before then, the single word 'sex' – which dates from the sixteenth century – referred indiscriminately to both sexual activity and the biological difference between males and females. The word 'sex' thus embodied an assumption that sexual activity could only take place between males and females. As a result, people have often assumed that being sexually attracted to women is a male or masculine trait while being attracted to men is a female or feminine trait.

These assumptions gave rise to the idea, widespread in the late nineteenth and early twentieth centuries, that homosexuals are 'inverts' – people whose personality traits are the opposite or 'inverse' of those normally expected of people of their sex. On this view, gay men must, because they desire men, be effeminate; lesbians, because they desire women, must have masculine traits. One 1922 author claimed that: 'Homosexual women have a well-marked tendency toward male habits and modes of dress. They smoke, drink . . . cut their hair short. . .' (see Clark 1987: 205). This idea of inversion rested on a failure to distinguish between having a particular sex (male or female), having a particular gender (masculine or feminine), and having a particular kind of sexuality (directed towards people of the same or the opposite sex).

This failure to distinguish between sex, gender and sexuality has influenced social activities and institutions so that they often treat sex, gender and sexuality as if they were inseparably connected. In principle one can be female and desire women, but in practice everyone is expected to have the sexuality that is assumed to 'fit' their sex and gender. Because sex, gender and sexuality really have become so closely connected, feminist philosophers in thinking about sex and gender have had to address sexuality too.

Yet whereas feminists pioneered philosophical inquiry into the nature of sex and gender, there is a long history of philosophical thought about sexuality, going back at least as far as Plato (although he speaks not of 'sexuality' but of 'eros'). This history of thought includes the theory of sexuality developed by Freud and his psychoanalytic followers. In contemporary Anglo-American philosophy too, the philosophy of sex is a growing area. As Alan Soble (1998) explains, philosophers of sex look at three main sorts of questions: (1) conceptual questions about what it is that makes some feelings, desires, acts and pleasures specifically sexual; (2) metaphysical questions about the meaning that sexuality has for us and its relation to other human activities and emotions; (3) ethical questions about what kinds of sexual activity are permissible.

Among these various approaches to sexuality, feminist thought about sexuality is distinctive in focusing on how sexuality is shaped by unequal power relations between men and women. Feminists ask how our sexual desires, feelings and activities might change if they were no longer shaped by these unequal power relations. This does not mean that feminists are interested only in ethical questions about sexuality, such as which sexual practices are consistent with treating people as equals. Thinking about the connection between sexuality and power leads into conceptual and metaphysical questions about sexuality. For example, some feminist philosophers have argued that unequal power relations between men and women influence people's ideas about what makes certain acts specifically sexual. These power relations lead people to assume that sexual acts are acts of male-dominated heterosexual intercourse. Feminists have rejected this idea of sex both because it is tied to unequal power relations and because it is implausibly narrow. Sex acts need not even involve the genitals, let alone heterosexual intercourse. But what, then, *does* make some acts and feelings sexual? Some feminists have suggested that sexual feelings and acts are ones that communicate emotions and create intimacy. But does this define too many of our feelings and acts as sexual?

We will return to these questions. For now, we should note another feature of feminist thinking about sexuality. As Jacquelyn Zita (1998b) points out, many of those contributing to this field are not professional philosophers. Some are writers and artists who explore female sexuality through novels and other artworks. Others are academics but work in disciplines other than philosophy such as law, literary theory or cultural studies. And many of the most important questions about sexuality and male power were raised by feminist activists in the context of heated debates about sexuality which took place within feminist political movements in the 1970s and 1980s. These debates are known as the 'feminist sexuality debates'. Although most of those who took part in these debates were not professional philosophers, they still 'work[ed] with philosophical assumptions about the nature of sexuality, power, and freedom', as Ann Ferguson says (1984: 107). The opposing positions within the feminist sexuality debates rely on implicitly philosophical arguments about what sexuality is, its place in human life, and how it should be practised. Sections 2–5 reconstruct these debates and the arguments about sexuality which were at stake in them.

2. Must feminists be lesbians?

The first set of feminist sexuality debates took place in the 1970s, especially in Britain, France and the United States. They concerned **political lesbianism**, a political position that arose out of radical feminism. For radical feminists, men as a group dominate women and male domination is the fundamental organizing feature of all societies. Those who advocated 'political lesbianism' added that what above all preserves male dominance is the fact that women are forced to enter into heterosexual relationships. This forces women to become loyal to the men with whom they have relationships. This loyalty makes it impossible for women to reject the male domination that, as radical feminists see it, inevitably colours these relationships. As a result, women feel equally unable to reject the same domination as it exists in society as a whole. Charlotte Bunch (1972), the Leeds Revolutionary Feminist Group (1981) and the Radicalesbians (1970) – amongst others – concluded that women can successfully reject male-dominated society only by becoming lesbians.

The idea that someone might choose to become a lesbian on political grounds may seem odd. One's sexuality seems to be something over which one has little control. It usually feels as if it is just in one's nature to be heterosexual, homosexual or bisexual. The political lesbian claim is that these appearances simplify a more complex reality. Our social institutions make heterosexuality 'compulsory' (as the US poet and feminist thinker Adrienne Rich puts it). 'Compulsory' may seem rather strong. Certainly, most of the films and advertisements that feature couples or show sex acts depict heterosexual couples and heterosexual sex acts, which conveys a message that heterosexuality is normal and natural. But this suggests that institutions encourage, rather than strictly enforce, heterosexuality. Arguably, though, cultural artefacts which presume that heterosexuality is the norm are part of a whole continuum of practices and institutions some of which *do* involve physical force (e.g. gay- and lesbian-bashing) or which do literally prohibit homosexual sex (some US states banned sodomy up until 2003. Today heterosexual couples can legally marry in most countries whereas homosexual couples cannot). Because the institutions which merely encourage heterosexuality are on this continuum with institutions that do enforce or compel heterosexuality, Rich refers to the whole continuum as forming a system of **compulsory heterosexuality**. It follows that heterosexual desires can never be merely natural, because they also have political support and sanction from this system of compulsory heterosexuality.

Advocates of political lesbianism claim that compulsory heterosexuality maintains male domination. This claim can be interpreted in stronger and weaker ways. The stronger version is that men deliberately created and uphold compulsory heterosexuality in order to enforce their domination over women. The weaker version is that this system benefits men by enabling them to dominate women, but that men did not deliberately create this system. Rather, (on this second view) the system of compulsory heterosexuality has built up due to a range of causes, and it now persists partly just because it has been around for so long, and partly because it benefits men to leave it unchanged. In either case, political lesbians agree that the first step towards overthrowing this system is for women to break out of sexual relationships with men. On this view, choosing one's sexuality on political grounds is not odd: sexuality is always a political matter anyway, but feminists need to resist and challenge the heterosexist – and male-dominant – political institutions that currently surround it.

One problem with these claims is that gay and bisexual men do not obviously benefit from heterosexuality being 'compulsory'. To solve this problem, Sarah Hoagland (1988: 28) argues that prohibiting men from having non-heterosexual sex is intended to protect men from the shame of occupying (what patriarchal societies see as) the 'female', subordinate position during sex. Thus, political lesbianism sees the oppression of gay men as a side-effect of a more basic subordination of women.

Another problem is that political lesbianism implies that all feminists must be or become lesbians to be consistently feminist. A woman who is in a heterosexual relationship cannot fully reject male domination and, it seems, must be an inferior, half-hearted, feminist. But if being a feminist means having to abandon heterosexual relationships, then, since most women are (for whatever reasons) currently in heterosexual relationships, relatively few women are likely to become feminists.

Rich tries to solve this problem in her article 'Compulsory Heterosexuality and Lesbian Existence' (1980). She accepts the political lesbian view that compulsory heterosexuality exists in the service of male domination (Rich 1980: 647). But Rich goes beyond political lesbianism by drawing on Nancy Chodorow's ideas. Chodorow holds that in almost all societies women's role is to care for young children at home. As a result, Chodorow claims, mothers encourage their daughters to become properly feminine by remaining emotionally close to their mothers and attuned to the close caring relationships that take place in the home. Hence, Chodorow concludes (1978: 193), girls tend to form deep, close bonds with their mothers which last throughout their lives.

It is doubtful whether all mother/daughter relationships take the form Chodorow claims they do (see chapter 5, section 4). Nonetheless, Rich uses Chodorow's claims to argue that women tend to find their relationships with other women – who remind them of their mothers – the deepest and most emotionally meaningful relationships that they have. Effectively forced into heterosexual relationships, Rich says, many women lead a 'double-life' in which their friendships or associations with women are what they most value. Women's deep feelings for one another are not always overtly sexual, Rich claims, but they are all on a **lesbian continuum**. Sometimes these feelings are overtly sexual, sometimes women desire close but non-sexual physical contact with other women, and sometimes women only feel affection for one another. But the differences here are not sharp.

With the concept of the lesbian continuum, Rich aims to revise political lesbianism so that it does not imply that heterosexual women must be inferior feminists. For Rich, *all* women – both lesbians and heterosexual women – exist on the lesbian continuum, so no woman is fully absorbed in relationships of male dominance. Effectively, Rich expands the category 'lesbian' to include heterosexual women.

Rich's position has at least three problems.

1   She allows that heterosexual women can be feminists only insofar as they come close to being lesbians. She still does not think that heterosexuality in itself is compatible with rejecting male domination.

2   Rich over-extends the category 'lesbian'. On Rich's definition, it seems that even males could be lesbians if they retained close bonds with their mothers, felt deeply related to women, and joined in women's efforts to resist patriarchy (Zita 1998a: 90–1).[1]

3   By extending the category of lesbianism to cover affectionate relationships between women, Rich implies that lesbianism is not

essentially about women having sex with other women. But surely lesbianism *is* essentially about sex.

However, this last criticism assumes that sex consists of acts of physical, genital, contact. Rich would object that this view of sex is not true to women's experience. Implicit in her idea of the lesbian continuum is the further idea that women see no sharp division between sexual and non-sexual feelings about other people. Women, Rich thinks, perceive sexual activity to be 'a form of expression between people that creates bonds and communicates emotion' (Ferguson 1984: 108). People can also share and communicate emotions in other ways – by walking, talking or eating together, for instance. So because women see sexual activity as primarily about emotional intimacy, they do not feel that their sexual activities are sharply distinguished from these other activities that communicate emotions and create intimacy. Women hold what Ferguson calls a 'primacy of intimacy' conception of sexuality.

Some arguments made by Marilyn Frye, though, suggest that the 'intimacy' conception of sexuality is not really available to anyone in present-day society. Frye argues that a particular understanding of sexuality is central to this society, and on this understanding emotional intimacy is just not of primary importance in sex. Rather, because our society is based on male domination, sexuality is thought to consist in 'male-dominant, female-subordinate genital intercourse' (Frye 1983: 129). The *Chambers Concise Dictionary* does indeed define sex as 'sexual intercourse' and sexual intercourse as 'the uniting of sexual organs, especially involving the insertion of the male penis into the female vagina and the release of sperm'.

Frye (1990) also argues that because the standard view in our society is that sex consists of acts of male-dominant heterosexual intercourse, lesbian sex cannot be recognized as sex at all. For Frye, it is not surprising that people sometimes wonder what lesbians do sexually. An example is the man in Joanna Russ's science-fiction novel *The Female Man* who, meeting some women whom he takes to be lesbians, 'stares rudely, unable to conceal it: *What are they? What do they do? Do they screw each other? What does it feel like?*' (Russ 1975: 174).

Frye suggests that lesbians need to move beyond the conceptual vocabulary of sex, and to create new words and concepts that can express the meanings of lesbian 'arousal, bodily play, passion and relational adventure' (Frye 1990: 312). Lesbians may need to express their erotic feelings through something like an 'intimacy' conception of sexuality, then, but Frye denies that any such conception can yet exist.[2] Moreover, Frye thinks that if such a conception arose it would not be a conception of *sexuality*, because sexuality just means male-dominant heterosexual intercourse. To make intimacy important would be to move away from the concept of sexuality altogether.

In general, the radical feminist writings considered so far suggest that our society is patriarchal and shapes sexuality in two main ways. (1) Heterosexuality is made compulsory and this has the effect of tying women to relationships with men in which men dominate them, sexually and otherwise. (2) Sexual acts are taken to be acts of male-dominant heterosexual intercourse. Women and/or lesbians, though, need to understand their 'sexual' feelings and acts in terms of not the existing concept of sex but an alternative set of ideas centred on intimacy. Rich believes that insofar as women are on the lesbian continuum they already have this concept of intimacy. Frye, in contrast, believes that women have yet to create it.

These radical feminist accounts of sexuality make some important points, for instance that sexuality is often assumed, too narrowly, to consist in male-dominant heterosexual intercourse. But on the whole these accounts probably sound dated. They do not take discrimination against gay men seriously enough, nor do they allow that women could ever have heterosexual relationships without thereby succumbing to male domination. Two further problems are:

1   To call heterosexuality 'compulsory' is to describe the whole continuum of pro-heterosexuality institutions in terms that apply only to one end of it – the end where legal prohibition or physical force is used against homosexuality. Some theorists (e.g. Butler 1990a) think a more accurate way to describe the whole continuum is to say that heterosexuality is *normative* (or that society is **heteronormative**). Society sanctions and encourages heterosexuality by means that sometimes rise to the level of legal and physical force but that are usually more subtle and insidious.

2   The radical feminist accounts of sexuality rest on the belief that male domination over women is the most basic social relationship. But other feminists reasonably object that racial and class

divisions are equally basic features of society. Once we recognize these other social divisions, it becomes harder to think that heterosexuality simply serves male domination. For instance, by being in a sexual relationship with a black man, a black woman might be resisting racial domination as much as she is succumbing to patriarchal domination.

3. Are lesbians women?

The French theorist and novelist Monique Wittig proposed a different form of political lesbianism. Wittig writes from within the tradition of **French materialist feminism**, which developed in the 1970s (and is expressed most fully by Delphy 1984). According to this school of thought, all women are oppressed in that men exploit their labour, and this exploitation consists in women having to do unpaid work – housework and childcare – for their husbands. Even if women also do paid work outside the home, they still have to work for their husbands too, just as in feudal societies every serf was obliged to work for the local lord.

Because women do unpaid work for men, people form particular expectations about what behaviour and characteristics are appropriate for women and men (i.e. being selfless, hard-working and docile *versus* being masterful and entitled to service). Thus, men's exploitation of women's labour generates gender roles and expectations: 'it is *oppression which creates gender*', Christine Delphy says (1984: 144). On this view, men's exploitation of women pre-exists and produces norms or ideas of masculinity and femininity. Because it pre-exists and produces ideas, this relation of exploitation is 'material' rather than 'ideal'. French materialist feminists are 'materialists' because they see this relation as the basis of women's oppression.

Delphy and Wittig also argue that expectations about men's and women's gender roles generate the belief that there are two biological sexes. Wittig denies that any physical property or group of physical properties in itself makes someone male or female. Certain physical properties – those which enable heterosexual sex and reproduction – are only thought to make people sexed against the background of particular assumptions about gender – namely, assumptions that women's role is to have reproductive sex with men and bring up men's children. Wittig says:

> What we believe to be a . . . direct perception [of someone's sex] is only a sophisticated and mythic construction . . . which reinterprets physical features (in themselves neutral . . .) through the network of [social] relationships in which they are perceived. (Wittig 1981: 11–12)

Wittig also argues that, if women are to be made to work for their husbands, then first they must be tied into marital relationships with men. Thus, a social system based on the exploitation of women needs women – and men – to be heterosexual, so that they will be motivated to enter into heterosexual marriages. However, Wittig says, lesbians escape this system as they have no husbands by whom to be exploited. Moreover, since being exploited by one's husband is what makes someone feminine and a woman, lesbians are not women, Wittig concludes.

> Lesbian is the only concept I know of which is beyond the categories of sex (woman and man), because the designated subject (lesbian) is *not* a woman, either economically, or politically, or ideologically. For what makes a woman is a specific social relation to a man, a relation [of] servitude. (Wittig 1981: 20)

Wittig agrees with US radical feminists that men oppress women as a group and that this oppression occurs in heterosexual relationships. But for Wittig this oppression takes the form of exploitation, and it *makes* those who are exploited into women. The process of exploitation creates expectations about feminine behaviour such that those who fulfil those expectations, by being exploited, count as feminine and as women. For Rich, on the other hand, oppression by men *prevents* women from expressing their own feminine sexuality, which is focused on intimacy and which emerges in lesbianism and affectionate relationships between women. For Rich heterosexuality *restricts* femininity, while for Wittig it *produces* femininity.

So, whereas Rich thinks that lesbianism releases femininity, for Wittig lesbians are neither feminine nor, in turn, female – since being female depends on being perceived to be female in virtue of satisfying feminine gender norms. Lesbian desires are, though, *sexual* desires, Wittig believes, unlike Frye. But these are not desires for women or for females. Rather, for Wittig, lesbians desire lesbians – individuals who escape male domination and are neither feminine nor female. Thus, Wittig thinks that lesbian sexuality anticipates what sexuality in general might be like in a future society which no longer rests on men's exploitation of women and so does not distinguish people by gender or sex.

Wittig explores this idea that lesbian sexuality prefigures the genderless, sexless sexuality of the future in her avant-garde novel *The Lesbian Body* (1973). The main characters are two lesbian lovers. Although they do not exploit one another, their sexual feelings for one another are not feelings of tender intimacy. Wittig rejects the intimacy conception of sexuality in favour of what might be called a 'passional' conception. The lovers experience their sexual feelings for one another as violent passions that they cannot control. The novel starts: '. . . say your farewells m/y very beautiful one . . . to what they . . . call affection, tenderness or gracious abandon' (Wittig 1973: 15). Throughout the novel, Wittig writes *je* ('I') as *j/e* and *mon* or *ma* ('my') as *m/on* or *m/a* ('m/y'). She does this to suggest that sexual passions challenge one's understanding of oneself as an autonomous person – an 'I' – who chooses and controls how one lives.

Being outside our control, our passions for other people make us vulnerable to those people, and we are prone to react against this by being aggressive and dominating (like the *j/* leaning forward to dominate the *e*). Early in the novel, the lover first bristles with jealousy and tears the skin from her beloved, then collapses in shame before the beloved's look and dies and rots away – only to be brought back to life by the beloved and for another cycle of aggression and vulnerability to begin. So for Wittig, sexuality in a non-exploitative society would still involve feelings of humiliation, confusion, aggression, and profound ambivalence towards other people. Indeed, because exploitative relations would no longer limit these sexual feelings they would be more intense and passionate than they are now.

Wittig is insightful about the complex emotions that surround sexual feelings and acts. But again there are problems with the theory of gender which supports her view of sexuality.

1   Wittig believes that men's actual exploitation of women pre-exists and produces ideas about gender and sex. But how can this exploitation occur unless people already believe that there are male and female individuals and that the appropriate (feminine) way for females to behave is to marry and work for men?
2   Arguably, one does not stop being a woman by abstaining from heterosexual relationships (MacKinnon 1989: 141–2). Outside the

bedroom, lesbians continue to live amongst a whole range of social institutions that constantly define them as women.

3   Wittig argues that we only think that certain physical properties make people sexed because we live amongst gender rules that state that women and men must have heterosexual sex and reproduce. We therefore classify people in terms of just those properties that enable heterosexual sex and reproduction. But Wittig's argument here presupposes (i) that people have certain physical properties – the genitals, gonads, etc. – which, together, really do enable people to engage in reproductive sex. (ii) And for it to be possible for reproduction to become a social norm, these properties must non-accidentally tend to occur together. Thus, Wittig's own argument implies that the genitals, gonads, etc. really do cluster together: they encourage one another's presence and when they co-occur they have an important causal effect – they enable people to reproduce. Given that these properties cluster, people are male or female if they have enough of the properties in either cluster. So contrary to what Wittig claims, her own arguments imply that most people really are male or female, regardless of what our gender norms lead us to think about them.[3]

4. MacKinnon on gender and sexuality

The second set of feminist sexuality debates built on the first and took place during the 1980s. On one side in these debates were those who saw male domination as, basically, male *sexual* domination, and who saw sexuality as the central sphere in which male power is exercised. Many of these feminists argued that we should avoid any sexual activities which are linked to male domination or which, like sado-masochism, involve domination generally. Others (e.g. English, Hollibaugh and Rubin 1987) took the contrasting view that any sexual activities, including activities that involve domination such as sado-masochism, are legitimate as long as all the people involved have consented to these activities and find them pleasurable.

The first of these two perspectives on sexuality is most fully developed by the US legal theorist Catherine MacKinnon. MacKinnon develops her position on sexuality in the context of outlining a comprehensive theory of gender. MacKinnon holds that the beliefs and institutions that organize modern western societies (and indeed almost

all societies) shape individuals into two genders that are hierarchically defined. Women are the subordinate gender, men the dominant
gender. 'The man/woman difference and the dominance/submission
dynamic define one another' (MacKinnon 1983: 635).

The defining feature of MacKinnon's theory of gender is her view
that society's gender hierarchy is a *sexual* hierarchy. Women are those
who are defined as sexually subordinate, men are defined as sexually
dominant (MacKinnon 1989: 130). Society defines femininity in terms
of sexual availability, which can be manifested by various traits such
as attractiveness, vulnerability, or being soft and pregnable. To be a
woman is to be a **sex object** – a mere thing that arouses other people
and exists to serve their sexual desires.

Meanwhile, MacKinnon thinks, society defines masculinity in
terms of sexual dominance: a masculine person is one who dominates
women, above all through sex. This definition of masculinity shapes
what men actually desire, so that men come to find it arousing to treat
women as sex objects and to impose their sexual desires upon women.
This is shown, MacKinnon believes, by such phenomena as rape,
prostitution, pornography and sexual harassment. Society's definition
of femininity also shapes what women desire, so that they find it erotic
to be submissive and sexually available. Nonetheless, because men's
role as a gender is to impose their sexuality on women, it is men who
define what sexuality is taken to be. In a patriarchal society, sexuality
basically means aggressive male sexuality.

Sometimes MacKinnon's writings give the impression that she
believes men to have an innate sexual urge to dominate women. But
more often she insists that it is men as a *gender* – a socially produced
group – who dominate women sexually (MacKinnon 1982: 532). Men
dominate sexually because this is their privilege, and because social
institutions have educated them to find this behaviour erotic.
Moreover, MacKinnon adds, because the feminine role is to be subordinate (where this is eroticized), any man who is subordinated by
other men – sexually or otherwise – is thereby made 'feminine'.

MacKinnon's theory of sexuality gives rise to her analyses of specific phenomena, for instance rape. She criticizes the view, which
some feminists hold, that rape is an act of violence, not of sex.
Although rape is violent, MacKinnon argues, any man who commits
rape does so because the act's violence arouses him sexually (1989:
134). And this violence arouses him because it is continuous with the

domination that all sex acts involve (given a patriarchal society) and which he like all men has been trained to find arousing. Rape and 'legitimate' sex both involve varying amounts of domination; they differ in degree, not in kind.

MacKinnon also criticizes the idea that rape is illegitimate because it is sex to which the victim has not consented. For MacKinnon, in a patriarchal society, whenever women consent to sex acts, they are in effect consenting to be dominated. Women's consent fails in two ways to make these sex acts morally legitimate. (1) The consent does not change the fact that these acts still involve an unacceptable level of domination. (2) When women consent, this is only because they have been schooled to enjoy their own subordination. This means, again, that rape and consensual sex differ not in kind but only in the degree to which they are morally suspect.

5. Problems with MacKinnon's theory of gender and sexuality

There are two main areas of potential difficulty within MacKinnon's theory of sexuality: (1) her theory of gender and (2) her understanding of what sexuality is.

(1) The central problem with MacKinnon's theory of gender is that it is over-simplified. She thinks that all societies define masculinity in terms of (sexual) dominance and femininity in terms of (sexual) sub-mission. Yet some groups of men are subordinated to others, e.g. black to white men. MacKinnon recognizes this, but claims that black men – and men of other subordinate groups – are 'feminized'. Angela Harris (1990) points out a problem with this claim. In the US, black men have often been viewed as dangerous, rapacious, sexual predators and so have often been unjustly punished or even killed for alleged rape. A major source of these views was the law against interracial sex which existed under slavery and which counted any sexual relations between black men and white women as rape. At least in the US, then, the subordina-tion of black men has not rested on their being defined as feminine. Instead it has rested on their being assumed to have the wrong sort of masculinity, and to have too much of it. This suggests that no society contains one single masculine role. Rather, in each society many forms of masculinity exist, and there are hierarchical relations between them.

Arguably, there are also different norms of femininity in every society. MacKinnon claims that the basic feminine role is to be sexually available, and that other feminine roles manifest or radiate out from this basic role. But consider the widespread idea that women's role is to give birth to and care for young children. The idea that women have special childcare responsibilities does not obviously derive from the idea that women are sex objects. In fact, women who fulfil their role of childcaring, by being visibly pregnant or being seen with young children, are often seen as 'above' sex, not sexually available at all. Or consider the still widespread belief that women are less skilled at science than men. (In 2005, the Harvard professor Lawrence Summers claimed that innate sex differences explain why there are few women professors in science and engineering.) Women are often believed to be more emotional than men and less able to observe, reason, and conduct experiments impartially. These beliefs have no obvious connection with the view that women are sex objects. We may conclude, against MacKinnon, that various *different* norms of femininity – and of masculinity – exist in each society.

(2) Now, since MacKinnon sees sexuality as 'determin[ed]' – shaped and moulded – by the 'sexist social order' (1989: 288), and since her view of the 'sexist social order' is over-simplified, plausibly she will also take an over-simplified view of sexuality. But what exactly does it mean to say that sexist society shapes sexuality? Here MacKinnon insists that sexuality is not a biological urge but is social: 'sexuality is whatever a given culture or subculture defines it as' (1989: 130). For MacKinnon, what people desire and find arousing is what their society encourages them to desire and find arousing. In almost all known societies, gender hierarchy is defined as erotic. So in these societies, people come to take erotic pleasure in gender hierarchy.

Some readers of MacKinnon (e.g. Herman 1993; Nussbaum 1995: 265–71) suggest that her view of sexuality comes at least in part from Kant. Kant (1997: 155–9) thought that sexual desires are dangerous because they compel us to treat other people not as persons but as objects – things, mere bundles of body parts, which are there for us to use. Kant thought these dangers could be overcome, and that sexual desires could safely and legitimately be satisfied, only within marriage, because marriage ensures that the spouses respect one another as persons. MacKinnon's views are like Kant's in that she stresses that sexual desires generally objectify people and that this makes sexual desires dangerous. But unlike Kant, MacKinnon (1) thinks it is primarily men who sexually objectify women and (2) she thinks that men only have these objectifying sexual desires due to living in a male-dominant society.

MacKinnon, then, thinks that sexuality is only dangerous to women because society is male-dominant. But some feminists (e.g. the contributors to Vance 1984) think that she exaggerates how much sexuality endangers women even in present conditions. Linda Gordon and Ellen duBois (1984), for example, suggest that MacKinnon overlooks the fact that sexual feelings, desires and acts can be – and often have been – not only dangerous but also pleasurable for women. Ann Ferguson says that these and other like-minded critics of MacKinnon hold a 'primacy of pleasure' view of sexuality. On this view, sexuality 'is the exchange of physical erotic and genital . . . pleasures' (Ferguson 1984: 109). According to this 'primacy of pleasure' view, sexual pleasure is good in itself and any practice that gives people sexual pleasure is also good, as long as those people have consented to engage in that practice.

But pointing out that women often derive pleasure from sex does not necessarily refute MacKinnon's theory of sexuality. MacKinnon can accept that women often take pleasure in sex, but she argues (1989: 135–6) that this is because women have been socialized to find their own objectification erotic and enjoyable. For MacKinnon, neither women's pleasure in, nor their consent to, sex acts makes those acts legitimate if they involve an unacceptable level of domination – as all sex acts do under patriarchy.

Nor does MacKinnon believe that women can escape from these patterns of eroticized domination through lesbianism. MacKinnon believes that patterns of domination largely reproduce themselves in lesbian relationships, with one partner assuming the dominant, male, position – e.g. the butch, or the sadist in a sadomasochistic relationship. For MacKinnon, lesbian sex is not necessarily politically progressive.

MacKinnon's critics can reasonably reply, though, that the pleasure that women take in sex – with women or men – is not always pleasure at being dominated. Women sometimes take pleasure in feeling sexually powerful or feeling equal to their sexual partner(s). Moreover, women sometimes enjoy being dominated sexually – by women or men – without thereby wishing to be subordinated in other contexts. Some women are aroused by fantasies of being dominated or raped, but this rarely if ever means that they want to be raped in reality.

Women's – and indeed men's – feelings about sex seem already to be more complex than they could be if MacKinnon's theory of sexuality were true. (Unlike MacKinnon, then, I suggest that lesbian sex need be no more politically progressive than heterosexual sex because sex of *both* kinds always involves a whole range of feelings – including the feelings of ambivalence of which Wittig wrote.)

We may conclude that MacKinnon's over-simplified view of gender has indeed led her to take an over-simplified view of our sexual feelings. And we might conclude that these feelings are complex because they are actually shaped by a range of diverse norms of femininity and masculinity. But this would be too hasty, because we still have not thought enough about what it really means to say that the gendered social order 'determines' the shape of people's sexual feelings. To try to clarify this, let us return to MacKinnon's claims.

MacKinnon takes it that when men, due to our 'sexist social order', desire to dominate women, this desire is a specially sexual desire. Men do not desire to dominate women in the same way that they might desire to go shopping. Men expect this domination to bring them a specially sexual type of satisfaction. But what *makes* this satisfaction specially sexual? MacKinnon's account of sexuality is ambiguous between two answers. Answer (i) is that the satisfaction men get from dominating women is specially sexual just because society has *defined* dominating women as something that is satisfying in a specially sexual way. That is, society has specified that the pleasures of gender domination belong to a special sexual class of pleasures (1989: 129). On answer (ii), the satisfaction men get from dominating women is specially sexual because men (like all human beings) naturally have some urges that are of a specially sexual nature, and although these urges in themselves go in no particular direction society channels them in a certain direction – towards dominating women.[4]

These two answers reflect two different views of sexuality. The first view, which may be called 'strong social constructionism', is that just in themselves none of people's energies and urges are specifically sexual. Rather, people only come to think of and experience some of their energies or urges as sexual if those energies or urges are defined or classified as sexual in the society in which these people live. The second view, which may be called 'weak social constructionism', is that human individuals naturally have certain specially sexual energies or urges, but that these energies or urges in themselves do not aim in any particular direction, and are only guided in particular directions (i.e. towards dominance in men's case) by society. On this view, men's and women's desires for dominance/submission are sexual because they result from the moulding of pre-existing sexual energies or urges.

To progress further in thinking about how gender shapes sexuality, we need to consider these two views of sexuality. Foucault and Freud, respectively, defend versions of the strong and weak social constructionist views. Let us start with Freud's weak social constructionism.

6. Freud and Foucault on sexuality

Freud's major work on sexuality is *Three Essays on the Theory of Sexuality*, first published in 1905. Freud rejects what he calls the 'popular' belief in the 'sexual drive', an urge for heterosexual intercourse which is thought to be innate in all individuals (Freud 1905: 45, 61). Freud does not deny that most adults have this urge. But he argues that it has been built up, by a complex process, out of quite different sexual feelings which – controversially – he claims begin in infancy.

These feelings start when an infant feeds at its mother's breast. Initially, this gives the infant pleasure in that it satisfies the infant's hunger. But while sucking to satisfy its hunger, the infant has had its lips and mouth stimulated – rubbed in a pleasurable way and made more sensitive. The infant then starts to want more of this stimulation for its own sake, regardless of whether it drinks any milk as a result. This want is felt within the infant's lips and mouth as a tension that only more stimulation can remove. By having been sensitized and charged with tension in this way, the mouth has become what Freud calls an **erotogenic zone**.

This wish for oral stimulation is, according to Freud, the infant's first sexual 'drive'. **Sexual drives**, Freud says, are both physical and mental. Their physical aspect is the tension, located in a particular body part, which the infant feels and which it needs to relieve. The mental aspect of a drive is the direction of this feeling of tension towards an 'object' – something that the infant remembers has brought relief before (e.g. the breast) and from which it hopes to gain relief again.

At first, the infant's main erotogenic zone is its 'oral' zone, its lips and mouth. After this 'oral' phase, infants enter an 'anal' phase, in which they mainly want anal stimulation, their anus having become sensitized while learning toilet control. By the age of four, the child's sexual feelings have become focused on its genitals (its penis or clitoris – Freud thinks infant girls are unaware of their vaginas) and on masturbation. The genitals have been sensitized by being rubbed during washing and cleaning. At this time, too, the child's sexual feelings and fantasies become more and more directed towards its mother, the main carer (Freud assumes) who has been ever-present in the child's life.

At first Freud called this masturbation-focused phase the child's 'genital' phase. But the word 'genital' did not make it clear that Freud saw this phase as distinct from the later focus on genital heterosexual intercourse which adults acquire. For Freud, young children do not yet desire heterosexual intercourse with their mothers. Young children have only a very confused idea of what intercourse might be (1905: 115). So to clarify that the 'genital' phase differs from adult sexuality, Freud (1905: 118) renamed the former phase the 'phallic' phase.

From age five, Freud says, the child's sexual feelings become much weaker, but they return at puberty. Society now insists that the adolescent must subordinate all his or her drives to a desire for heterosexual intercourse. This involves partly (1) learning to satisfy the other drives in the context of foreplay – for instance, satisfying the oral drives by kissing – and partly (2) learning to 'repress' these other drives.

To be more precise on this last point, the adolescent must repress any awareness of what the *objects* of these early drives are. This leaves him or her with sheer feelings of physical tension which need relief. These left-over urges become directed towards new objects that resemble those of which awareness has been repressed. For example, urges left over from repressed oral drives might become directed towards food. Thus, left-over sexual urges can take all kinds of new objects – new people, but also things such as food, feet, hair, clothing, shoes. Potentially anything can acquire sexual connotations.

According to Freud, then, society demands that adolescents impose a heterosexual organization on their early sexual drives. In fact, though, each child's parents had already begun to enforce this demand by trying to prohibit their children from fulfilling any of their early drives (because these are not yet focused on genital intercourse). Freud (1924) first looked at the effect of these prohibitions on boys. By age four, he says, every boy is in the throes of the 'Oedipus complex': his sexual drives are directed towards his mother and he sees his father as his rival. (The complex is named after the mythical Greek king Oedipus, who unintentionally killed his father and married his mother.) Adults threaten to punish the boy for his sexual feelings and activities with **castration** – by which Freud means cutting off his penis.

These threats hit home when the boy first sees the female genitals and assumes that females have suffered castration. Fearful of meeting the same fate, the boy gives up his desire for his mother and identifies with his father's authority. In puberty, when his sexual desires flood back, he has to build on what has been begun and keep these desires channelled away from his mother, towards other women, and into the socially acceptable form of desires for intercourse. But, Freud adds, some boys, having come to see women as castrated and mutilated, cannot find any woman sexually appealing. These boys become homosexual.

In several later articles (Freud 1925, 1931, 1933), Freud described what he saw as the more tortuous process by which girls come to subordinate their drives to a drive for heterosexual intercourse. The four-year-old girl has masturbatory fantasies about her mother. But on seeing the male genital, she realizes that her smaller clitoris cannot compete with it. She becomes stricken with **penis envy**. Ashamed of her clitoris, she turns away from sexuality and from her mother, whom she now sees as an inferior being like herself. At puberty, the girl's sexual feelings return, and two main patterns of development are open to her. (1) She may acquire a 'masculinity complex', wishing for a penis and endlessly emulating men. This can lead her to become a lesbian. (2) She may take the path of 'normal femininity', starting to desire her father in reaction against her mother and wanting him to give her (through intercourse) a child as a substitute for the penis. Gradually she transfers this desire onto other men.

We can pick out four key ideas from Freud's theory of sexuality:

1 Sexual drives are feelings of tension which are located in sensitized body parts and which are directed towards objects that are expected to provide gratification.
2 Each individual has many sexual drives but must impose a coherent organization on them in the process of negotiating a 'web of social or cultural constraints' (Minsky 1996: 4). Specifically, because society – via the child's parents – demands that the child become focused on heterosexual intercourse, the child must organize its

drives around that focus. So a 'sexuality' is a coherent organization of drives – with two aspects. (i) Consciously, individuals learn to give their drives different levels of importance (e.g. to prioritize genital over oral pleasure). (ii) This conscious structure of feelings rests on a mass of repressed desires, whose left-over energy can turn in many new directions.

3   Freud thinks that sexualities are 'socially constructed' in that individuals always construct them in the context of their family relationships, and specifically in the context of (i) the social constraints that their parents impose and (ii) mothers being the main carers while fathers are more distant authority figures. For Freud, these two features of family relationships do not vary.[5]

4   Each individual's sexuality takes its initial shape in childhood and is cemented in adolescence. One's adult experiences can only with difficulty alter one's sexuality. This is why people's sexual desires, although socially constructed, feel 'natural'. They feel deep-rooted and almost impossible to change.

Challenging Freud, Foucault puts forward a more strongly 'social constructionist' view of sexuality. In Volume 1 of *The History of Sexuality* (1976a), he denies that every individual, everywhere, has a sexuality. Rather, sexuality is a modern invention: only because of certain social institutions peculiar to the modern period does each person now think that he or she has such a thing as a sexuality. In the early modern period, the Catholic institution of confession began to encourage people to look within themselves and to monitor their 'inner life' and feelings, and especially to look out for feelings concerning various kinds of sex acts. (These acts have always taken place; they are not a modern invention.) Then, starting in the eighteenth century, a new concern with public order and population health arose in European states. In the interests of maintaining public health, the medical profession – including the emerging psychiatric profession – took over from priests the job of monitoring people's desires and feelings about sex acts. Foucault thus rejects the widely held view that in the Victorian era sex was heavily repressed, that is, hidden and not spoken about. Rather, Foucault says, in this era there was a burst of attention to, vigilance about, and regulation of sex.

For Foucault, only when people are encouraged to look in themselves and see how they feel about sex acts do those people start to see themselves as having their own personal sets of specially sexual feelings and desires. These same social pressures lead people to start seeing these 'sexual' feelings as peculiarly central to who they are, and as something over which they have a special responsibility to exercise control. Only in the nineteenth century, then, did the idea take hold that each individual has his or her own sexuality. The further idea then arose that there are different classes of people defined by their different types of sexual feelings, such as homosexuals or 'hysterical' women. So, for Foucault, each individual only has a sexuality insofar as they have been led to believe in the existence of their sexuality, to speak about it, and to watch out for it.

Foucault does say that all human bodies have 'forces, energies, sensations, and pleasures' (Foucault 1976a: 155). But just in themselves, none of these pleasures or energies is sexual. They only become sexual if we think that they are sexual. If we think of some of our pleasures as sexual then we attend to them more vigilantly, and this makes these pleasures feel more intense so that they really feel as if they are in a special class (1976a: 44).

Foucault denies, then, that any bodily pleasures in themselves have any features that mark them out as members of a class of specially sexual pleasures. Freud in contrast thought that some bodily pleasures *do* have inherent features that make them specifically sexual. These pleasures result from the stimulation (real or fantasized) of sensitized body parts by objects to which they have been sensitized or by other objects onto which those feelings of sensitivity have been transferred.

Freud and Foucault agree that individuals construct their sexualities – their personal patterns of sexual feeling – in ways that are influenced by the people and institutions around them. But for Freud individuals construct their sexualities from drives that are already sexual, whereas for Foucault individuals construct their sexualities from feelings that only become sexual once they start to be viewed in that way.

7. Sexuality versus gender

I looked at Freud and Foucault so as to clarify what it means for social norms of gender to determine or shape individuals' patterns of sexual feeling. However, neither Freud nor Foucault exactly thinks that our sexualities are constructed by or in the context of gender relations.

Foucault does not use the concept of gender and he does not integrate any understanding of the power relations between men and women into his account of sexuality.

Freud comes closer to using a concept of gender. He distinguishes between anatomical maleness/femaleness and mental maleness/ femaleness (Freud 1933: 147).[6] He also argues that mental maleness/femaleness is not simply caused by anatomical maleness/ femaleness, but must be *acquired* over time by a complex process. Becoming mentally male or female has two aspects, for Freud.

1   It means acquiring a male or female (active or passive) sexuality. As we saw, Freud thinks that girls and boys develop these different sexualities because of how they come to perceive anatomical sex difference – the presence or absence of a penis – in the context of their family relationships. Girls usually develop passive sexualities: they become focused on getting penetrated and impregnated by males whom they see as father-substitutes. Boys usually develop active sexualities: they become focused on penetrating females whom they see as mother-substitutes.

2   Based on their different sexualities, boys and girls develop further personality traits which differentiate them. For example, Freud says, women are dominated by feelings of envy while boys are able to become concerned about justice.

For Freud, though, the routes by which boys/girls form first active/ passive sexualities and then male/female personalities are complex enough that boys can sometimes develop passive and female traits while girls can form active and male ones.

Freud's concept of mental maleness and femaleness differs from the concept of gender in at least three ways.

1   For Freud children become mentally male or female under the influence of 'social customs' or constraints (1933: 149) – the prescription of heterosexual intercourse and the status of mothers as main carers. But as we saw earlier, Freud denies that these constraints can be changed.

2   Mental maleness and femaleness are at base *sexual* identities for Freud. The concept of gender does not put this stress on sexuality.

3   The concept of gender has it that we become masculine or feminine by learning to conform to the social expectations others have

of us. But Freud sees the ability to identify and fulfil other people's expectations as a complex ability that must be learnt over time. By the time a child has fully learnt this ability, it will *already* have begun to form a (male or female) sexuality, since this happens early in childhood. But then maleness and femaleness must be more basic to our minds than the concept of gender can capture.

Since neither Foucault nor Freud uses a concept of gender, it is not clear that either of their accounts of the social construction of sexuality can shed light on how exactly gender might shape sexuality. But despite Freud's and Foucault's non-use of the concept of gender, many feminists have found their theories of sexuality insightful – Freud's theory especially. This may seem surprising given Freud's notorious talk of 'penis-envy'. Nonetheless, many feminists believe that even if some details of Freud's theory such as his account of penis-envy are incorrect, he makes three general points that are true and important.

1   Improving on MacKinnon, Freud acknowledges the complexity of our sexual feelings, complexity which exists because our sexualities are put together from diverse elements by a complex process.
2   Yet Freud recognizes that despite the complexity of our sexualities, they end up mainly organized into male-dominant, female-submissive patterns.
3   Improving on political lesbianism, Freud recognizes that our sexualities become established early in life and cannot be changed at will. No adult can rationally decide what kind of sexuality to have.[7]

But Freud can only make these points as part of his broader theory of sexuality, which is organized by the concept of mental maleness/femaleness and not that of gender. So this concept of mental maleness/femaleness allows Freud to gain insights into sexuality. Some feminists have inferred that they might progress further with thinking about sexuality by moving away from the concept of gender. This need not mean abandoning the idea that sexuality is structured by unequal power relations between men and women. Rather, it means finding a new way to grasp these power relations and their impact on sexuality without using the concept of gender. Some feminists argue that the concept of 'sexual difference' shows the way forward here (e.g. Braidotti 1998). Chapter 4 will assess this concept.

For now, we should note that however insightful Freud's three points about sexuality may be, they also create problems for feminists. Together points 2 and 3 imply that it will be very hard if not impossible for us to change the male-dominant patterning of our sexualities, which is set in place in our childhoods. Even if one is a feminist who wants to challenge the subordination of women, one's own patterns of sexual feeling – and those of the other people one knows – will be very hard to change. A feminist might battle against subordination by day but be unable to act other than submissively within the bedroom. And this fixation of sexual patterns is likely to limit how far people will want to challenge women's subordination in the first place. If by an early age most women's sexualities have become passive, then women will be more likely to enjoy than be repelled by images that depict them as sex objects. Thus, Freud leaves feminists with a puzzle about how our sexualities could ever change in the direction of equality.

8. Conclusion

Feminist thinking about sexuality contributes to several existing areas of philosophy. These include:

1   Practical ethics. What sexual practices are legitimate? How far does consent ever make a sexual practice legitimate? What distinguishes sex from rape?
2   The self. Much feminist work on sexuality, as well as Freud's work, suggests that having a sexuality is central to having a coherent self that persists over time. But then how does it affect one's self if one undergoes a serious sexual assault or rape? (See Brison 1997.)
3   The philosophy of emotion. This asks what emotions are, how rational they are, and how they relate to other mental capacities such as perception. Feminist accounts of sexuality are relevant here because they suggest that sexual feelings are always bound up with complex judgements about and emotional responses to other people – responses of trust, vulnerability, hostility.

Feminist debates about sexuality have also opened up a set of new philosophical questions. Is sexuality biological, socially constructed, or somewhere in between? What is the relationship between gender inequality and the injustices that gays and lesbians suffer? Are lesbians those who desire women, females, or neither; or is lesbianism best left undefined? Are there sexual practices that should be avoided (or promoted) because they are connected to (or free from) gender and other inequalities? Can we understand sexuality as shaped by gender relations, or must sexuality be understood in terms of a theory of 'sexual difference' and not a theory of gender? The next chapter will explore this question.

Notes

1 Zita herself has some sympathy for the idea that there could be male lesbians.
2 But Frye does not stress intimacy as much as Rich. Frye's conception of lesbian 'sex' straddles Rich's intimacy conception and Wittig's 'passional' conception (as I will call it).
3 Chapter 1, section 7 explains these points more fully.
4 MacKinnon tends to favour (1). But she herself claims that 'what is sexual is what gives a man an erection' (1989: 137). This claim implies that (for example) pornographic images of men dominating women become erotic because these images viscerally seize onto men's penises and 'make the penis shudder and stiffen with the experience of its potency' (1989: 137). But if these images can act directly on male bodies in this way, then presumably this is because they channel pre-existing sexual energies within men's bodies. This agrees with answer (2).
5 Some feminists have challenged this. For example, Chodorow (1978) argues that we could introduce shared parenting and that this would transform what kinds of personalities girls and boys develop.
6 In fact the English translation distinguishes between mental *masculinity/femininity* and anatomical maleness/femaleness. But Freud, writing in German, uses one word *Männlichkeit* for both masculinity and maleness, and one word *Weiblichkeit* for both femininity and femaleness. So I think it is more accurate when translating Freud to distinguish between anatomical maleness/femaleness and mental maleness/femaleness.
7 Rich would say that the roots of lesbianism *are* laid early in childhood for all women, stemming from girls' very close bonds with their mothers. But to say this Rich has to rely on Chodorow, whose claims about mother/daughter relationships have problems. (See chapter 5, section 4.)

Further Reading

Varieties of political lesbianism   Rich 1980; Frye 1990; Wittig 1981.
The feminist sexuality debates   Bar-On 1992; Ferguson 1984.
MacKinnon on sexuality   MacKinnon 1989: ch. 7.
Freud, psychoanalysis and feminism   Minsky's introduction to Minsky ed.
  1996 is a good way in to this large and complex area.

4 Sexual Difference

1. Irigaray and sexual difference

As well as the concepts of sex, gender and sexuality, feminist philosophers often use the concept of sexual difference. Some (e.g. Rhode 1990a) use 'sexual difference' simply to refer to the difference between gendered individuals – individuals who have taken on feminine or masculine norms. Others use 'sexual difference' to refer to the difference between gendered bodies, bodies that have absorbed gender norms. But most feminists who talk of 'sexual difference' treat it not as a synonym for 'gender' but as an alternative to the concepts of sex and gender. These feminists believe that the concept of sexual difference captures something the concepts of sex and gender omit: namely, that as human beings we always live and experience our bodies as imbued with *meaning*, never as bare biological things.

Moreover, 'sexual difference' feminists hold that the meanings that we find in our male and female bodies are given by the cultures in which we live – by the symbolic associations that these cultures attach to maleness and femaleness. For example, in the Christian religion the male body has often been used to symbolize humanity's status of being made in God's image, while the female body has symbolized sin, as in the story of the Fall. So whereas 'gender' refers to norms of thought and behaviour, and 'sex' refers to biology, **'sexual difference'** refers to the meanings and symbolic associations which cultures, and the individuals who live in them, give to being male- and female-bodied. The sexual *difference* in question is both (1) the difference between male and female as it is symbolized culturally and (2) the resulting difference in how men and women live their bodies.[1] This concept of sexual difference originates with the philosopher Luce

Irigaray, who is Belgian-born but has worked mainly in France and Italy. This chapter introduces Irigaray's concept of sexual difference and relates it to broader debates about difference – and about difference-versus-equality – in feminist philosophy.[2] Irigaray uses the concept of sexual difference instead of those of sex and gender. I myself will argue in this chapter that the concept of sexual difference should supplement but not replace those of sex and gender.

Irigaray trained not only as a philosopher but also as a linguist and psychoanalyst. At first a follower of the French psychoanalyst Lacan, she later became highly critical of him. However, her key concepts, including that of sexual difference, emerge out of Lacanian concepts. So to understand Irigaray we must first look at Lacan's thought. Looking at Lacan is also worthwhile because, while not a feminist himself, he has influenced many feminist philosophers and theorists.

However, Lacan's thought is hard to understand. It changes over time, his writing style is obscure and he invents many technical terms. It is often hard to follow his trains of thought and to see why he makes the claims that he does. Sections 2 and 3 try to reconstruct his key claims and his reasoning for them.

2. Lacan on the mirror-stage and the symbolic order

We saw in chapter 3 how Freud claims that our sexualities are complex but, overall, are structured in a male-dominant way: female sexuality is passive, male sexuality is active. And for Freud our sexualities are formed early in life and cannot readily be changed. Freud's explanation for these facts is that (given certain social constraints) girls and boys come to see the clitoris as an inferior or 'castrated' version of the penis. Lacan gives a different explanation for the facts that Freud identified. Lacan's explanation is that *language*, which we enter at a young age, produces *desire* in us, and that since language is fundamentally patriarchal it fixes our desire into male-dominant patterns.

Freud himself did not put much stress on the concept of desire. So Lacan gives his own account of desire. To understand this account, we must start from his view of very young infants. He holds that before six months each infant depends utterly on its mother and has no ability to coordinate its movements and no sense of having a unified self or body at all. Instead the infant is flooded by sensations and impulses. The **mirror-stage** in child development runs from six to eighteen months and begins when the infant, seeing its image reflected in a mirror, recognizes that image as *itself* (Lacan 1966: 2). For Lacan, the child gains a sense of its self only by identifying with the reflection of its unified body that it sees in the mirror. Lacan sees the mirror-stage as part of what he calls the '**imaginary** order'. This is one aspect of human existence – an aspect that involves us identifying with images, an aspect that begins with the mirror-stage but persists to varying degrees throughout each person's life.

The child's self-recognition in the mirror pleases it, by giving it its first awareness of itself as a unified being, and by suggesting to the child the possibility of its being able to coordinate and control its own movements. However, since this is still beyond the child's actual powers, the child's self-recognition is also a *mis*recognition. The child gains a sense of itself only by mistakenly identifying with an image which is different from it and which has a unity and a capacity for control which it actually lacks. Hence, for Lacan, the self is 'alienated' or 'split' from itself (Lacan 1966: 19).

As the child becomes more aware of itself, it becomes more aware of being distinct from its mother, although it still depends on her to satisfy all its physical needs. The child also gains some degree of awareness that it does not measure up to its mirror-image: that its sense of itself as unified is a fantasy. The child clings to that fantasy by demanding love from its mother, since this demand for love is, at root, a demand that the mother see the child as having the completeness and perfection that it actually lacks. The child conveys its demand for love by demanding that the mother see to its physical needs; the child regards the mother's acts of satisfying its needs as proofs of her love (Lacan 1966: 286).

Eventually the child must learn to participate in social life beyond its relation to its mother, which for Lacan means that the child must acquire language. This means not merely learning to utter a few sounds or words, but learning to use language constantly and to let language guide all one's thoughts and actions. By 'entering' language in this comprehensive way, the child exits its formerly one-to-one relationship with its mother. Because language expels the child from its bond with its mother, Lacan calls language the 'Name-of-the-father' (Lacan 1966: 67). Language acts like a traditional father – an authority figure who enforces society's demands.

Lacan's understanding of language draws on the influential linguistic theory of Ferdinand de Saussure. Saussure argued that language is a system of **signs**, and that each sign connects a **signifier**, a visual or auditory image (e.g. the letters *cat*) to a **signified**, a concept or meaning (the concept of a cat). Which signifiers get connected to which signifieds is arbitrary – *cat, gato, chat, Katze* all mean cat in different languages. *Cat* means cat not because the letters somehow resemble a cat as we conceive it. Rather, Saussure argues, *cat* means cat because *cat* differs from *car, cut, act, chat*, and, ultimately, from all the other words in the English language. Signifiers, then, only have meaning because of their difference from all the other signifiers: 'In language there are only differences *without positive terms*' (Saussure 1916: 120). Hence different languages, which embody different systems of differences between signifiers, make available different sets of meanings and concepts. What people can think depends on what language they use.

Lacan moves away from Saussure by giving much more weight to the fact that the total set of signifiers in any language constantly changes as people produce new expressions and phrases. No linguistic system is ever complete: languages exist over time and are constantly changing. New words and combinations of words are appearing, others are dying out. Every such change alters the total set of differences which distinguishes the meaning of each word from those of all the others. So the meaning of any word, even *cat*, keeps changing, however minutely. Over time, series of gradual, minute changes in the meanings of words build up to major changes. Consider *terrific*: in the eighteenth century it meant 'terrifying', but now it means 'excellent'. Lacan concludes that the meaning of any signifier is not fixed but is endlessly 'deferred' until the time when the set of signifiers in the language is completed – a time that never comes.

Lacan infers that any encounter with language is frustrating. Any words and phrases that one encounters promise to be meaningful, yet have no definite meaning. This propels us to try to find meaning in these words by acquainting ourselves with other words and phrases (for it is in relation to these other words that the first set of words get their meanings). But to identify what those other words and phrases mean, we have to acquaint ourselves with still other words and phrases: 'no signification can be sustained other than by reference to another signification' (Lacan 1966: 150). We have got caught up in an endless chain of signification. As such, when any child enters language, it becomes gripped by a new force: *desire*, specifically the desire

for meaning. For Lacan desire is not a biological force; rather, it is produced in the individual by language. Desire is, as it were, the register
within the individual of the endless unfolding of language. 'The
passion of the signifier now becomes a new dimension of the human
condition in that . . . in man and through man *it* [i.e. language]
speaks' (1966: 284).

By entering language one enters what Lacan calls the '**symbolic
order**' (or just the 'symbolic'). He uses this term to mean both (i) language as a structured set of symbols and (ii) the desiring aspect of
human existence which results from entering language. Entry into the
symbolic forces the child to abandon its fantasy of having a complete
and unified self. This happens because language makes available
many new signifiers – words and phrases – in terms of which the child
can identify itself. But as these signifiers have no stable meaning,
none of them offer the child a coherent sense of itself. The child is con-
demned to pursue meaning endlessly and in so doing to endlessly
pursue the prospect of gaining a complete sense of itself. Ideally the
individual will acknowledge that this is their situation. Yet we all cling
to our fantasies of coherence to some extent: we remain in the imaginary order as well as the symbolic order.

Another aspect of desire, for Lacan, is its difference from 'need' and
'demand'. Formerly the child demanded from its mother both love
and physical need-satisfaction. But now, having entered language, the
child is aware that it cannot be complete and perfect, and yet it still
longs to be so, so its demand for love – its demand that its mother see
it as complete and perfect – becomes unsatisfiable and insatiable.
From this point on, no amount of physical need-satisfaction can meet
the child's demand for love. And as the 'demand [for love] becomes
separated from need' 'desire begins to take shape' (Lacan 1966: 311).
That is, in becoming insatiable, demand takes the form of an unap-
peasable desire which cannot be satisfied by any particular objects or
acts. However, having entered language, the child may not direct this
desire towards its mother. It has had to exit its one-to-one relationship
with its mother. As such the child must repress its early feelings for
her. These feelings return in the form of the child, and later adult,
directing its desire to other substitute women. Or, at least, this is what
men learn to do; we will turn to women shortly.

To sum up: for Lacan, the symbolic order is (1) language as an
endless chain of signifiers, (2) which breaks up the mother–child unit,

and (3) which generates desire in each individual. (4) Moreover, Lacan claims that, in all societies, the symbolic order fundamentally organizes people's culture and way of life (Lacan 1966: 148; Grosz 1990a: 145).

3. Lacan on the phallus and sexual difference

We have seen how, according to Lacan, language generates desire in each individual. But in what way is language patriarchal for Lacan? He argues that language is necessarily phallocentric (phallus-centred) and that in every possible language the **phallus** must be the 'master-signifier'.

In his very difficult 1958 paper 'The Signification of the Phallus' (included in Lacan 1966), Lacan claims that the phallus is the 'signi-fier' – roughly, the symbol – of the desire which language produces in us.[3] Normally the word 'phallus' means the erect penis as a symbol of male sexuality and fertility. So at first Lacan might seem to be saying that the erect penis must be our symbol for desire. But matters are more complex.

Specifically, Lacan thinks, the phallus symbolizes (1) the hope-lessness of desire. The phallus symbolizes how we each reach towards other people, desiring their love – but remain endlessly reaching, never being satisfied that our desire is met. Now, it might seem that the phallus can only symbolize this feature of desire if the phallus is the erect penis, since the penis remains erect just as long as sexual union is not achieved but deflates at the point of orgasm. (2) The phallus also symbolizes language: because, for Lacan, each word only has meaning in relation to other words, each word end-lessly reaches out, as it were, towards the other words that would complete it.

Lacan's view, then, is that in every language the phallus must be the central signifier because it symbolizes language itself. So all language is 'phallocentric' – phallus-centred. Feminists have been uneasy about this claim, since Lacan seems to be suggesting that every culture must make the male sex organ into its central symbol. Yet Lacan often insists that the phallus is not the same as the penis. Why not?

For Lacan, one need not have a penis anatomically in order to enter into language and begin to desire (Lacan 1982: 118). Anyone, whether biologically male or female, must enter language and everyone must do so on the same terms. Whether or not one has a penis, one must recognize that the phallus is the only adequate symbol for one's hopeless desire. On its own this argument will not appease feminists, though. If the *content* of the phallic symbol is the erect penis, then all that the argument shows is that women as well as men must represent their desire in terms of an erect penis. (For Lacan, to take the phallus as the symbol or 'signifier' of one's desire is not *consciously* to think anything; rather, it is to organize one's mental life in a certain way as a precondition of entering language and becoming capable of conscious rational thought at all.)

But Lacan also suggests that the content of the phallic symbol is not necessarily the erect penis but is *any* organ that is taken to symbolize the striving involved in desire (Grosz 1990a: 12). This might be the penis or the clitoris, Lacan says (1966: 285). Still, he also says that the erect penis 'can be said to be the most tangible element in sexual copulation' (Lacan 1966: 287). Yet Lacan is only saying that the erect penis *can be said* to be most tangible – which implies that other organs, such as the clitoris or breasts, might be said to be equally tangible and suitable as symbols of desire.

So Lacan does not simply equate the phallus with the penis. Yet neither does he totally disconnect them. Other aspects of his thought reconnect the penis and phallus. Recall that by entering language, the child loses the symbiotic unity that it formerly had with its mother's body. This means that when the child comes to symbolize its new status as someone who speaks and has desire, the mother's body and body parts cannot provide appropriate symbols of this status. The mother's body unavoidably suggests the unity that the child has lost, as opposed to its new status of having lost that unity. But the mother's body is, of course, female. So it must be the opposite kind of body to the mother's body which appropriately symbolizes the condition of being someone who desires and lacks. This kind of body is male. And the most salient distinguishing feature of male bodies is that they have penises. So the male organ best symbolizes the individual's status as a lacking, desiring, and linguistic being.[4]

Now, Lacan would say that it is a mistake to equate the phallus with the penis on the basis of the penis's salience. Yet this confusion does not seem to be avoidable. Given the way that language breaks our early bonds with our mothers, it is inevitable that we will come to confuse the phallus with the penis.

In sum, when Lacan says that all individuals must take the phallus to signify their speech and desire, he does to a significant extent mean that they must symbolize their desire in terms of the male penis. The female body cannot signify speech and desire, because this kind of body suggests a pre-linguistic absence of desire.

Lacan is not saying that biological females have to regard themselves as male-bodied. Entering language requires understanding oneself as either female or male (Rose 1982: 49). Most biological females will come to regard themselves as female; most biological males will come to regard themselves as male.[5] But women cannot identify themselves as female without applying to themselves the idea of what it means to be female which is embodied in language. This is the idea that the female body is the symbol of lost, pre-linguistic, unity: 'the woman . . . is produced . . . as what he [the man] has to renounce' (Lacan quoted in Rose 1982: 49). That is, female bodies are seen as: (1) lacking in desire, since desire does not exist before language; (2) in a state of pre-verbal muteness. Muteness and passivity are not positive qualities: the female is understood solely in contrast to the male, as lacking the desire and speech that are defined as male. Still, female-bodied individuals must make sense of their femaleness in these negative terms. Thus, women acquire a split self-understanding. They must make sense of their femaleness by seeing themselves as speechless objects of male desire, but must also make sense of the fact that they do speak and have desire by seeing themselves as in that respect phallic and male. Male individuals face no such difficulties.

This brings us to Lacan's concept of sexual difference. Although he does not use the phrase 'sexual difference', his work does develop a concept of **sexual difference** as

1   the ideas about the male/female difference which are embodied in language (According to these ideas the male body has the phallus and symbolizes speech and desire. The female body lacks the phallus and symbolizes mute passivity.)
2   and the difference between men and **women**, that is, male and female individuals who have applied to themselves these ideas about what it means to be male or female and who experience themselves in terms of these ideas.

This concept of sexual difference blurs the distinctions between sex, gender and sexuality. After all, Lacan first developed his views in the

1940s and 1950s before the sex/gender distinction was formulated. How exactly does his concept of sexual difference relate to the concepts of (1) sex, (2) gender and (3) sexuality?

1   Sexual difference is not the same as sex difference, the biological difference between males and females. Sexual difference is an *interpretation* of sex difference which is embodied in language. However, sexual difference is an interpretation not of what sex difference is or consists of biologically but of what it means or *symbolizes* – either speech and desire (male) or mute passivity (female).

2   Lacan avoids any concept of gender for at least three reasons.

   i   He thinks he can adequately explain men's and women's social positions without referring to social norms or expectations (Brennan 1991: 128). Sexual difference as embodied in language directly implies that there are specific ways in which males and females should think about themselves and act. For example, if maleness symbolizes speech and desire, then it is fitting for men to be assertive in conversation and to initiate sexual relationships with women.

   ii   But sexual difference is a set of ideas which is embodied in *every* language. These ideas must therefore prevail in every culture and society and cannot be changed. In contrast, if gender expectations exist then they vary in different societies and so they can (potentially) be changed.

   iii According to the concept of sexual difference, one must enter language, and therefore also take on a position within sexual difference, in order to become capable of conscious thought at all (Brennan 1991: 123.) 'Conscious' thought is thought that 'obeys the laws of reason and rational logic' (MacCannell 1992: 441). Now, to take on gender norms a child must already be conscious and rational enough to accurately receive and act on messages that other people send out about those norms. So for gender theorists individuals are conscious and rational before becoming masculine or feminine. But for sexual difference theorists individuals only become conscious and rational *by* adopting male or female positions.

3   Sexual difference is the interpretation of male and female bodies as signifiers of, respectively, desire and the status of being a passive

object of male desire. As such, sexual difference interprets *sex* difference as basically a difference in *sexual* positions. Therefore, sexual difference shapes men's and women's patterns of sexual feeling into either active or passive form.

4. Lacan, feminism and Irigaray

How helpful is Lacan's thought for feminists? Some feminists find Lacan's thought off-putting due to its obscurity and its focus on the phallus. But others (e.g. Mitchell 1974) prefer his concept of sexual difference to that of gender, especially because (they think) the concept of gender falsely implies that social and sexual relations between men and women can be easily changed. In contrast, Lacan explains why sexual relations between men and women are both male-dominant and hard to change, without resorting to the view that biology determines men's and women's sexual positions (Mitchell 1974: 17). For Lacan language, not biology, sets the meanings of maleness and femaleness.

Yet for Lacan the basic meanings of maleness and femaleness are not merely *hard* to change. They cannot be changed *at all*. And these meanings privilege the male sex organ and position women as passive sex objects. Since feminists seek to change women's status for the better, it is not obvious how feminists can support Lacan's view that language fixes these meanings of male and female. (On this conflict between Lacan and feminism, see Brennan 1991: 114–27.)

Still, it need not follow that feminists should reject Lacan's thought as a whole. It might be possible to revise Lacan's concept of sexual difference so that it explains why it is difficult to change women's inferior social and sexual position, but no longer implies that this position cannot be improved at all. Irigaray revises Lacan's concepts in this way. She begins by criticizing Lacan's reasoning as to why any language must embody a 'phallocentric' interpretation of sex difference.

As we saw, Lacan thinks that because each child must break away from its mother, the female body necessarily signifies passivity and pre-verbal muteness, not desire and speech. Irigaray agrees that the *mother's* body must always acquire this meaning for each of us. But there is more to being a woman (a female human being) than being a mother. So it need not follow that, because the mother's body signifies pre-linguistic passivity, the female body in general must take on the same meaning. Children will only infer that the female body, in general, means mute passivity if their culture gives them no way to conceive that the female body is distinct from the maternal body. Only if children live in a cultural environment that defines being female – reductively – as being a mother (or a potential mother) will children be unable to distinguish female from maternal bodies.

Western culture, Irigaray holds, is just such an environment. In her view, western culture – Judaeo-Christian religion, European art and literature, modern science, etc. – has a long history of claiming that there is no more to being female than being able to bear and raise children. And this claim itself forms part of a broader western approach to thinking about femaleness.

According to Irigaray, this approach starts by defining what it is to be male and then defines what it is to be female in relation to maleness. It is assumed that anything male exists, and can be understood, independently of anything female. Conversely, it is assumed that anything female exists and can be understood only in relation to something male. Take the Russian folk saying 'I thought I saw two people but it was just a man and his wife'. Being female, the second individual is taken to exist not as a person in her own right but only in relation to her husband.

Irigaray's idea that the female has always been defined in relation to the male goes back to Simone de Beauvoir, who writes in *The Second Sex*:

> The terms *masculine* and *feminine* are used symmetrically only as a matter of form . . . In actuality the relation of the two sexes is not quite like that of two electrical poles, for man represents both the positive and the neutral, as is indicated by the common use of *man* to designate human beings in general; whereas woman represents only the negative . . . She is defined and differentiated with reference to man and not he with reference to her; she is the incidental, the inessential as opposed to the essential. He is the Subject, he is the Absolute – she is the Other. (Beauvoir 1949: 15–16)

For Beauvoir, women are always seen as **Other** or secondary to men. Irigaray agrees: 'The "feminine" is always described as deficiency, atrophy, lack of the sex that has a monopoly on value: the male sex' (Irigaray 1977a: 69).[6]

(However, Irigaray (1995) disagrees with what she takes to be Beauvoir's view that women should become the same as men by taking on the positive traits that men have reserved for themselves. Irigaray instead thinks that we should recognize women to be genuinely different from men, as this chapter will explain later.[7])

Because women have been thought to exist only in relation to men, it has been thought right for women to serve men. And the chief service that women, *as* women, can provide for men is to carry and bear their children. This counts as service for men if it is assumed that children are their fathers' products and 'belong' to their fathers. In western culture, Irigaray suggests, women are indeed assumed to contribute little or nothing to the make-up of children. For instance, Aristotle thought that the mother merely contributes matter to the foetus while its form – its soul and animating principle – is contained in the father's sperm. The assumption that children are their fathers' products is reflected in the convention (which still exists in many countries) for children to take their fathers', not their mothers', names. For Irigaray, what all this amounts to is that there is an entrenched belief that women's nature or 'function' (1991: 50) as women is to serve men by bearing children.

To return to Irigaray's arguments against Lacan: she concludes that western culture has over time erased any notion that being female might involve more than being an actual or potential mother. Within this culture, when children start to see the maternal body as a symbol of pre-verbal passivity, they cannot avoid seeing the female body in the same way. And children must therefore see language and desire – by contrast – as male and phallic. But this is not a result of the child's entering into language as such, as Lacan thought. It is the result of the child entering into a *particular* culture, one that ranks females second. This culture has a long history but it is still just one particular culture, and so it could be changed.

Irigaray worries that this cultural trend to reduce being female to being a mother damages daughters' relationships to their mothers. In her prose-poem 'And the One Doesn't Stir Without the Other' (1979), a daughter addresses her mother, lamenting the failure of their relationship. The daughter could only see herself as a woman if she saw herself as a mother, like her mother. But then she felt suffocated and overwhelmed by her mother. To break away from her mother, the daughter felt that she must turn towards her father and other men, aspiring to be like them. She was forced to leave her mother alone, abandoned.

Another (fictional) example of a daughter with a troubled relationship to a mother is Lily Briscoe in Virginia Woolf's novel *To the Lighthouse*. Lily's relationship is with Mrs Ramsay, who is not Lily's biological mother but whom Lily has adopted as a mother-figure. Mrs Ramsay, the mother of eight children, seems entirely happy to support her academic husband and bear and nurture his children. She seems to embrace femaleness as it is traditionally understood (i.e. as consisting in motherhood and service to men). Lily feels drawn to Mrs Ramsay because Mrs Ramsay so embraces femaleness. Yet Lily herself feels unable to live like Mrs Ramsay and pursues the life of a modernist painter. In the early parts of the novel, Lily feels that by rejecting motherhood, she is rejecting being female. She feels dry, lonely, not properly female. These feelings affect Lily's work on a painting that features Mrs Ramsay and her son. Lily reduces the mother and child to an abstract 'purple triangular shape' (Woolf 1927: 52). Lily cannot complete the painting, because when painting she feels cut off from her femaleness and her ties to Mrs Ramsay. Because Lily cannot distinguish being female from being a mother, she cannot see herself as a specifically female artist, and this strangles her creativity.

5. Irigaray on western philosophy

Irigaray believes that western culture's ideas about the female sex can be changed, but with difficulty because this culture has a long history. The ideas about sex expressed in western religion, art, literature, philosophy, etc., have influenced and reinforced one another over time.

Irigaray thinks that philosophers' versions of these ideas have been especially influential. This might seem unlikely: compared to poets or religious writers, philosophers have rarely made explicit statements about the meaning of sex difference. But Irigaray argues in her book *Speculum of the Other Woman* (1974) that philosophers have constantly used male and female bodies as symbols of metaphysical principles, e.g. of reason and emotion. So to see what philosophers think about sex difference, we need to look beyond their overt claims and arguments. We need to look at the symbolism and imagery which, Irigaray insists, exist in even the driest philosophical texts.

One of Irigaray's examples is Plato's myth of the cave in his *Republic* (Irigaray 1974: 243–48). Plato describes some prisoners who are chained in an underground cave, watching images of things projected on a screen. One prisoner is dragged into the outside world, where he sees and learns about real things, not mere images. Irigaray argues that Plato portrays the cave as a womb – a round, dark, chamber which can only be exited by a narrow passage. Plato is using the female body as the symbol of a state of ignorance and illusion. He implies that, in order to achieve knowledge and gain access to reality, one must leave the female body behind. Thus, Plato contrasts illusion to knowledge and symbolizes these as female and male respectively.

Irigaray believes that Plato's cave myth typifies a way of thinking which runs through the history of western philosophy. First the philosopher distinguishes between two metaphysical principles or basic elements of reality. One element is judged to be basic and superior – e.g. knowledge – and the other is judged to be secondary and inferior – e.g. ignorance. Many philosophers make whole series of these distinctions. Plato, for example, distinguishes reality from illusion, reason from desire, justice from self-interest, etc. (Many feminist philosophers refer to these distinctions as **binary oppositions** because they define one term as positive, the other as negative.) When setting up these binary oppositions, philosophers map whichever elements they take to be basic and superior onto the male body and map the secondary, inferior, elements onto the female body. Philosophers disagree on what the basic elements of reality are, but they always symbolize the superior and inferior elements as male and female respectively (Cixous 1975: 64).

This symbolism that pervades philosophical theories has spread through western culture as a whole. But no one who has lived and grown up amid this inherited symbolism of male and female can simply start to think differently. So how can the symbolism be changed? Irigaray proposes (1977a: 76) a strategy of **mimicry** (or *mimesis*), which she carries out in some of her own work. The strategy is to mimic, i.e. reproduce, traditional images of the female sex. This strategy works in two main ways.

1   Because we can only become conscious rational individuals by taking on our cultural horizon, necessarily this horizon is something of which we are largely unconscious. But mimicry makes us more conscious of this horizon, and this enables us to criticize it.

2   Irigaray often mimics traditional imagery in ways that subtly change its content. For example, she holds that the philosophical

tradition has used the female body to symbolize formlessness. The pre-Socratic philosopher Pythagoras associated the female with 'limitlessness' – boundless chaos. Female bodies have been thought to be formless, or shapeless, because they change shape dramatically at puberty and during pregnancy, and because there are no sharp boundaries between a pregnant mother's body and that of the foetus inside her. Irigaray (1991: ch. 4) takes up this imagery of the formless female body. But she shifts the emphasis onto the fact that females do not have one unchanging bodily form but pass through many different forms as part of a process of growth and development. So she redefines female 'formlessness' as not a lack of form but the valuable quality of advancing through multiple forms over time.

Mimicry, then, is a way to move towards positive images of the female body. In a culture which contained such images and which did not reduce femaleness to motherhood, women could take their female bodies to symbolize their condition of being speaking, desiring, individuals. Famously, Irigaray suggests that an aspect of the female body which could nicely symbolize women's desire and speech is women's two sets of lips – their labia and the lips of their mouths (Irigaray 1977a: 26, 1991: 175). The lips symbolize a female kind of speech – a 'speaking-as-woman' – which is 'always in the process of weaving itself, of embracing itself with words, but also getting rid of words in order not to become fixed, congealed in them' (Irigaray 1977a: 29). In this culture, then, women could understand themselves to be female not only when they bear children but also when they speak and desire. And in doing so, they would also be regarding their speech and desire as being of a distinctly female kind.

A culture with positive images of the female body would improve mother/daughter relationships. On entering this culture, girls would still leave their initial state of bodily closeness with their mothers. But girls would learn from this culture that their mothers are not only mothers, but are also female individuals with whom they can form special woman-to-woman relationships. Daughters could then feel distinct from, but still specially related to, their mothers. Later in Woolf's *To the Lighthouse*, Lily comes to relate to Mrs Ramsay in this more positive way (belatedly, as Mrs Ramsay is now dead). Realizing that Mrs Ramsay was not merely a subservient mother but also exercised power and initiative in a specially female way, Lily is able to embrace being female and paints with a new visionary creativity.

To sum up: Irigaray thinks that western cultural images of male and female bodies are both hierarchical and very deep-seated because they are tied to the history of philosophy. She suggests that we 'mimic' philosophical images of the female body to give it positive significance. At this point, we can clarify how she has revised Lacan's concepts of the symbolic order and sexual difference.

6. Irigaray on the symbolic order and sexual difference

For Lacan, the 'symbolic order' meant language. For Irigaray the **symbolic order** means a culture's inherited set of ideas and images, which form the horizon of people's thought. So for her the symbolic order goes beyond, but includes, language, since ideas are generally articulated in and co-evolve with language.

On sexual difference, Irigaray agrees with Lacan that we have a basic horizon of images of what male and female bodies mean. But Lacan held that maleness symbolizes speech and agency while femaleness symbolizes silence and passivity. Irigaray thinks that these particular symbolic patterns are just part of a broader pattern of imagery. This pattern takes the male body to be superior and to symbolize whatever is thought to be metaphysically basic or most valuable (e.g. knowledge, speech).

Irigaray agrees with Lacan that these images shape men's and women's sexualities and generate expectations about how men and women should act. Thus, like Lacan, Irigaray does not use the concept of gender. She thinks that our expectations of men and women flow not from shifting social norms but from deeply entrenched cultural symbolism. For example, she would say that the (traditional) expectation that women should bear children and be subject to their husbands flows out of the symbolic idea that female bodies are secondary to male bodies.

Lacan thought that these ideas about the symbolic meanings of male and female constitute sexual difference. Irigaray revises this claim. She argues that (paradoxical as it may sound) the ideas and images which define sexual difference in western culture *deny* sexual difference. They deny that the female sex is a sex in its own right. Instead these ideas define sexual difference as a hierarchy or a binary (positive/negative), rather than a genuine difference between two equally positive terms. Whereas Lacan considered this situation inevitable, Irigaray argues that it can and should be changed. In her view, we need to put in place – gradually, through mimicry – a new cultural horizon that construes sexual difference as a genuine and not a pseudo difference. This new culture would take male and female bodies to embody different, but equally basic and valuable, metaphysical principles, such as male form and female metamorphosis.

Irigaray's concept of **sexual difference** captures several things that the concepts of sex and gender omit:

1   there is a deep-rooted horizon of ideas about the symbolic meanings of male and female bodies;
2   entering into western culture, and learning to speak any associated language, requires understanding oneself in terms of these ideas;
3   this horizon of ideas shapes how we experience and live our bodies; and
4   this horizon of ideas shapes our sexualities. Like Lacan, Irigaray thinks that having desire requires entering language/culture. But since our culture equates being female with being maternal, women cannot understand themselves, *as* women, to desire actively. To the extent that women take up what they see as a female position in sexual relations, they will be passive. Thus patterns of male-dominant sexuality are entrenched in our culture.

Irigaray is not the only feminist philosopher to say that we always live and experience our bodies as meaningful, not merely biological, items. Some others who make this point will be discussed later (chapter 6, section 4), but one whom we encountered in chapter 2 is Moira Gatens (1983). Gatens argues that each society contains an 'imaginary' composed of ideas about the imagined significance of biology and of various body parts. These 'social imaginaries' shape the body-images in terms of which we 'map' our bodies to ourselves. Both Irigaray and Gatens, then, think that the meanings we find in our bodies are shaped by social/cultural horizons.

Unlike Gatens, though, Irigaray thinks (as does Lacan) that humans are biologically male or female but that culture decides what meanings to give to this biological difference. In contrast, for Gatens biology alone does not make anyone male or female; rather, culture leads us to interpret our biology as differentiated by sex. Moreover, Irigaray stresses more than Gatens does the importance of cultural ideas concerning the *symbolic* meanings of male and female bodies and, especially, of the symbolic meanings that *philosophers* have attributed to male and female bodies. For Irigaray, how we live our bodies as men and women is deeply shaped by the western philosophical tradition. Does Irigaray overestimate how much power philosophy has had? Not necessarily. After all, the thought of Plato and Aristotle has exerted a huge influence on Christianity, which in turn has had a huge influence on western thought and social life as a whole.

But there are problems with Irigaray's attempt to entirely replace the concept of gender with that of sexual difference. These concepts pick out different things. As I argued in chapter 2 (section 6), the concept of gender picks out the fact that gender norms, which are embodied in social institutions and practices, specify what actions and roles are appropriate for people of a given sex. Meanwhile the concept of sexual difference picks out the fact that we have a web of ideas about the cultural and emotional meaning of male and female bodies. These ideas are about the meanings of bodies *themselves*, not about what it is appropriate for people to do or think *given that* these people have male/female bodies.

This difference between gender norms and sexual symbolism becomes visible when they conflict. They conflict, for instance, when our gender norms prescribe that menstruation should be kept out of sight, while our symbolic horizon loads menstruation with emotionally rich meanings (dirt, pollution, fertility . . .).[8] Since the concepts of gender and of sexual difference pick out different things, we need to retain and use both concepts. The concept of sexual difference should not replace but should be added to and integrated with the concepts of sex, gender and sexuality.

It is worth clarifying that symbolic ideas about the cultural and emotional significance of different bodily properties also differ from scientific ideas about what these properties consist of at a biological level. Science aims to understand the biological make-up of these properties without reference to any human significance that these properties might take on. To be sure, cultural symbolism often influences scientific ideas by providing metaphors and images in terms of which scientists describe the phenomena they study. For instance, influenced by the symbolic idea that women's function is to reproduce, scientists have sometimes imagined that menstruation is a failed attempt to produce a baby. Scientists have therefore described the menstrual process of shedding the womb lining as a process of 'degenerat[ion]', 'decline', 'lack', and 'deteriorat[ion]' (Martin 1987: 47). But although ideas about the symbolic meaning of sex influence scientific beliefs about sex and vice versa, we should retain the conceptual distinction between them.

7. Equality, difference, care

Irigaray's position is described as **sexual difference feminism** (e.g. by Braidotti 1998).[9] Irigaray's position is *feminist* because she believes that women are currently subordinated to men and that this can and should be changed. Her account of this subordination is that western cultural traditions take the female body to be secondary to the male body, which negatively affects women's self-understandings, sexualities, and social positions. Irigaray is a *sexual difference* feminist because the kind of change she recommends is cultural change to recognize the sexes as genuinely different. Irigaray claims that feminists should not aim for women to achieve equality with men (see Irigaray 1991: ch. 1). Like some other feminist thinkers, she argues that feminism should instead aim to obtain recognition for women's difference(s) from men. What does this difference/equality contrast mean?

Debates about the merits of difference versus equality have been central to feminist thought in many countries since the 1980s. These debates have developed differently in France and Italy – where Irigaray has worked – and in Britain and North America. Let us look first at the Anglo-American debate. Section 8 will turn very briefly to the French debate and Irigaray's place in it.

Equality for women was the central goal for the liberal feminists who fought for women to receive an equal education and for legal recognition of women's equal rights to own property, enter professions, and vote. More recent liberal feminist groups, such as the National Organization of Women (NOW) in the US, fight informal barriers and prejudices that still render women unequal within the public worlds of work and politics. However, it is a simplification to say (as I did in the Introduction) that only liberal feminists aim for women's equality. So do many socialist and some radical feminists – but they argue that reforms to existing institutions will never bring about equality, because the basic principles on which present-day society is organized disadvantage women.

For these radical and socialist feminists, achieving equality for women requires transforming the basic way in which society is organized. For socialist feminists this above all means transforming our work relationships and the way in which different jobs are allocated to men and women. For radical feminists it is above all sexual, reproductive and family relationships which must be transformed. Shulamith Firestone, for example, claims in *The Dialectic of Sex* (1970) that women are disadvantaged by their responsibilities for childbearing and childcare. To remove these disadvantages, she thinks, new technologies must be used to gestate all foetuses outside the womb, and the nuclear family must be abolished and replaced by communes. Firestone remains an equality feminist: her goal is still for women to be able to participate equally in social life. But she thinks that far-reaching social transformation – in fact, a social revolution – is needed before this goal can be achieved.

What liberal, radical and socialist kinds of **equality feminist** share is a belief that women should be able to participate equally in society and should have equal access to the benefits and positions that society makes available. Some equality feminists want women to be able to participate equally in existing social institutions, while others think that society needs to be radically transformed before equality can become possible. Between these extremes ranges a spectrum of equality feminist positions pursuing more or less far-reaching social reforms. (It should be noted that some liberal feminist positions are quite ambitious and come close to socialist or radical positions.)

It might seem odd to lump all these positions together as 'equality feminism'. Surely there is a world of difference between pursuing women's equality within *existing* social institutions and pursuing women's equality within *transformed* social institutions? Yet in wanting women to be able to participate fully in social life, all these equality feminist positions share a desire for women to be able to participate fully in *public* life in its whole range – rather than being marginalized in the family or confined to narrow areas of life such as nursing, service professions or sex work, which are seen as compatible with women's basic family role.

Difference feminists start from a different set of concerns. They believe that women have distinctive values or perspectives the worth and importance of which have not been recognized. Difference feminists want women's values or perspectives to be acknowledged and taken on board throughout society much more than they are at present. Some radical feminists, such as Rich (1976) and Griffin (1984), are difference feminists. But not all difference feminists are radical feminists. Two well-known (non-radical) difference feminists are Sara Ruddick and Carol Gilligan.

In *Maternal Thinking* (1989) Ruddick argues that mothering should be recognized to be a highly skilled activity with its own aims. These aims are to preserve children, nurture their growth and train them to behave in socially acceptable ways. Mothering as an activity is guided by an ideal of non-violence. (Actual mothers may not live up to this ideal.) Ruddick argues that mothers can become motivated, *as* mothers, to engage in political activism. One of her examples is the Argentine 'mothers of the disappeared': a group of mothers who held marches and vigils demanding information about their children who had been kidnapped, tortured or killed by the military dictatorship in the 1970s. Mothers can also become motivated to take part in peace politics, because war as an activity has an aim – inflicting violence – which conflicts with the aims of mothering.

Carol Gilligan's *In a Different Voice* (1982) came up in the introduction. To repeat: Gilligan argues that men's approach to moral reasoning typically takes the form of an 'ethic of justice'. According to the ethic of justice, individuals are self-sufficient and have rights; moral problems arise when there are conflicts among these rights, and moral reasoning works out which rights take priority. Gilligan argues that traditional moral theories express men's experience and so articulate this ethic of justice. These theories do not capture women's typical approach to moral problems. This approach – the ethic of care – is one that women tend to adopt because of their traditional responsibility for caring for other people (especially family members). Faced with moral problems, women do not use general principles to decide whose rights take priority. Instead women try to work out what is the best way, in some specific situation, to meet the needs of the people involved and to preserve the networks of relationships around these people. Gilligan gives a now-famous example. She asked two children whether a man should steal an unaffordable drug for his sick wife. Jake quickly answers 'yes, because the right to life trumps the right to property'. Amy vacillates but eventually tends towards 'no, because the theft could cause difficulties for the chemist and damage his relationships in turn'.

What unites Ruddick and Gilligan, and defines them as difference feminists, are the following beliefs. (1) Traditional gender expectations specify that women should mother and/or carry out activities of care. (2) Given these expectations, women tend to take on mothering and caring activities and to adopt the corresponding values – non-violence – or approach to moral reasoning: the ethic of care. (3) Yet neither traditional moral theory nor social and political institutions – which are often entwined with the military or have the task of distributing various goods in a just way – recognize women's distinctive values/perspective.

Difference feminists, then, reject the view that women above all need equal access to the public sphere as it is presently arranged. Presently, the public sphere is shaped by masculine values such as militarism or justice. But these are not the only legitimate values. Women's family-focused values and perspective deserve respect in their own right, and women should not have to comply with masculine values or to fit into public spaces based on those values.

Do difference feminists also oppose the kinds of equality feminism which seek women's equal access to radically transformed social institutions? Arguably, yes. Equality feminists seek to transform social institutions just so that women can participate equally in social life. As such, the equality feminist's political project rests on the belief that women need to leave their marginalized place in the family or in certain 'caring' or stereotypically 'feminine' jobs. So, difference feminists think, this project still fails to see the worth of the caring perspective which women's traditional place in the family produces.

A problem with difference feminism is that it could well reinforce women's traditional (mothering/caring) gender role and, with it, women's subordination to men. After all, according to Ruddick and Gilligan women's peaceful values or moral voice arise out of women's traditional place of being excluded from public life and forced to focus on personal relationships at home. But if women's values and moral voice are valuable, then by implication the marginalized position that gives rise to these values and voice is also valuable, and should be preserved as it is. Interestingly in this context, the Virginia Military Institute used Gilligan's work to defend its policy of not admitting women. The Institute argued that women's special moral voice made them unsuited for admission to its leadership training programme (Moi 1999: 108). In this way difference feminism threatens to strengthen – or can be used to strengthen – traditional barriers keeping women out of the public world of work and politics. Whether difference and equality feminisms can be reconciled is a question to which chapter 7 will return.

8. Difference feminism and sexual difference feminism

Irigaray's sexual difference feminism arose in the context of the French equality–difference debates. In the 1990s equality feminism became the dominant form of feminism in France, in the shape of the campaign for 'parity': for laws (which were passed in 2000) requiring equal numbers of female and male candidates on all election ballots. Yet in the 1970s and early 1980s, many French feminists were highly critical of any equality feminist project of this kind. But their objection was not that any such project must overlook or devalue women's special family-based values. Rather, French difference feminists argued that even if women gained full equality with men, both in the public sphere and in terms of financial and material well-being, this would leave in place a male-centred *symbolic* order. This order is what must really be challenged, and struggling for legal, political or economic equality is actively harmful because it distracts from this real task. Or so, at least, argued the *Psych et po* – 'Psychoanalysis and Politics' – group led by Antoinette Fouque. *Psych et po* drew on Lacan to argue that the symbolic order (in Lacan's sense of language) defines all speaking agents as male. Thinkers linked to *Psych et po* such as Hélène Cixous (1975: 86) suggested that avant-garde writing is the way to challenge the phallocentrism of language. This is because it employs language in ways that are transgressive and unorthodox, and that therefore are 'feminine' rather than phallocentric.

Irigaray agrees that the real problem for women is the existence of a symbolic order (in her sense of an entrenched culture) which defines being female as something merely negative. This symbolic order gives women a split sense of self and makes women homeless within culture. Irigaray's view here contrasts with Gilligan's view that women do have their own moral perspective. Unlike Gilligan, Irigaray thinks that women's traditional roles are not the source of a distinctive and valid perspective, but merely reflect western culture's denial of a positive female identity and its definition of mothering as a mere 'function'.

This contrasts, too, with Ruddick's view that mothering is a skilled activity. So whereas Anglo-American difference feminists seek recognition of women's *already* existing difference, Irigaray wants to *create* a difference between women and men which, she thinks, has never genuinely existed. Thus:

- Anglo-American difference feminism: because of gender roles, women are different from men; their difference deserves recognition.
- Irigaray's sexual difference feminism: because of cultural symbolism, women have no positive female identity; this identity should be created.

(Feminist philosophers use the word 'identity' in a variety of ways that are rarely spelled out. Roughly, for Irigaray, western culture 'denies a positive female identity' in that it gives women no way to understand and experience themselves to be female-bodied without also seeing themselves as passive, secondary to men, etc. A culture that provided a 'positive female identity' would permit women to take themselves to be both female-bodied and active, equivalent in worth to men, etc.)

Since Irigaray does not urge that we should recognize an *existing* gender difference, she might seem to escape Gilligan and Ruddick's problem of reinforcing women's traditional gender role. Yet Irigaray's feminism does tend to reinforce traditional images of the female body. Irigaray thinks that we can only create new images of the female body by building on and 'mimicking' past images. For example, Irigaray reaches her positive idea that female bodies are in a process of growth by revising the traditional idea that the female body is chaotic and formless. But this means that even as Irigaray revises that traditional idea, she also reinforces it by continuing to make it important – albeit in revised form – for how we understand what it means to be female.

Irigaray would deny that this is a problem with her position. Given that our cultural horizon is very deeply ingrained, we can only change it via mimicry. For Irigaray, if we tried to make a more radical leap outside of our pre-existing culture and to introduce symbolic patterns that are wholly new, then actually we would only end up *reproducing* old symbolic patterns without realizing that we are doing so. We just cannot jump outside of our traditions in one go.

Irigaray's view that traditional imagery must be repeated (with a difference) is called **strategic essentialism**. Traditional symbolism around sex is 'essentialist' in that it assumes that maleness and femaleness each have an essential nature or meaning – maleness is essentially rational, femaleness is essentially chaotic, etc. A 'strategic essentialist' is someone who strategically reproduces essentialist ideas in order to subtly give them a different, non-hierarchical, meaning and so work towards cultural change.

Earlier in this chapter I suggested that the concept of sexual difference should not replace but should be added to the concepts of sex and gender. But if sexual difference exists as well as sex and gender, then a question arises as to whether it is possible to eradicate gender as some feminists have advised. Recall that Butler (amongst others) thinks it would be desirable to eradicate the social expectation that there should be two genders, or that males and females should act in systematically different ways. This would be desirable because societies that insist on two genders necessarily (i) oppress people who are gender-ambiguous and (ii) see heterosexuality as normal and natural, since gendered individuals appear to need people of the opposing gender to complement them.

Now, Irigaray argues that we should retain sexual symbolism but give equally positive symbolic meanings to male and female bodies. But perhaps a culture that did this would inevitably generate different – although non-hierarchical – norms for how male- and female-bodied people should act. For example, if the female body were taken to symbolize growth and change then this might generate a social expectation that women's lives should involve more dramatic changes than men's. It seems that sexual difference feminists must think that it would be impossible to remove gender norms altogether, and that we should instead aim to restructure gender non-hierarchically.

Butler might object that this commits sexual difference feminism to the oppression of non-heterosexuals and of people of ambiguous gender. Moreover, could there ever really be different norms for males and females without one sex being subordinated to the other? Take the harmless-sounding idea that women should have more life-changes than men. In practice this could well translate into the idea that women and not men should leave work when they have children. So feminists need to be able to attach non-hierarchical symbolism to male and female bodies without this conveying an expectation that men and women should act in systematically different and power-imbalanced ways. But it is not obvious how this is possible.

9. Conclusion

This chapter has shown how Irigaray's concept of sexual difference derives from Lacan. I have also argued that Irigaray's concept of sexual difference usefully highlights one aspect of the social reality that shapes women's and men's lives. But we must also look at how sexual symbolism co-exists and entwines with varied sets of gender expectations that are embodied in social institutions. Moreover, recognizing sexual difference as well as gender raises a question about whether gender can be removed and, if not, whether gender could ever be defined non-hierarchically.

Feminist discussions of difference and sexual difference bear on several areas of philosophy, such as:

1   History of philosophy. Like other feminist historians of philosophy such as Lloyd (1984), Irigaray shows how all philosophical theories and concepts are shaped by imagery and metaphor. This imagery cannot be ignored, since it guides how philosophers understand and construct their theories in the first place. Irigaray also claims that there is a constant history of sexed binary oppositions in philosophy. But is this too simplified a view of philosophical history, which after all is very diverse?

2   Ethics and political philosophy. Difference feminists suggest that key moral and political concepts such as justice and individual rights, and central traditions of thought such as Kantian ethics or social contract theory, are 'masculinist': they reflect men's perspective exclusively. So do we need to reconceive justice or rights in less masculinist ways? How might this be done?

3   Philosophy of language. Some radical feminists have claimed that language is male. One such radical feminist, Dale Spender (1980), argues that men have commandeered languages and shaped them so that they draw distinctions that support male dominance. For instance, English gives negative connotations to words for women – like 'witch' or 'spinster' compared to the benign term 'bachelor' (Saul 2005). Lacan offers a different way to see language as male: for him, all language must be 'phallocentric'. How plausible are any of these claims? In what sense might 'female' speech or language be a desirable or meaningful possibility?

Aside from how they bear on existing philosophical fields, feminist discussions of difference and sexual difference open up a range of new and important questions. Do cultures contain basic patterns of symbolism regarding male and female bodies? Is this symbolism written into the nature of language, or can it be changed? What is the relation between gender and patterns of sexual symbolism? Should feminists aim to create a genuine sexual difference or to dissolve gender – or are these aims compatible? Is recognizing women's difference compatible with pursuing women's equality? Questions such as these mark out the field of feminist philosophy of difference and sexual difference.

Notes

1 Some sexual difference feminists talk about the difference between 'masculine' and 'feminine' as it is symbolized culturally. I prefer 'male' and 'female' because the symbolism in question surrounds bodies.
2 This chapter looks only at Irigaray's earlier work (especially Irigaray 1974, 1977a). Her later work, from the mid-1980s onwards, is different and would need separate discussion.
3 For ease of comprehension I will speak of the phallus as the 'symbol', rather than the 'signifier' (as Lacan usually says), of language and desire.
4 Ragland-Sullivan (1986: 275, 281, 299) suggests a similar interpretation of Lacan.
5 For Lacan biological females (or males) can sometimes adopt the symbolic male (or female) position. Moreover, for Lacan, the complexity of our emotions before entering the symbolic means that *everyone* wavers between the male and female positions to some degree.
6 The words in Beauvoir and Irigaray that are translated as 'masculine' and 'feminine' are *masculin* and *féminin*. In Beauvoir and Irigaray these words have different connotations to the English words 'masculine' and 'feminine', which refer to the two gender roles. Some French feminists such as Delphy and Wittig do use *féminin* and *masculin* to refer to gender roles. But Beauvoir and Irigaray use *masculin* and *féminin* to refer to the meanings that being male-bodied and female-bodied take on within human culture. See chapter 6, section 4 on this issue in Beauvoir.
7 Chapter 7, section 2 will argue that Beauvoir's own position is more complex than Irigaray believes.
8 Chapter 2, section 6 argues this at more length.
9 Irigaray is reluctant to call herself a feminist. See chapter 7, section 5.

Further Reading

Lacan   Grosz 1990a is a full-length introduction. Brennan 1991 is more advanced but still illuminating.

Irigaray   Irigaray's essay 'This Sex Which Is Not One' in Irigaray 1977a is classic, as is Irigaray 1979 (on mother/daughter relationships). Irigaray 1995 is a useful later article that explains some of her earlier ideas. Grosz 1989: ch. 4 is a good introduction to Irigaray.

Sexual difference feminism   Braidotti 1998, though difficult, bursts with ideas.

Difference feminism   Gilligan 1982: ch. 1; Ruddick 1980. Eisenstein 1980: xv–xx clearly explains the intellectual origins of Anglo-American difference feminism.

5 Essentialism

1. Feminist debates about essentialism

One of the liveliest areas in recent feminist philosophy is the set of debates that has taken place since the 1970s about essentialism. These debates have been heated: feminists have often criticized other feminists for being 'essentialist', and those criticized have defended themselves sometimes by denying that they are 'essentialist' and sometimes by defending 'essentialism'. But different feminists mean very different things by 'essentialism'. Some of the main things for which feminists criticize one another when they make the accusation of 'essentialism' are:

1   making biological determinist claims, i.e. claiming that women's biology gives rise to their social position(s) or their values or ways of acting;
2   making universal claims about all women which actually only apply to some women;
3   making any claim that certain experiences, situations or concerns are common to all women;
4   assuming that the word 'woman' has one single meaning.[1]

Different feminists emphasize different problems from this list when they use the word 'essentialism'. So one key feature of the essentialism debates is that the 'essentialism' that is under debate has a range of meanings. When reading feminist literature on 'essentialism', one should be aware that different authors use this term differently.

Nonetheless, this chapter will argue that the different feminist senses of 'essentialism' are connected, and the chapter will track some of these connections. I believe that these connections arise because the essentialism debates are in fact organized around three core questions (although in much of the literature these questions remain in the background). These three questions inform how most feminists, despite their different understandings of the term, think about 'essentialism'. The first question is: (1) Is there any property, or set of properties, which all women share?

A tempting reply is: yes – all women have the property of being female. After all, in everyday language 'woman' often just means 'female human being'. But many feminists are reluctant to say that what women share is femaleness. Consider that in everyday language, 'woman' not only suggests a female human being. It also suggests someone who occupies a specific social role, as in the phrase 'a woman's place is in the kitchen'. And it suggests someone with a specific set of psychological traits, such as being liable to cry (hence the phrase 'boys don't cry'). In short, the word 'woman' is ambiguous between sex and gender. This is unsurprising: the word predates the sex/gender distinction, and so it embodies the pre-feminist view that women's status and psychology are neither social nor changeable but are fixed by biology. But since many feminists distinguish sex from gender, they want to redefine 'woman' to make it less ambiguous.

Many feminists, therefore, take it that what it is to be a **woman** is to be a member of the feminine *gender* (e.g. Spelman 1990: 134). On this view, an individual is a woman if she satisfies social expectations about femininity.[2] Being a woman, then, is different from being biologically female. In principle, one could be both a biological female and a man – although this is rare, since society presses females to become feminine. A fictional example of a female man is Evelyn in Angela Carter's *The Passion of New Eve*. Evelyn is a sexist man on whom radical feminists inflict a male-to-female sex-change, and who directly afterwards combines female flesh with a man's mind (Carter 1982: 78).

When feminists ask whether there are any properties which all women share, they are asking whether there are any properties which all women have *as women*, just in virtue of belonging to the feminine gender. But any properties that women have as members of the feminine gender must be properties they have acquired due to social expectations. So if women share any properties, this must be because all societies impose similar expectations on them. Societies seem very varied, but perhaps at a deeper level they hold the same expectations about femininity. For example, Charlotte Witt suggests, foot-binding in China and cosmetic surgery in Europe and the US both rest on the same expectation 'that women [should] mutilate themselves in pursuit of . . . culturally defined notion[s] of physical beauty' (Witt 1995: 329).

Other feminist theorists object that women's lives are really, not just apparently, very diverse. These theorists argue that expectations about femininity are fundamentally different in different societies, and in different groups within each of those societies – in different classes, races, and ethnic and subcultural groups. As a result, women in different societies and social groups develop very different sets of psychological traits and bodily habits. Given women's diversity, many feminist theorists conclude that there are no properties which all women as women share.

Why are these debates about whether women have any common properties known as debates about 'essentialism'? In philosophy, essentialism is the belief that objects have both 'essential' and 'accidental' properties. Essential properties are properties that objects must necessarily have in order to belong to a particular kind. For example, for a lump of metal to be a piece of gold it must have an atomic number of 79. If something lacks this property, then it cannot belong to the kind gold but must be an object of a different kind. In contrast, the size and weight of the piece of gold are 'accidental' properties: they could change, but the object would still be a piece of gold. So essentialism about *gender* is the view that there is some socially acquired property, or set of socially acquired properties, which one must necessarily have in order to belong to the feminine – or masculine – gender. Perhaps, in order to be a woman, one must have been socialized into caring for one's friends and family.

Now, it seems that one could claim that all women share certain common – socially acquired – properties without claiming that these are properties women must necessarily have in order to be women. Recall Catherine MacKinnon's claim that all women, as women, are sexually subordinated. Surely, one might think, MacKinnon takes this status to be an accidental rather than an essential property of women. Surely she must believe that women could, and should, lose their sexually subordinate status but still remain women. Perhaps, then, the feminist debate about common properties has been misnamed and is not really a debate about gender *essentialism* at all.

But remember that, for many feminist thinkers, what it is to be a woman is just to fulfil the feminine role as it is defined in a given society. If there is (as MacKinnon, among others, thinks) just one basic cross-cultural feminine role (for MacKinnon, the role of being sexually subordinate), then in order to be a woman one must fulfil that role. And one must have the traits and habits that go with that role. Any person who lacks these traits and does not fulfil the feminine role is not a woman. From this perspective, a woman who was not sexually subordinate would just not *be* a woman any longer.

Given the way in which many feminists understand 'woman', then, those feminists who claim that there are common social expectations about femininity, and that all women have common properties as a result, are also claiming that these expectations and properties are essential, i.e. necessary, to women. They are expectations and properties which all women must fulfil or possess in order to count as women. Thus, the feminist debate about common properties is simultaneously a debate about the question: (2) Is there any property, or set of properties, which women must necessarily – essentially – have in order to be women? Those feminists who answer 'yes' are **essentialists**.

Other feminist theorists deny that there are any universal social expectations about femininity. These theorists, who deny that there is any single set of expectations which every woman must necessarily fulfil in order to be a woman, are **anti-essentialists**. They highlight facts such as this: white upper-class women in nineteenth-century America were expected to stay at home and tend their families, while their black women slaves were expected to do heavy manual work outside the home. But, anti-essentialists point out, women of both kinds were still women: they did not need to share any common feature in order to qualify as women. These anti-essentialist arguments raise a third question. (3) If women have no common properties, then what makes them members of the same kind? *Are* we justified in claiming that women are of the same kind at all?

Because feminists understand 'essentialism' in varying ways, they do not all explicitly frame their discussions of essentialism in terms of these three core questions. Nonetheless, these three questions are in the background, implicitly or explicitly, throughout the essentialism debates. Thus, bearing these questions in mind will help us to steer through the history of these debates, in which diverse uses of 'essentialism' are in play.

One reason why these essentialism debates became heated is that some feminists thought that if women share no patterns of experience or values or social position, then they cannot have any motivation to act together in pursuit of political change. That is, anti-essentialism seemed to imply that feminist politics is impossible. I think that this concern about anti-essentialism is misplaced. I see the question of how political action by groups of women or feminists is possible as a practical one, embracing questions such as:

1   In what circumstances can solidarity exist amongst people – including women – who have different interests, experiences and levels of power?
2   What methods can people find by which to discuss and agree on shared political goals without the more powerful people dominating those who are less powerful?
3   How can different political groups form coalitions with one another?

These questions can only be answered from practical political experience, not by answering the philosophical question of whether women have anything in common and, if not, what does make them members of the same kind. This philosophical question is the focus of this chapter.

2. Socialist feminism, radical feminism and their black feminist critics

In the 1970s, feminist movements in many countries such as the US, Britain and France were largely divided into liberal, socialist and radical wings. At this time it was mainly socialist feminists who used the term 'essentialism'. They used this term to refer to (1) anti-feminists who claimed that women's social position is fixed by their biology. Why did socialist feminists classify these people as 'essentialists'? People who believe that there are essential properties often think that a thing's essential properties cause or explain its other properties. For example, the atomic mass of a piece of gold is what causes and explains its surface properties such as its colour and texture. The biological determinists to whom socialist feminists objected seem to have been 'essentialists' in this sense. They thought that women's biological properties caused and explained their subordinate social role and low status.

Socialist feminists also (2) classed some radical feminist thinkers as 'essentialists'. These radical feminists (e.g. Griffin 1984) suggested that men have a biological tendency to set up dominance relationships, and that women have a biological tendency to create more caring and non-hierarchical relationships. This position is essentialist because it takes men's and women's biology to explain their other characteristics. Radical feminists such as Griffin did not conclude that it is futile to try to change men's and women's positions. Instead they argued that we should go over to a 'female' form of culture and society. Socialist feminists (e.g. Segal 1988) asked how this cultural transformation could be possible if male biology necessarily leads to male domination.

Generally, socialist feminists understood essentialism to be the same as biological determinism and to be objectionable – like biological determinism – because it implies that social change is impossible. From the perspective of later feminists, though, much of 1970s socialist feminism is *itself* essentialist. Clearly 1970s socialist feminists were not essentialists in the sense of being biological determinists – they opposed biological determinism. When other feminists accused socialist feminists of being essentialist, they used 'essentialism' in a new sense. The kind of 'essentialism' to which socialist feminists tended to subscribe is the belief that all women have a common property – the property of being exploited or oppressed by men.

This new use of 'essentialism' can be confusing given that much feminist writing equates 'essentialism' with 'biological essentialism', i.e. biological determinism. But the feminists who make this equation are mistaken. To be an essentialist, one does not have to believe that women's common properties are biological or are biologically determined. If one believes that all women share certain features because of how they are treated or socialized, and that women cannot be women without acquiring these features, then one is an essentialist.[3]

Socialist feminists, then, are essentialists because they believe that all women, *as* women, share the property of being exploited or oppressed by men. Socialist feminists defended this belief in opposition to traditional Marxism. Marxists argued that working-class and middle-class women have opposed interests because of their opposed locations within the class relations that, for Marxists, form the basic structure of any society. Working-class women are exploited, while middle-class women exploit the work of others or at least benefit from being married to men who carry out this exploitation. So working-class women's interest is in struggling for the abolition of capitalism together with working-class men. Meanwhile middle-class women's interest is to preserve capitalism. As middle- and working-class women have no common interests, they have no basis on which to join a common feminist movement.

To refute this traditional Marxist view, socialist feminists needed to show that despite their different class positions all women as women have a common situation: they are all exploited or oppressed by men. For example (as we saw in chapter 3), Christine Delphy claimed that all women – whatever their class – are exploited by their husbands, for whom they have to do domestic work. If Delphy is right, then all women do share an interest in struggling together to throw off this burden of exploitation. So for socialist feminists there are *two* forces that shape all women's lives: (1) their shared exploitation by men and (2) their different places in class relations.

Radical feminists agreed that women all suffer oppression by men, but they maintained that this oppression shapes women's lives more fundamentally than their class. Radical feminists also stressed that men oppress women sexually, for example through rape or by forcing women into heterosexual liaisons. Socialist feminists instead emphasized that women are exploited and that this takes place in the family, where women are forced or expected to do unpaid domestic work and childcare.

By the late 1970s, both approaches were being criticized by groups of women whose lives did not fit the patterns that socialist and radical feminists described. Black feminists, from the US especially, were among the most forceful critics. They challenged (1) the socialist feminist emphasis on women's exploitation within the family. For black women who usually rely economically on work outside the home, the workplace and not the family is the central place of exploitation. Moreover, for black women and women of colour, families are never merely a place of exploitation because they also provide respite from the racism of the surrounding environment. As Barbara Smith says: 'Home has always meant a lot to people who are ostracized as racial outsiders in the public sphere. It is above all a place to be ourselves' (Smith 1983: li).

(2) Black feminists also criticized the radical feminist claim that all women as women suffer sexual domination by men. When black women suffer sexual domination, this is never merely sexual but always has racial dimensions as well. For instance, in the US during

slavery, it was not a crime for a white man to rape a black woman (and legal and political thinkers promoted the idea that black women are in any case sexually insatiable and promiscuous). In the decades after slavery, many black women worked as domestic servants for white families and often suffered rape or sexual harassment at the hands of their employers. In these cases sexual and racial domination were entwined in the idea that black women were there to be used, sexually and otherwise. Still, as Patricia Hill Collins points out, black women are most likely to be raped by black men. But even here the sexual domination that black women suffer is not simply sexual but is also animated by racist ideas. For example, acts of rape by black men may often be informed by the idea that black women are sexually insatiable, an idea that is a legacy of slavery (Hill Collins 1990: 179).

These black feminist criticisms imply that any attempt to create a theory of women's common social position (such as their shared exploitation within the family) will always exclude some women. There will always be some women whose lives do not conform to the theory (e.g. because to these women families are never simply exploitative but are also a haven in a racist world). The point is not just that there will always be some exceptional individuals whose lives do not fit a given theory. Rather, there will always be whole groups of women whose lives systematically fail to conform. In short, theories that claim that all women share a common social position will always be *falsely over-generalized*, claiming to apply to all women when at best they only apply to some.

Moreover, socialist and radical feminists generally claimed that their theories had the virtue of having been developed out of women's experience. But evidently their feminist theories did not readily correspond to black women's experience. Seemingly, feminists had derived their theories from the experience only of white, usually middle-class, women. And these theories had had the effect of silencing less privileged groups of women by suggesting that, as their lives did not match the theories, they were anomalies or were not 'real' women. Arguably, then, theories that claim that all women share a common social position are not only false; these theories also *oppress* those women who fail to share the supposedly common position.

When black feminists pointed out that socialist and radical feminists had made false and oppressive over-generalizations, the problem to which they were pointing (without always using the term) was that socialist and radical feminists were 'essentialist'. Socialist and radical feminists were 'essentialist' in that they made claims about the common position/experiences of all women – claims which actually only applied to some women. Moreover, anti-essentialist feminists would add, those claims *necessarily* only applied to some women, since there just *is no* common position/experience that all women share.

We should note that these criticisms of essentialism do not make it impossible to make statistical generalizations such as 'on average, in the UK (full-time) women workers earn 82 per cent of what (full-time) male workers earn'. Generalizations of this kind do not falsely claim that *every* woman worker earns 82 per cent of what every male worker earns. However, anti-essentialist criticisms do imply that when making any such generalizations about (e.g.) 'women's average earnings' we

1   should acknowledge that these generalizations cut across the differences between the (average) earnings of white women, black women, Indian women, and many other groups of women; and
2   we should seek to gain a fuller picture by finding out about the different earnings of women in these various groups.

If we are careful, we can construct some limited generalizations without over-generalizing. But, plausibly, any claims about *all* women *will* be both falsely over-generalized and oppressive to some women.

3. Essentialism and sexual difference

So far we have seen how the problem of essentialism has arisen for some forms of feminism which use the concept of gender. As we saw in chapter 4, though, some feminist philosophers use the concept of sexual difference and not that of gender. Do issues of essentialism still arise for sexual difference feminists?

Some feminists (e.g. Moi 1985: ch. 7) have accused Irigaray, the originator of sexual difference feminism, of being an essentialist. To understand these criticisms, we must first recall that Irigaray thinks we cannot easily think past our horizon of cultural symbolism about what it means to be male and female. She therefore suggests that we 'mimic' this symbolism in ways that alter it. This mimicry is strategically essentialist. It reproduces or mimics inherited ideas about the essential natures of males and females strategically, in order to alter them and to make them more open to criticism.[4]

But critics such as Moi accused Irigaray of being an essentialist in a different sense. They targeted Irigaray's image of women's 'two lips' (Irigaray 1977a: 26). As we saw (chapter 4, section 5), Irigaray suggests that women's two sets of lips – their labia and their mouths – could provide a symbol of women's status as speaking and desiring agents. Irigaray's critics, though, thought she was claiming that one of women's biological properties – their labia – necessarily causes them to speak differently to and less coherently than men. These critics concluded that Irigaray believed that women's biology makes them necessarily different from, and liable to be subordinated by, men. Irigaray's critics, then, took her to be an essentialist in the sense of being a biological determinist. This criticism is inaccurate: Irigaray is an essentialist in the different sense of being a strategic essentialist.[5]

Other feminist thinkers have extended the notion of strategic essentialism beyond the context of Irigaray's thought. For instance, Denise Riley suggests that 'it is compatible to suggest that "women" don't exist – while maintaining a politics of "as if they existed" – since the world behaves as if they unambiguously did' (1989: 112). What Riley means is this. Anti-essentialists are right that women inhabit different places in society and have different values and experiences. But at the symbolic level women are thought about as if they were all the same – as when Hamlet states 'Frailty, thy name is woman'. Because these symbolic ideas about woman's nature deeply shape people's thought, sometimes the only way to challenge these ideas is not to reject but to 'mime' them, to reproduce them with a difference. To do this is to combine strategic essentialism in relation to the symbolic order with anti-essentialism in relation to gender.[6]

We might object that symbolic ideas about women's nature must surely affect women's social positions so that all those positions *do* acquire common features. For instance, if the idea exists that women's function is to bear children then surely all women will find themselves expected to do this work. But strategic essentialists can reply that the same symbolic ideas will have very different effects in different circumstances. What exact kind of childrearing work women do will vary relative to their class and race. For example, Hill Collins (1990: ch. 6) argues that, compared to white women, US women in black communities and neighbourhoods give one another much more extensive help with childcare – so that in these communities the work of 'bloodmothers' is regularly supplemented by help from 'othermothers'.

Still, we might wonder whether many symbolic ideas about women rest on a hidden presupposition that they apply only to some but not all women. For example, Hélène Cixous reports that women have long been seen as a 'dark continent' (1975: 68) relative to men.[7] According to Cixous, women have been seen – like Africa as many Europeans came to perceive it in the nineteenth century – as an unknown, dangerous and uncivilized region. Yet this imagery is only meaningful if people who are (or are thought to be) of African descent are also seen as a 'dark continent' relative to white Europeans. In that case, black women form a dark continent within the dark continent of women. But then it is really only *white* women who are seen merely as the dark continent relative to men and not also as a dark continent relative to other women. Symbolic imagery which appears at first sight to apply to all women is actually about one privileged subgroup of women, whom it falsely equates with women as a whole. If feminists reproduce this imagery, even with a difference, then they also reproduce this equation of the most privileged women with women as a whole.

Strategic essentialism, then, has similar problems to the forms of 'gender' feminism which make claims about 'all women' which really only apply to some, privileged, women. Likewise, strategic essentialists assume that traditional essentialist ideas concern all women when actually these ideas only concern some privileged women. There may be ways for strategic essentialists to overcome this problem. But we should now return to the problems with the kind of essentialism that affects some forms of 'gender' feminism, since these latter problems have been at the heart of the feminist essentialism debates.

4. MacKinnon, Chodorow and the problems with essentialism

'Gender' feminists might respond to the criticisms of essentialism made by black feminists by defending a more nuanced version of essentialism. That is, one might defend a more nuanced version of the claim that women share a common social location as women. One might agree that women are never just women – they are always white or black, middle-class or working-class, heterosexual or homosexual, able-bodied or disabled. Each woman's social location as a woman is combined with a social location in terms of race, class, etc. But this is consistent with there being a general *form* or pattern of gender oppression from which all women suffer. This general form of oppression manifests itself or gets modified in a number of particular ways when it is combined with, or is intersected by, other forms of oppression.

The concept of **intersectionality** has been developed by black (and other) feminist sociologists and legal theorists, including Patricia Hill Collins and Kimberlé Crenshaw (1989). The concept means that societies contain several different 'systems of domination' which 'intersect' with one another (or which 'interlock', as Hill Collins 1990: 222 puts it). So when another form of oppression intersects with gender oppression, it affects and modifies the form that gender oppression takes. Perhaps, for example, all women as women do an unfair share of domestic work within the family. But when this exploitation is intersected by racist oppression as it is for black women, this exploitation takes on a particular manifestation as work that at least creates a space of respite from racism.

Along these lines, one might try to defend MacKinnon's claim that all women occupy a common position of sexual subordination to men. Angela Harris (1990) has criticized MacKinnon's claim, arguing that for black women sexual subordination is always racial subordination at the same time. But in defence of MacKinnon, perhaps black women are still – like white women – sexually subordinated as women, but their sexual subordination as women manifests itself in a particular form because it intersects with and is affected by racist oppression.

Harris's arguments imply, though, that MacKinnon's theory cannot rightly be defended in this way. Harris's arguments expose two problems with the 'nuanced essentialist' view that black and white women undergo different modifications of the same general form of oppression as women.

(1) This 'nuanced essentialist' view implies that there are some women who are oppressed solely in terms of gender and not also in terms of class, race, sexuality, or any other non-gender system of domination. The gender oppression which these women suffer is not intersected or affected by any other kind of oppression. So these women suffer gender oppression in its pure form and not under some particular modification. This implies that these – privileged – women are the paradigm cases of women, whose lives reveal the workings of the gender system in its pure form (Spelman 1988: 186). And since these women experience gender oppression in its pure form, their experience must yield the most insight into the nature of gender oppression. So 'nuanced essentialism' implies that the experience of white, middle-class women

should form the starting-point for feminist theory. It seems, then, that if feminist theorizing is premised on 'nuanced essentialism' then it will inevitably be exclusive and oppressive.

(2) Harris argues that actually black women do not undergo a particular modification of the same general form of oppression that white women also undergo. According to MacKinnon, that general form of oppression is sexual subordination to men as a group. But, Harris objects, black women are not sexually subordinated to men as a group. They are sexually subordinated in one way to white men and in another significantly different way to black men. In the US, if a white man rapes or harasses a black woman, then (regardless of his intentions) this act carries specific meanings because of its continuity with the historical legacy of slavery. A different set of meanings comes into play if a black man is the perpetrator. For example, the woman might feel worried about complaining because she is aware that historically many black men were falsely accused of rape.

Harris's second argument suggests that the 'nuanced essentialist' view is false. That is, it is false to say that there is one general form of gender oppression which gets modified into various particular manifestations. An alternative view would be that there are several *different* forms of gender oppression each corresponding to different class and race locations. To clarify what this view might amount to, we can look at some criticisms of Nancy Chodorow, another feminist theorist who is an 'essentialist' in that she believes women to share a common social role as childcarers.

Chodorow claims that, systematically and cross-culturally, women have primary responsibility for the care of young children (Chodorow 1978: 215–17). As a result, mothers treat their children differently depending on whether they are male or female. Mothers know that their female children will one day be responsible for childcare too, so they treat these children as the same as themselves. This behaviour causes female children to form a sense that their selves and emotions are very similar to those of their mothers. So girls develop, and retain as women, a fluid and relational sense of self. That is, they feel that their selves and feelings are not clearly distinguished from those of their mothers and of other people generally. For Chodorow, this property of having a relatively fluid and relational sense of self is one that all women share as women, because of how their mothers have brought them up.

Chodorow has been criticized for ignoring the fact that women of different classes and cultures mother their children in different ways. To defend herself, Chodorow might appeal to a form of nuanced essentialism. She could argue that different forms of mothering all foster close mother–daughter relationships, but that they do so in a variety of class- and culture-specific ways.

Carolyn Steedman's *Landscape for a Good Woman* (1986) casts doubt on this defence. This partly autobiographical, partly theoretical book reflects on Steedman's relationship to her mother as a working-class girl growing up in 1950s London. Steedman remembers a time when a middle-class health visitor humiliated her mother. Her mother 'cried . . . And then she stopped crying, . . . got by . . . [and thought] it shouldn't be like this; it's unfair; I'll manage' (Steedman 1986: 1–2). She was determined to restrain her unhappiness and to cope and be self-sufficient. She urged her daughter to achieve the same self-sufficiency: 'I must never, ever, cry for myself' (1986: 30). Rather than encouraging emotional dependency and closeness between mother and daughter, Steedman's mother encouraged emotional independence and resilience.

So it would be false for Chodorow to claim that working-class mothers, like middle-class mothers, treat their daughters as closely connected to them, but do so in a class-specific way. Women of different classes have different ideas about appropriate feminine behaviour and they mother their daughters in correspondingly different ways. Girls from different classes will develop correspondingly different senses of self. Middle-class girls may have a relational sense of self, but working-class girls may feel more self-sufficient and stoical. As Elizabeth Spelman concludes, 'females [always] become not simply women but particular kinds of women' (Spelman 1988: 113).

We must conclude that in all societies, there is not one single system of gender oppression – or one single form of femininity – which takes on a range of modifications. Rather, in each society there are many different forms of femininity (and masculinity), and many different sets of expectations about appropriate feminine (and masculine) behaviour. Since a gender is defined by a set of expectations about appropriate behaviour, this means that each society can be said to contain several different feminine (and masculine) genders (Spelman 1988: 175). Each of these genders exists relative to a particular race, class, and culture. Thus, black femininity is not a modification of one general form of femininity. Black femininity, white femininity, middle-class femininity, Jewish femininity, etc., are all different forms of femininity which follow no common pattern. Each of these class-, race- and culture-relative forms of femininity is oppressive for women insofar as that form of femininity is defined as subordinate to some form(s) of masculinity. But these kinds of oppression do not follow any single pattern, because different definitions of femininity imply different forms of subordination.

Yet if women of different groups are feminine in different ways and have different values, experiences, etc., then what makes them all *women*? If their ways of being feminine do not follow any common pattern, then what is it that makes all of them ways of being *feminine*? All the participants in the feminist essentialism debates accept that black women, white women, Jewish women, working-class women, etc., are all women. But the philosophical question is, what is it that makes all these women members of a single kind (the kind 'woman'), if their social situations, values, and experiences follow no common form? Several feminist philosophers have proposed answers to this question. Sections 5 to 7 critically assess answers proposed by Cressida Heyes, Iris Young and Sally Haslanger.[8]

5. Family resemblances

So far I have assumed that women can only belong to the same kind if they share some common property. But perhaps this assumption is false. Perhaps women are of the same kind not due to any common property but because there is a network of resemblances between them. So Cressida Heyes (2000: ch. 3) argues, drawing on Ludwig Wittgenstein's notion of 'family resemblances'.

Wittgenstein introduces this notion in connection with games. He argues that we should not assume that there must be a property which all games (ball games, word games, card games) share and in virtue of which they are all called 'games'. We must 'look and see' whether there is any such property. Wittgenstein suggests that in the case of games – and some other entities – there is not. Rather, 'games form a *family* the members of which have family likenesses' (Wittgenstein 1969: 17). Family members resemble one another in criss-crossing ways. Amy has her aunt's build, her mother's eyes and her cousin's hands, while her cousin has her mother's nose and her mother has her aunt's hair. They are all said to belong to the same family because of these criss-crossing similarities. Games, likewise, are all called 'games' on the basis of a criss-crossing set of resemblances between them.

A simplified model can show how Heyes applies these points to women. Individuals Ann and Bess have XX chromosomes but Cat is a male-to-female (MTF) transsexual with XY chromosomes. Bess and Cat present themselves as conventionally feminine whereas Ann acts butch. Ann and Cat care full-time for their families while Bess has no family and pursues a business career. There is no single property (XX chromosomes, feminine self-presentation, care duties) that all three people share. And none of those three properties would on its own suffice to make any of them a woman. Rather Ann, Bess and Cat belong to the category 'woman' because they have enough overlapping similarities with one another (Heyes 2000: 84).

In hard cases it is unclear whether someone resembles other women enough to fall under the category. Some feminists believe that MTF transsexuals do not have enough similarities to count as women (e.g. they have not had a life-time of vulnerability to rape and sexual violence), so that MTFs should not be allowed into women-only spaces and events. For example, the Michigan Womyn's Music Festival admits only 'womyn-born-womyn', excluding MTFs who were born male. Heyes, on the other hand, argues (2000: 92–4) that MTFs *do* have enough similarities to count as women. Throughout their lives, MTFs have often encountered threats of violence; MTFs struggle – as many women do – to conform to feminine ideals; and they have felt deep unhappiness with their biological bodies – again like the many women who resort to cosmetic surgery, just as MTFs turn to sex-change surgery.

There is a problem with Heyes's approach. This problem reflects a wider problem with resemblance theories of what it is for something to be a certain kind of thing. Any one thing resembles many other things in an indefinite variety of ways. Suppose that Ann and Bess resemble one another in having freckles, Bess and Cat in that they like brussels sprouts and Ann and Cat in that they holidayed in France as children. Presumably *these* resemblances are not relevant to their status as women, whereas the resemblances mentioned earlier were. But how do we know which resemblances are relevant to determining whether someone is a woman?

To know that the earlier resemblances were relevant, we need background knowledge that all women are expected to do care duties and to fulfil certain ideals of feminine appearance (slenderness, youthfulness, etc.). These body ideals and expectations of care are feminine gender norms – norms that are applied to individuals who are (or who are taken to be) female. But if we know that these norms exist, then we also know by implication that women are those who conform sufficiently to these norms. In that case being a woman ultimately depends *not* on having enough similarities to other women but on fulfilling a given society's norms of femininity. Inevitably those who fulfil these norms sufficiently will thereby come to resemble one another, but these resemblances are a consequence, not a condition, of their being women.

6. Are women a series?

Iris Young's account of what makes women members of the same kind is that all women belong to what she calls a series. She explains what a series is in her article 'Gender as Seriality: Thinking About Women as a Social Collective' (1994). She takes the concept from a distinction between *groups* and *series* made by the existentialist philosopher Jean-Paul Sartre (1960: 256–9).

For Sartre, a **group** is a set of people (e.g. French resistance fighters during the Nazi occupation) who have common values and a shared identity and who organize activities together to promote those values. In contrast, a **series** is a set of people who have no shared values and identities, but who are passively cast into identical circumstances by the objects that structure some aspect of their lives. For example, a set of people who are waiting for a bus are a series. They are all cast into the same situation, that of having to wait for the bus. They are cast into this situation by the bus timetable, the bus stop, the road network and the route that the bus takes. Sartre says that these objects – the timetable, the bus stop, etc. – are 'practico-inert'. Although only inert objects, they have a practical effect: they organize people's lives.

Now, Young agrees with anti-essentialists that there are no 'specific attributes that all women have' (Young 1994: 733). Women occupy very different social locations and so there are no values, experiences or sense of identity that all women share. For Young, this means that women are not a group in Sartre's sense. But this is consistent with women being a series. To be a series, their lives must all be organized by the same set of 'practico-inert' objects. And Young claims that women's lives are indeed organized by the same objects. These objects are 'visual and verbal representations' – such as romantic films, gossip magazines or 'chick-lit' – and artefacts that are 'flooded with gender codes' (1994: 729) – such as women's clothes, make-up, hairdryers and depilatory tools.

These objects are 'gender-coded' due to a background assumption that there should be a sexual division of labour. That is, it is assumed that women should do certain activities or jobs such as childcare or nursing. Particular objects are then designed for and targeted at women under the assumption that they should be doing these activities. For example, in contemporary western countries women's clothes and shoes are usually designed to make the wearers look sexy or fashionable rather than to enable them to accomplish practical tasks. Thus, 'feminine-coded' objects channel women to do the sorts of activities that are expected of them.

So, for Young, in any particular society all women's lives are organized by the same set of gender-coded everyday objects. Which objects these are varies in different societies, depending on what activities they expect of women. For instance, different objects organize women's lives in traditional agricultural communities and in modern urban societies. But in every society, Young holds, there *is* a specific set of feminine-coded objects structuring women's lives. However, these women's shared 'practico-inert' realities do not cause them to have the same kinds of experience, to form the same values or even to engage in the same activities. Each woman makes sense of and responds to her circumstances in a unique way (Young 2005: 16–17). Common 'practico-inert' realities translate into diverse individual experiences and lives. This is why Young denies that there are any 'specific attributes that all women share'.

To sum up: for Young, all women's lives are organized by sets of objects which convey assumptions – specific to particular societies – about women's place in the sexual division of labour. Young's view has a problem, as Mari Mikkola (2005: 104–6) shows. Today, many women work in occupations – lecturing or medicine, for instance – which until relatively recently were judged suitable only for men. These women find themselves in working environments and surrounded by objects that inherit a masculine code. For instance, women lecturers work amidst lecture theatres, desks and computers which, on Young's analysis, encode an expectation that their users will be men. This is reflected in that much of this equipment – e.g. the lecterns in lecture theatres – is the wrong size for most women.

But for Young what makes someone a woman or a man is just whether their lives are organized by masculine- or feminine-coded objects. It looks as if, on Young's account, women who work in traditionally 'masculine' occupations count as men. Young might reply that these women's lives are not only structured by the objects in their work environments but also by feminine-coded objects such as cosmetics, sanitary towels and hairdryers. Yet suppose – not unreasonably – that these women spend most of their time at work. If so, then they have at least as much claim to be men as have 'men' who have opted to spend all their time at home looking after young children, and dealing with 'feminine'-coded objects including nappies, prams and day-care centres. Yet this conclusion – that the working 'women' are really men – is implausible, since most of these 'women' *are* identifiably women (and not only female) by other criteria. Generally these women understand themselves to be women, they have typically 'feminine' personality traits and they have feminine modes of embodiment.[9]

I conclude that we should not accept Young's thesis that women belong to the same kind because their lives are all structured by feminine-coded objects. This thesis cannot account for women whose lives are largely structured by masculine-coded objects yet who remain recognizably women. We need an alternative account of what makes women members of the same kind.

7. Are women subordinated on the basis of their sex?

Haslanger's article 'Gender, Race: (What) Are They? (What) Do We Want Them To Be?' (2000) develops a theory of gender which simultaneously identifies something that all women have in common. Haslanger holds that the differences between women's social and cultural locations should not obscure the fact that in almost all societies males are systematically privileged over females. She infers that what women have in common, despite their differences, is that they are 'socially positioned' as 'subordinate' to men on the basis of their sex. As she puts it:

S is a woman iff [i.e. if and only if] S is systematically subordinated along some dimension (economic, political, legal, social, etc.), and S is 'marked' as a target for this treatment by observed or imagined biological features presumed to be evidence of a female's biological role in reproduction. (Haslanger 2000: 39)

Haslanger's definition of what it is to be a **woman** has four main parts:

1   To be 'socially positioned' in a given way is to be perceived and treated in a given way by others and for social institutions to structure one's life in accordance with those perceptions.

2   To be 'subordinated', or 'oppressed', is to be put at a disadvantage relative to people of some other group – in this case, men. (On this definition of oppression see Frye 1983: ch. 1.) One can be disadvantaged along various 'dimensions', e.g. economically – if one is pushed into a relatively low-paying job – or sexually – if one is made vulnerable to sexual violence. According to Haslanger, to be a woman, one need not be subordinated along all dimensions of social life. As long as one is subordinated in at least some respect, and on the basis of sex, then one belongs to the kind 'woman'.

3   In any society many systems of oppression exist. Being a woman is distinctive in that the oppression it involves is imposed on people because they are or are taken to be female-sexed. In contrast, Haslanger suggests, to be black is to be oppressed on the basis of physical features – skin colour, facial structure, etc. – which, others presume, indicate African origin or ancestry. Women, Haslanger says more precisely, are oppressed based on being 'observed' or – in the case of some intersexed and transgendered people – 'imagined' to have the biological properties of a female. Moreover, even those people who unambiguously are biologically female are usually treated oppressively not because others have actually seen their anatomy but because others presume they are female given their clothes, posture, and demeanour.

4   Why should actual, presumed or imagined female biology provide a basis or warrant for oppressive treatment? Haslanger argues that there must be a prior assumption that having female biology makes people inferior and so appropriate 'targets' for subordinate treatment. The oppression of women thus depends on ingrained

cultural ideas about the inferior status of the female body (Haslanger 2000: 40). For this oppression to cease, male and female bodies would first need to be seen as of equal worth.

For Haslanger, what women have in common such that they are all women is that they are all oppressed on account of their actual or presumed sex. What particular kind of oppressive treatment they receive varies across different cultures and subcultures (Haslanger 2000: 39). Upper-class Victorian women were oppressed by being prevented from working outside the home. Working-class Victorian women were oppressed by having to combine such work with care for their often large families. But women are all women because, whatever kind and degree of oppression they suffer, it is imposed on them on account of their actual or presumed sex.

Haslanger has more success than (say) MacKinnon at identifying a property common to all women because Haslanger does not argue that women have in common a particular form of oppression, such as being sexually objectified. For Haslanger, what women have in common is the higher-level property of suffering any one of *many* forms of oppression and doing so based on their observed or presumed sex.

But Haslanger's account of gender has a problem. Since, for Haslanger, women are by definition subordinate, it follows that feminism's aim is for women to cease to exist (Haslanger 2000: 46). Indeed, any woman who challenges her subordinate status must by definition be challenging her status as a woman, even if she does not intend to. The problem is that these claims of Haslanger's leave no room for what Natalie Stoljar calls 'revaluing . . . [i.e.] the positive project of developing new and different conceptions' of femininity (Stoljar 1995: 281). This project of 'revaluing' is the project of redefining femininity in ways that free it from its traditionally subordinate status. In Haslanger's view this is impossible. Although Haslanger certainly thinks that we can and should change our gender norms, in her view any positive change to our gender norms would involve getting rid of the (necessarily subordinate) feminine gender.

Haslanger herself might not think that the fact that she does not allow for revaluing is a problem. She would probably stress that the feminine traits that one might try to revalue, such as caring, are moulded by contexts of oppression. As a result of this moulding, we cannot revalue feminine traits without – undesirably – having to preserve the oppressive contexts that produce them. In the case of caring traits, this context is that of family life, which for Haslanger is one of the 'dimensions' of social life along which females are perceived and treated as subordinate. In the family, this treatment takes the form of the expectation that females should bear an unjustly heavy burden of caring.

But let us think about Haslanger's notion of 'dimensions' of social life in light of the Foucaultian approach to gender which I endorsed in chapter 2. According to this approach, each of the various dimensions of social life which Haslanger identifies – work, sexual relationships, etc. – actually consists of a multiplicity of social institutions and relationships which each involve different sets of norms of femininity and masculinity. In each case, these sets of norms are bound up with a particular set of power relationships. Generally, these power relationships are (as Haslanger says) relationships in which women are subordinated to men based on their sex. But this general pattern of feminine subordination exists as a result of the co-existence – and mutual influence – of all these different norms, which each subordinate women in particular ways. Haslanger would presumably agree, since she thinks that different women are oppressed in different ways that are always specific to the times, places and social contexts in which these women live.

But once we accept that there is this multiplicity of social norms that subordinate women, then – I believe – it follows that it *is* possible to 'revalue' femininity. It follows from the Foucaultian view of gender that, because each power relationship and set of norms has its own dynamic, those who are subordinated within a given relationship always have the capacity to resist it. More specifically, those people can resist that power relationship not by totally rejecting it (this is impossible and unrealistic) but by reinterpreting or revising the norms that cement this relationship. For instance, within family relationships, women might reinterpret the norm that women should perform more care to argue that they deserve to be respected and recognized as carers or to be financially rewarded for their caring work. Or women might argue that if caring is so important then men should share this work and should learn to take on the associated 'feminine' virtues.

Thus, the implication of the Foucaultian view of gender is that norms can always be reinterpreted and fought over at a 'micro-level'.

These struggles to reinterpret what is expected of women (and of men) simultaneously shift the balance of power between women and men. Indeed, the Foucaultian view implies that women must always have engaged in ongoing resistance to subordination, even though contingently an overall pattern of masculine domination has tended to remain in place.

This means, though, that to be a woman is not *necessarily* to be subordinated. For if femininity can be redefined in ways that reduce or remove the power inequality between men and women, then femininity is not necessarily a subordinate status. Contingently, femininity has tended in most societies to be a subordinate status, but this state of affairs can be changed.

So, if Haslanger's view of women's subordination is (as I have suggested) consistent with a Foucaultian approach to gender, then Haslanger's view is also consistent with the possibility of femininity being 'revalued', or redefined so that it is non-subordinate. Yet Haslanger's definition of women denies this possibility. According to her definition, what it is to be a woman is to be subordinated based on one's actual or assumed sex. On this definition, if one is not so subordinated then one is not a woman, and if one successfully challenges one's subordination then one is challenging one's status as a woman. Haslanger's definition, I conclude, should be rejected: because norms of femininity can be and constantly are being revised, women can be women without thereby being subordinate.

If Haslanger's definition of women is rejected, then all that remains to unite women is that they are all expected to act in ways that are considered appropriate for people who are or are perceived to be female-sexed and that they all conform (sufficiently) to these expectations. That is, we are left with a weakened version of Haslanger's definition of women:

> S *is a* **woman** iff S is expected to act (and think, value, etc.) in certain distinctive ways, and does so act, where this is expected of S because S is observed or imagined to have biological features that are presumed to be evidence of a female's biological role in reproduction.

This definition is essentialist in that it picks out a property (the property of fulfilling social expectations which apply because one is or is taken to be female-sexed) which all women have in common and which they must necessarily have to be women. But this is such a high-level property that the definition is consistent with the *anti-essentialist* claim that the actual expectations made of women vary across cultures and subcultures, so that women do not share any concrete social position, values, patterns of experience, etc.

This definition has not reverted to the mistaken view that what women have in common is that they are female. That view is mistaken because it falsely conflates being a woman with being female. Rather, on my definition what women have in common is that they fulfil specific social norms which other people and institutions apply to them because they are or are taken to be female.

To accept this definition one does not have to agree with my earlier arguments that sex difference is biological. Suppose one agrees with Warnke and Wittig that people only pick out certain biological features as making people sexed given social norms which prescribe opposed masculine/feminine roles in reproductive sex. One may then say that women are those who fulfil specific social norms that are applied to them because they have or are assumed to have certain biological properties – breasts, vagina, womb, etc. – which are taken to make them female-sexed given a social climate in which norms of femininity/masculinity prevail.

In section 4, we saw that feminist criticisms of essentialism suggest that no society contains one single feminine or masculine gender. Spelman (1988) claims instead that each society contains several feminine and masculine genders, i.e. different sets of class-, race- and cultural-specific norms of femininity and masculinity. Yet in chapter 2 I argued that if gender exists then necessarily there are two genders, because gender just is the norm that males should act masculine and females feminine. Against that argument, feminist criticisms of essentialism seem to imply that if gender exists then necessarily there are *more* than two genders, because males/females are always expected to act masculine/feminine in a range of class-, race- and culture-specific ways.

But we can now see that these different feminine 'genders' (for simplicity let's focus on femininity) have a common property: they are all applied to people because those people are or are assumed to be female. Norms of femininity vary by class, race, etc., but this fact that they are all applied to females is what makes them all norms of *femininity*. And this means that all these norms contribute to defining one single feminine gender. These norms do not follow any common pattern in terms of their content, but they each define a part of a society's total set of expectations about what it is (in a whole range of contexts) to be feminine. So, after all, I suggest that diverse norms of femininity and masculinity contribute to defining two genders rather than defining a multiplicity of feminine and masculine genders.

If so, then although in any given society males/females are not all expected to act in the same ways, there is still a higher-level expectation that females should act feminine (according to some class-, race-, culture-specific set of norms) and males masculine. As such it is still the case that females are expected to act systematically differently from males. Thus, at the present time it remains true that, as Butler argues, diverse forms of femininity and masculinity exist only *within* an undesirably two-gender set-up.

8. Review and conclusion

This chapter began by asking whether all women share any property that makes them all women. Anti-essentialist feminists, especially black feminist critics of socialist and radical feminism, have convincingly argued that women have no such property, because women occupy very different places in society and so have no common social role, self-understanding, values or patterns of behaviour and experience. The question then arose, what *does* make all women women? I have argued that women only have in common the high-level property that they are expected to act (and do act) in distinctive ways because of their actual or perceived sex.

Like other areas of feminist philosophy at which we have looked, feminist debates about essentialism bear on several existing areas of philosophy – notably:

1   questions in social philosophy: questions of what social groups are, and what it is that makes any given set of people (e.g. women) into members of a group that occupies a distinctive place within society.
2   issues in political philosophy about whether and how it is possible for people to act collectively in pursuit of social change. In what circumstances might a set of people – e.g. women – who have no shared experience or values become motivated to join together in a social movement?

3   arguments in metaphysics about whether any things have essen-
     tial properties and what it is for a property to be essential. Feminist
     debates about whether any properties are essential to women rep-
     resent one particular area to which these philosophical arguments
     apply.

But feminist debates about essentialism do not merely result from
applying philosophical arguments about essential properties to the
case of women. Rather, these debates result from feminist theorists
drawing on philosophical concepts of essences and kinds to think
through political issues about the nature of women's oppression and
about power inequalities between women. This means that the
feminist essentialism debates take philosophical arguments about
essences in newly political directions, producing some new questions: What are women? Do women have any common properties?
Are women necessarily oppressed? How can feminist theorists avoid
privileging some women over others? These questions mark out
feminist thought on essentialism as a new and important area of
philosophy.

Notes

1 Simone de Beauvoir has yet another understanding of what 'essentialism'
   is. For her it is both (1) the claim that each human individual has a fixed
   nature, 'essence' or set of defining characteristics and (2) the more specific
   claim that women have a fixed nature. She denies both claims (as we will
   see in chapters 6 and 7) and in that sense is an 'anti-essentialist'.
2 This definition of 'woman' differs from that of: (1) Lacan and Irigaray. For
   them, a **woman** is a biologically female human who has come to identify
   herself as female, by understanding her body in terms of inherited symbolism regarding what it means to be female. (2) de Beauvoir. For her, a
   woman is a biological female who has given meaning to her female body
   over time. See chapter 6, section 4.
3 As Heyes (2000: 37) and Witt (1995: 324–5) argue, biological determinism
   is only one form of essentialism.
4 Irigaray herself does not use the phrase 'strategic essentialism', which
   Gayatri Chakravorty Spivak (1984–5) coined in a different context. This
   does not prevent Irigaray from *being* a strategic essentialist.
5 As in chapter 4, I am speaking only about Irigaray's earlier work.

6 However, Riley thinks that sometimes feminists can best challenge ideas of women's nature not by miming them but just by saying that they are false (Riley 1989: ch. 4).

7 Cixous has in mind Freud's saying that 'the sexual life of adult women is a "dark continent" for psychology' (Freud 1926: 313).

8 Others including Frye (1996), Stoljar (1995) and Zack (2005: chs. 1–3) also offer answers that I lack space to discuss here.

9 Young argues that the female body is one of the feminine-coded objects which serialize women (1994: 729). So she might reply that the women in question are, indeed, women just because in gender-divided societies all those who have female bodies are women. This reply is unsatisfactory because it makes it impossible for anyone to be both female and masculine.

Further Reading

Definitions of essentialism   Grosz 1990b: 333–5; Heyes 2000 ch. 1; Witt 1995: 321–2.

Criticisms of essentialism   Lugones and Spelman 1983; Spelman 1990 offers the most in-depth criticism of essentialism (see, especially, ch. 6); Harris 1990 criticizes MacKinnon's essentialism.

Accounts of what makes all women women   Heyes 2000 ch. 3; Young 1994; Haslanger 2000.

More advanced texts on essentialism   Stoljar 1995; Witt 1995.

Essentialism and sexual difference   Grosz 1990b.

6 Birth

1. Feminist philosophy and birth

Many of the feminist philosophical debates considered in this book have touched on the topic of birth. For instance, some care ethicists such as Virginia Held (1993: 80–4) argue that physically bearing children gives mothers a particular bond with their children. This, Held thinks, is partly why women – at least if they are mothers – place great importance on care. And in chapter 4 we encountered Irigaray's criticisms of (what she sees as) the traditional western view that childbearing consists in passively containing a male-implanted seed as it grows to independent life. Irigaray suggests, as other feminists have, that childbearing should be reconceived as a creative process, not a passive function.

Birth, then, has become a theme within various strands of feminist thought. Building on this, some feminist philosophers and theorists have reflected on birth more systematically. This chapter looks at some of these reflections.[1] First we should distinguish birth from three related phenomena:

1 *pregnancy and gestation.* Not all pregnancies come to term. As Amy Mullin (2005) argues, pregnancy is not valuable only if it ends with the birth of a child; it is a life-enriching experience in its own right. Mullin warns that feminist philosophers of birth sometimes overlook pregnancy and its distinctive value. Despite Mullin's warning, this chapter will discuss gestation and women's experiences of pregnancy under the heading of birth. I do so because many feminist insights into pregnancy overlap with insights into birth and vice versa: the two areas of inquiry inform one another.

2 *childcare* is the activity of looking after a child once it is born. Childcare might come from adoptive rather than biological parents,

and it need not come solely from the child's biological or adoptive mother. Care may come from a combination of people, e.g. parents plus paid childcarers.

3   *mothering.* A pregnant woman may be described as a mother (of her foetus). But 'mothering' also refers to childcare that is carried out *after* the child's birth. In short, 'mothering' is ambiguous between gestation and childcare. Many biological mothers indeed feel that their activity of caring for their young children flows out of their activity of caring for their developing babies when they were pregnant. But the ambiguity of 'mothering' is not wholly helpful, for it can – falsely – suggest that only the biological mother of a child can properly care for it.

This clarifies that childcare (and 'mothering' in the sense of childcaring) is distinct from gestation and childbirth (and from 'mothering' in the sense of gestation). The rest of this chapter will focus on the latter: on gestation and childbirth.

2. Birth, medicalization and male domination

Radical feminists were the first feminists to see birth as a political and philosophical issue. They hold that male domination of women takes the central form of male control over women's bodies: specifically, over women's sexuality and women's reproductive powers (their capacity to gestate and bear children). According to radical feminists, male attempts to control women's reproductive powers have taken many forms, but in modern western countries one important form they have taken is that of a medicalization of birth.

Until the seventeenth century, midwives looked after women in labour. Thereafter, doctors – exclusively male until recently – took control of childbirth and (falsely) dismissed midwives as ignorant practitioners of magic (Rich 1976: ch. 6). Doctors propounded a medical model of pregnancy and birth: they understood pregnancy as an illness and birth as a dangerous crisis, both needing management by doctors. Hence doctors moved the place of birth from the home to the hospital, where birth can occur under medical supervision. This process has been completed only recently: in 1900 less than 5 per cent of US women gave birth in hospital, by 1940 55 per cent, and by the 1970s 99 per cent – a figure unchanged in the US today (Mullin 2005: 111).

Similarly, in the UK and Canada 97–99 per cent of births now happen in hospital.

One might think that the medicalization of birth has benefited women. After all, many women gladly avail themselves of modern procedures such as anaesthesia and caesareans. But radical feminists suggest that these positive things are mere side-effects of a process of medicalization which men have fostered not out of concern for women's welfare but so as to increase their control over women. Medicalization, radical feminists argue, has taken control over birth away from women – whether as mothers or as midwives – and has given control to men – both as doctors and as scientific 'experts' who can advise women on how to navigate the perils of pregnancy and birth.

Adrienne Rich in *Of Woman Born* (1976) was among the first radical feminists to criticize the medicalization of birth. In Rich's view, men have striven since prehistoric times to control women's reproductive powers. Men naturally feel fearful of women's power to create or destroy foetal life (1976: 71). Men's fear motivates them to try to seize 'power-over' women's power. Rich distinguishes 'power-over' from the kind of power that women naturally have – transformative power (1976: 99). This is the power to transform an embryo into a baby and to transform food into milk when breast-feeding. Women's power is 'power-*to*' – power to create, from one thing, something new and different. Men's biology, Rich argues, does not give them this kind of power, so as a substitute they seek power *over* women's reproductive powers (1976: 64).

According to Rich, centuries of men's exercise of power-over have transformed motherhood. (Under 'motherhood' she includes both childbearing and the work of caring for young children. I shall focus on what she says about the childbearing aspect of mothering.) Since the eighteenth century, men have developed specialist scientific knowledge about childbearing to which women were not allowed access, depriving women of the means to make sense of their own experiences while pregnant. As a whole, Rich says, men have *alienated* women's own reproductive powers from them (1976: 13). She means that men have turned these powers into something women find alien and can neither understand nor control.

In chapter 3 we saw that it is not always clear whether Rich thinks that all men deliberately aim to dominate women. *Of Woman Born* is clear: all men do aim to dominate women, but this aim is rarely conscious or deliberate. Because men fear women's powers (1976: 11), and because fear is unpleasant, men repress their awareness of this fear. Men then also have to repress their awareness of their desire for power-over women, otherwise men would be reminded of why they have this desire, i.e. because they fear women's powers. So, Rich believes, men desire and pursue domination over women, but men are unaware of doing this.

Has Rich given us a plausible explanation for men's dominant social position? Arguably not. Why don't women who are too young or old to give birth or who are infertile seek 'power-over' other women? Why wouldn't men pay attention not to the powers they lack but to those they *do* uniquely have, such as powers to produce and expel sperm? Moreover, Rich assumes that we need to explain the universality of male domination with reference to one single motivation to dominate which all men must share. But surely, because there are diverse forms of male domination, we need specific explanations of why each different form has arisen. Thus, Rich does not explain what we actually need explained (the diverse forms of patriarchy). Nor does she adequately explain what she does seek to explain (the universality of patriarchy).

To return to Rich's account of childbearing, she calls the alienated, male-controlled, form of motherhood 'motherhood as institution', which she distinguishes from 'motherhood as experience'. She defines the latter as women's 'potential relationship to [their] powers of reproduction and to children' (1976: 13). Potentially, Rich thinks – in a non-patriarchal society – women could understand these powers, 'freely and intelligently undertake' to use them (1976: 175), and feel empowered by them. The point of Rich's distinction between motherhood as institution and as experience is to suggest that although many women might now feel that childbearing is alien and unpleasant, this is solely down to the *institution* of motherhood. It is not inherent in childbearing to feel alien and oppressive. In the right conditions, it could feel creative and empowering. Here Rich is arguing against Firestone, who saw childbearing as inherently barbaric – no more meaningful than 'shitting a pumpkin' (Firestone 1970: 189) – and as the direct cause of women's oppression. In contrast, Rich attributes women's oppression not to female biology but to male control over female biology.

Rich's claims about the extent of male control over childbearing may sound outdated. In many European countries, pregnancy is now treated – to a much greater extent than it was forty years ago – as a normal process, not an illness, and it is mainly midwives rather than doctors who provide antenatal care. However, this does not mean that birth has been 'de-medicalized'. Pregnant women are subjected to a huge range of tests, which not only identify various potential problems but also reflect an assumption that pregnant women are in an abnormal state needing special monitoring and attention. Because of the same assumption, hospital births are carefully monitored and controlled using a range of procedures: continuous electronic monitoring of foetal heart-rates, for example, or giving mothers synthetic hormones to speed up their contractions. And the proportion of women giving birth by caesarean section continues to rise: in the US, 29.1 per cent of all births were by caesarean in 2004, compared to 20.7 per cent in 1996 and 5 per cent in 1970.

The general feminist conclusion – that medicalizing developments such as these do not always benefit women but, actually, often *disempower* women – is surely plausible. When advised or told to have caesareans, many women feel angry, disappointed, and as one woman put it 'out of control . . ., like everything was just totally out of my control' (Martin 1987: 82). And although the medical techniques that are used to control and regulate labour undoubtedly have benefits for women, these techniques also tend to make yet more medical monitoring and interventions necessary. This has the effect of transferring control over the birth process from the mother to medical personnel (see Rouse 1987: 233–4, 239–40). For instance, foetal monitoring immobilizes the mother, making it more likely that she will need anaesthetic and that her contractions will slow down so that synthetic hormones and, sometimes, caesarean or forceps deliveries become necessary.

Yet would it really be a good thing for pregnancy to be considered normal rather than abnormal? Diane Taylor (2006) reports that US federal guidelines issued in 2006 ask all women of childbearing age to treat themselves as 'pre-pregnant'. Women are asked to take vitamin supplements, to avoid smoking or drinking regularly, and to take various other precautions for the sake of their merely potential children. Taylor takes this to be evidence that US women are meant to behave more as incubators than as persons. Still, perhaps these 'pre-pregnancy' guidelines do not so much treat pregnancy as normal as treat *all* women as abnormally vulnerable to illness and to (sometimes self-inflicted) dangers. If so, then perhaps genuinely treating pregnancy as normal remains a desirable feminist goal.

3. The phenomenology of pregnancy

Feminist critics of the medicalization of birth insist that we need to listen to women's own accounts of their experiences of pregnancy and birth. Pregnancy and birth are not merely biological processes about which only doctors or scientists can have real knowledge. These processes occur to individual women, for whom these processes are always meaningful. Some feminists try to articulate, philosophically, how pregnant women experience their condition. These feminists are doing what is called the phenomenology of pregnancy.

Phenomenology is a tradition of philosophy which flourished in mainland Europe in the early to middle twentieth century, founded by Edmund Husserl. Phenomenologists aim to give plausible descriptions of the forms of human experience. The aim is not to explain why experience takes the forms it does or to argue that experience must take certain forms. Nor do phenomenologists aim exhaustively to describe every single human experience. Instead they try to identify and describe basic patterns into which all experience is organized. For example, all human experience presents itself as ordered temporally: one's awareness of what is in the present is always suspended between one's anticipation of the future and one's remembrance of the past. However, phenomenologists believe that how we experience is seldom if ever self-evident to us. The forms of our experience are so obvious – after all, they are ever-present whenever we have any experience at all – that we find it next to impossible to notice these forms. As Hegel put it, 'the familiar, just because it is familiar, is not known' (1807: 18).

Some feminist philosophers such as Carol Bigwood (1991), Gail Weiss (1999) and Iris Marion Young (1984) try to describe women's experience of pregnancy in a way that is informed by phenomenology. Rather than trying to describe all the different experiences of pregnancy that individual women have, they aim to identify patterns that manifest themselves across a whole range of ways in which women experience pregnancy. Generally, though, feminists do not try to find patterns that are common to all experiences of pregnancy everywhere. Plausibly, no such patterns exist. Instead feminists tend to focus – as Young does – on patterns that are common to how women in 'technologically sophisticated Western societies' experience pregnancy (Young 1984: 161).

Young's article 'Pregnant Embodiment' (1984) remains the classic feminist phenomenological study of pregnancy. In experiencing pregnancy, women are of course experiencing their bodies and the changes taking place within them. Thus Young finds it helpful to draw on Merleau-Ponty (1945), because he argues that our experience always includes a dimension of awareness *of* our bodies. (See chapter 2, section 5.)

Merleau-Ponty thinks that ordinarily my awareness of my body is in the background of my consciousness. As I am writing now, I do not notice my hand holding my pen, only the words I am writing. Now, and usually, I use my body to carry out plans, and I attend only to those plans and treat my body as invisible. However, other phenomenological authors have argued that my awareness of my body moves into the foreground of my consciousness in circumstances when my body is unable to carry out my plans – perhaps I am too tired or unwell. I can no longer concentrate on my plans, because my body as a material presence has absorbed my attention.

Young argues that pregnancy, as experienced in modern western societies, does not fit in with this claim that one becomes consciously aware of one's body only when it becomes obstructive. A pregnant woman is aware of her body as engaged in processes of its own which she cannot control: perhaps she feels her breasts or belly growing. But this awareness does not prevent her from carrying out tasks: she continues with these while also attending to her bodily processes. Young mentions her own experience of searching for a library book while noticing a hardening in her belly (1984: 162). The pregnant woman's attitude towards her body, Young concludes, is *aesthetic*: she contemplates – and enjoys contemplating – its changes. She can enjoy these changes just because they are compatible with and do not impede her regular activities (given that she lives in a technologically advanced society).

Young notes two further features of modern western experiences of pregnancy as well as aesthetic enjoyment of the changes in one's body.

1   When pregnant, I feel another life within me. In part, this life presents itself as a separate life, engaged in its own processes and

activities – hiccupping, kicking – which I cannot control. But this life is also *within* me so that I am specially aware of its movements. The boundary between my body and that of the foetus is thus blurred (Young 1984: 162–63. Kristeva 1977 also makes this point).

2   A pregnant woman feels uncertain where the outer boundaries of her body lie, because the size and shape of her body are changing so rapidly (Young 1984: 163). Hence women in late pregnancy often feel clumsy and keep bumping into things. The pregnant woman's 'imaginary body' – her mental 'map' of the properties and dimensions of her own body – cannot keep pace with the rate at which her body is changing.

Several feminist philosophers have criticized Young's account. Gail Weiss (1999: 52–4) disagrees with Young's claim that the changes of pregnancy are so rapid as to prevent the pregnant woman from forming a coherent, unified body image. Weiss objects that the pregnant woman has a different *kind* of image of her body, *as* something that is changing, growing and expanding (Weiss 1999: 53). This is the kind of body image, Weiss suggests, with which we would all be better off: a kind of image which is sensitive to, rather than conceals, the body's constant changes. After all, all bodies *are* constantly changing, even if less obviously than in pregnancy.

There may also be a problem with Young's claim that the three features of the experience of pregnancy which she describes are universal in modern western societies. Against Young, Mullin argues that even within these societies there are no universal features of the experience of pregnancy. According to Mullin, the ways in which pregnant women respond to their changing biology are always affected by their different places in class, race and other social divisions (Mullin 2005: 91–2).[2]

Mullin (2005: 47–8) also disagrees with Young's claim that pregnant women respond to their biological changes in a fairly passive way by observing and enjoying them aesthetically. Mullin argues, instead, that pregnant women are constantly active in giving meaning to these changes, and that they give different changes different levels of importance, in part by comparing these changes to other past events. For instance, a pregnant woman might compare the rapid growth in her breasts to similar growth spurts that she remembers from puberty.

If pregnant women actively give meaning to their biology, then the phenomenology of pregnancy belongs within a broader field of feminist inquiry: inquiry into women's 'lived bodies', that is, into how women give meanings to their own bodies. So we should look at this feminist concept of the lived body.

4. Lived bodies

Toril Moi (1999) and Young (2002) trace the feminist concept of the lived body back to Simone de Beauvoir. For Beauvoir, each human individual is always free to choose the direction of her life. Beauvoir denies that anyone ever makes their choices based on their 'nature' (e.g. as a 'naturally caring person'). One only acquires a 'nature' insofar as one commits oneself to certain ways of acting through the choices one makes. Nor does one make choices based on one's values. Rather, *by* making choices I commit myself to particular values. For example, (as Beauvoir sees it) I do not choose to have an abortion because I believe that abortion is legitimate. Instead I choose to have an abortion and in so doing I commit myself to the position that abortion is legitimate.

For Beauvoir, individuals inevitably make their choices against the background of their **facticity**. This is a set of given facts about each individual:

1   she has a particular past;
2   she is in a certain place, time and country;
3   she is viewed in specific ways by others (e.g. as a Jew, as a woman);
4   her body has certain physical properties (size, age, sex, skin colour).

In light of the values by which an individual chooses to live, these facts, including the fact of what bodily properties that individual has, take on particular meanings. The 'facts . . . in themselves have no significance. . . . [Their] meaning . . . is revealed as such only in the light of the ends man proposes' (Beauvoir 1949: 67). For instance, if I choose to conform to prevailing norms of feminine appearance, then my body may seem too fat. One study has found that 75 per cent of women perceive their bodies to be bigger than they really are (Bordo 1993: 55–6).

For Beauvoir, then, my **lived body** is not a set of bare biological facts but a set of *meaningful* facts whose meaning derives from my choices over time. At least some of these choices will affect my body's physical properties, for example if I choose to diet and lose weight. In such cases, meanings become embodied in the physical properties of my body – perhaps my reduced size signifies to me that I am attractive by prevailing standards. So when I give meaning to my body, the properties on which I bestow meaning actually *already* embody meanings and are not merely biological. My new choices may perpetuate or change the meanings that my body has already taken on.

Consider in this light Beauvoir's famous phrase 'One is not born, but rather becomes, a woman' (1949: 295). One is born either female (*femelle*) or male (*mâle*). But no female or male body is born with an innate meaning. Each of us creates our body's meaning in an ongoing process. By giving meaning to my female body over time, I become a **woman** (*une femme*) – a human female whose female body has meaning. To be *féminin* (or *masculin*) is to have biology that has acquired meaning as opposed to having bare biology.

So the concepts *féminin* and *masculin* function differently in Beauvoir's thought to the concepts 'feminine' and 'masculine' within feminist theories that centre on the concept of gender. In those theories, to be 'feminine' is to have learnt to fulfil the relevant gender role. For Beauvoir, on the other hand, to be *féminin* is to have given meaning to one's female biology over time.[3] Thus, Beauvoir's distinction between bare biology and humanly meaningful (or lived) biology is not the same as the distinction between sex and gender (Heinämaa 1997).[4]

To relate this back to pregnancy: part of a pregnant woman's facticity is the dramatic bodily changes she is undergoing. But each pregnant woman freely decides what she values. For instance, if she values being a mother above all, then the changes in her body may appear endlessly fascinating and very welcome. A woman who has chosen different values might find the very same changes to be a disruptive nuisance.

Other feminist philosophers whom we have come across – notably Irigaray and Gatens – also use the concept of the lived body, but differently to Beauvoir (and to Moi and Young, who rely on Beauvoir). All feminist lived-body theorists agree that in everyday life we always see our bodies as infused with meaning. But feminists disagree on what shapes these meanings. Irigaray and Gatens think that the meanings of being female and male are set in place by the symbolic order (or the social imaginary) rather than being created by individuals who freely choose their own values. For Irigaray and Gatens, to even *become* an agent who can choose values, one must first take on a language and culture and, with them, a male or female identity. Hence one cannot easily choose to revise or discard the meanings one learns to attach to one's being male or female. These meanings are so fundamental to our self-conceptions that we can only with great difficulty imagine them being revised.

It may seem that Beauvoir overstates how much freedom of choice we have while Irigaray overstates how much power culture has over us. But Irigaray believes that we can gradually change cultural symbolism by 'mimicking' it. As for Beauvoir, she believes that women tend to accept the meanings that are already given to their bodies in a culture that (she thinks) has been almost wholly made by men. This largely man-made culture portrays women as beings who are trapped in their bodies, unable to make free choices because their biology compels them to act in certain ways – e.g. to be 'hysterical' or 'nymphomaniacs'. Women tend to accept these ideas because these ideas deeply pervade western culture and because these ideas have shaped how women experience their bodies ever since they were born. So although in principle women could give their own meanings to their bodies, in practice they usually adopt the meanings men have already given to the female body. Since these meanings depict women as by nature unfree, they deceive women into not exercising the freedom through which they might confer new self-created meanings on their bodies.

As a whole, the concept of the **lived body** captures the fact that individuals always experience their male or female bodies as meaningful, where these meanings derive either from individual choices, publicly shared cultures, or some mixture of the two. How useful is this concept of the lived body?

Moi (1999) argues that this concept improves on the sex/gender distinction, which, she thinks, gives a poor account of lived individual experience. In lived experience, one's body is always meaningful. One's body never presents itself as a set of bare biological facts. Scientists, Moi says, may describe bodies as purely biological organisms, but these are specialized descriptions that move away from everyday experience. This does not mean that scientific descriptions are false: arguably, there *are* biological facts about bodies about which our best scientific theories inform us. Moi's point is that in everyday life we do not experience our bodies as the kinds of thing that scientists talk about.

Moi concludes that feminists should use *only* the concept of the lived body and not also those of sex and gender. Here Moi seems to assume that the sole aim of feminist philosophy is to give phenomenological descriptions of what it is like to be a woman – of what meanings being female-bodied acquires in various social settings. Yet feminist philosophers also need to explain *why* femaleness takes on particular meanings in certain climates. To do this, feminist philosophers need to examine the social, cultural and biological factors that shape these meanings. The real nature of these factors will seldom be apparent to living individuals. A woman might believe that her body is too fat, but unless she has studied feminist theory she will probably not see Descartes's mind/body dualism as the source of this belief (as Bordo 1993 suggests it is). Feminist philosophers need to explain as well as describe the forms of women's experience. This means using the concepts of sex, gender, sexuality and sexual difference to analyse the factors that shape women's experience.[5]

Phenomenological study of pregnancy and of other aspects of women's lives is valuable, but it is equally important that feminist philosophers study the factors that shape how women experience pregnancy and birth. One of these factors is the symbolic order, and specifically those elements of this order which attribute meanings to birth. Two feminist authors who examine western patterns of symbolism around birth are Grace Jantzen and Adriana Cavarero.

5. Birth, death and the symbolic order

Jantzen and Cavarero analyse western symbolism around birth from different perspectives. Jantzen is a British philosopher of religion who is critical of what she sees as the over-emphasis on death and the afterlife within traditional Christianity. Cavarero is an Italian philosopher who combines ideas from Irigaray (especially the idea that western societies are structured by a male-centred symbolic order) with some ideas from US radical feminism.[6] Still, Jantzen's and Cavarero's analyses overlap in content, partly because they are both influenced by Irigaray.

Both Jantzen and Cavarero build on a suggestion of Irigaray's that the western symbolic order is not only male-centred but is also preoccupied with death. Western culture, Irigaray (1989) claims, treats death as a more central feature of human existence than birth and values destruction over creation, as reflected in the vast sums spent on war and military technology. According to Jantzen, we can see that western culture is indeed preoccupied with death from the fact that this culture chooses to see human beings as defined by their mortality. 'The platitude that "all men are mortal" is not simply a statement of fact; it is part of a construction of human subjectivity which preoccupies western culture' (Jantzen 2005: 31).

It can be hard to know how to assess these very large-scale generalizations about 'western culture' – to which Cavarero refers in a range of ways: not only as 'western culture' (1990: 1, 4) but also as, amongst others, 'western thought', 'the logic of western language' and 'cultural tradition' (1993: 193, 196, 200). Even assuming that we can meaningfully talk about 'western culture' as one single thing, this culture still contains many different strands. On what grounds may we decide that a fixation on mortality cuts across all these strands?

One approach is to look at a narrower area within 'western culture' – say, the western philosophical tradition. We indeed find that philosophers have said much about death and remarkably little about birth. Philosophers have asked what death is, whether persons can survive death, and whether death is bad. Arguably philosophers' preoccupation with death dates back to Plato. In his dialogue *Phaedo*, Plato has Socrates describe philosophy as a kind of preparation for death. By contemplating timeless ideas, the philosopher learns that his intellectual and immortal soul is different from his body, into which his soul has 'fallen' – become imprisoned – at birth. He realizes that death only comes to the body, but that the body's death will free the soul from its prison. Thus, instead of fearing death, the philosopher should embrace it as a welcome release from the body. Socrates, therefore, willingly drinks the poison that will kill him.

Why has western culture been preoccupied with death? Cavarero argues that this is because men fear the maternal body. Imagine a culture which saw birth and being born – not death – as the central feature of human life. In that case, each person would see it as fundamental to who they are that they were born of their mother and, in turn, that their mother had the power to give or take their embryonic life (Cavarero 1990: 64–5). But this power to give or take life is unique to women. In a birth-centred culture, then, men would be aware of women's power and would therefore tend to fear women. So men prefer to regard death as the central feature of human existence. Death has no special connection with women; it affects everyone equally (1990: 68–9, 104–5). Men favour a death-centred culture because in it they have no reason to feel that women have a power that they lack. (Here we see Cavarero's debt to Rich, who also claimed that men naturally feel excluded from and afraid of women's 'power-to' give birth.)

Cavarero argues that once death is seen as the central feature of human existence, none of us can ever escape the awareness of our own impending death, which becomes overwhelmingly frightening (Cavarero 1990: 70). One way to alleviate this fear is to imagine that there is an afterlife or an eternal realm that is unaffected by death and into which the self can potentially escape. Plato adopts this solution when he claims that the soul is eternal and that death merely releases the soul from the body.

A different way to alleviate the fear of death is to conceal death. Historians and sociologists have argued that this concealment has become widespread in the twentieth century. Death now usually happens in hospitals, not at home; dead bodies are kept at the undertakers, not at home, before a funeral; and we use medicine to keep death away from ourselves and from our families for as long as possible. Most celebrities and film and pop stars are young, because young bodies do not remind us of ageing or mortality. This trend to make death invisible might seem to contradict Cavarero's and Jantzen's claim that our culture is death-obsessed: rather than being death-obsessed, modern societies seem to be death-denying. But Jantzen argues that people only try to avoid death because they find it terrifying, and in turn that people only find death terrifying because they actually see it as central to human existence (1998: 130–1).

Cavarero argues that because death has come to be seen as so all-important, birth has come to be understood with reference to death. Death is a going out of existence – going from being to nothing. Birth is then seen as the mirror-opposite of death, and so as coming into being out of nothing (Cavarero 1990: 70). Here birth ceases to be seen as a coming *from one's mother* (or as being 'of woman born', as Rich put it).

We have seen how Cavarero argues that, once death began to be seen as central to human existence, it made sense for Plato (1) to distinguish within each person between their intellectual, immortal soul and their unintelligent, mortal body. This picture of persons implies (2) that birth merely adds a transient mortal body to a pre-existing soul. Moreover, (3) intellect and body are associated with men and women respectively. From (2) and (3), the idea follows readily enough (4) that through their semen men create or transmit the soul of the embryo, while women merely provide its matter. Hence the view has become entrenched in western societies that men – not women – are the real parents who should have control over birthgiving processes (Cavarero 1990: 71).

How accurate is Jantzen's and Cavarero's picture of the western symbolic order? Despite the difficulty of assessing their sweeping claims, I think they are broadly right that much of western culture has focused on death rather than birth. And Cavarero neatly explains why any death-centred culture must also be male-centred. But do Jantzen and Cavarero do justice to the fearfulness of death? They suggest that in a birth- rather than death-centred culture, death would no longer be feared, because it would be accepted as just one part of the life-cycle (Cavarero 1990: 113–15; Jantzen 1998: 168). Plausibly, defining death as *the* central feature of human existence has made death seem more frightening. But even if death were seen as a less important aspect of existence than birth, surely death would remain a daunting prospect to most of us, even if less intensely so than at present. A birth-centred culture could reduce, but not remove altogether, the human fear of death.

Anyway, what would a 'birth-centred' symbolic order look like? It would stress (1) that each of us is born and (2) that each of us is born of a woman. This is because birth would no longer be understood, with reference to death, as a coming-from-nothing. Hence this order would recognize (3) that even if not all women can or do give birth, it is only ever women, and never men, who have the power to give birth. Cavarero and Jantzen also ask (4) how our understandings of what it *is* to be a self would have to be revised if it were generally accepted that the central feature of each self is that it is born.

One might think that we all appreciate already that each human self is born. But while no one denies this fact when it is pointed out to them, arguably the common-sense picture of human selves in our society is that they are full-grown adults. Consider that when political philosophers try to identify rules by which human beings can live together in society, they often talk as if adults were the only human beings who need to be taken into account. For example, Hobbes advises political thinkers to 'look at men [i.e. people] as if they had just emerged from the earth like mushrooms' (1647: 102). Feminist philosophers conclude that recognizing that being born is funda-mental to being a self *would* be a major change.

Cavarero's account of what is involved in rethinking selves as born, or as 'natals' rather than mortals, draws on Hannah Arendt's complex concept of 'natality', from Arendt's major work *The Human Condition* (1958). The word 'natality' comes from the Latin *nascere*, 'to be born'. However, as we will now see, Cavarero not only draws on Arendt's concept of natality but also criticizes some aspects of it.

6. Cavarero, Arendt and action

Arendt defines **natality** as 'the fact that human beings appear in the world by virtue of birth' (Arendt 1963: 211). Cavarero takes from Arendt the idea that our natality – the fact of our each having been born – gives each of us a unique *life-story* and that, in each case, it is one's life-story which makes one a unique self. However, Arendt con-nects this idea with the claim that each of us only acquires a unique life-story insofar as we 'act' within what she calls the 'space of appear-ances' (roughly, public space). So before we can understand how Cavarero and Arendt think about natality, we first need to examine these claims that Arendt makes about action. This section will focus on Arendt's view of action and Cavarero's criticisms of it; section 7 returns to natality.

Acting, for Arendt, differs from two other practical activities: labouring (maintaining one's body and meeting one's physical needs, e.g. by cleaning, grooming, preparing meals) and working (producing relatively long-lasting artefacts such as buildings, tools and art-works). **Acting**, for Arendt, consists in disclosing oneself to others – showing others who one is – through deeds and speech. Through one's deeds and speech, one strives to distinguish oneself in front of these others, to achieve excellence in their eyes. Arendt has in mind as an example the ancient Greek warrior Achilles, who won immortal fame for his courage and ferocity in the war against Troy. Arendt adds other, less violent, examples: displaying excellence as a healer, a music-maker or a play-actor (1958: 207), or as a speaker who finds the right words at the right moment (1958: 26).

For Arendt, then, action requires a plurality of others to whom one strives to appear. Action therefore depends on there being what Arendt calls a 'space of appearance' – a public space in which individuals can appear to one another. Arendt holds that the Greek city-state was one such public space, where citizens met and engaged in debate.

How, for Arendt, does my acting within the space of appearance give rise to my unique life-story? All actions, Arendt holds, have (unpredictable) outcomes and set off chains of consequences, in response to which I engage in further actions. The entire series of my actions and their outcomes and consequences makes up the story of my life.

But, Arendt claims, I cannot know my own life-story. Only *others* can know it, by narrating it. This is because (1) the meaning of my actions is only available to others. I might freely leap into a river to save someone from drowning, but only others can judge whether I have acted heroically or have foolishly put an additional life at risk. And (2) each action has many aspects, each of which can be seen by different spectators who each observe the action from different locations and circumstances. I, as one single agent, cannot see these many aspects of my action. As a whole, then, Arendt thinks of public space as filled with meaningful narratives that tell of the life-stories of individuals and their deeds.

Cavarero agrees with Arendt that each of us builds up a life-story through our actions and their effects, and that we rely to a considerable extent on others to hear our own life-stories narrated. But, against Arendt, Cavarero denies that we are *wholly* dependent on others for knowledge of our own stories. According to Cavarero, we are each partially aware of our own stories. We remember some of our actions and life-events and how they follow one another. But no one can remember their birth or early infancy, and their memories of later life are always partial and incomplete. Still, Cavarero says, we remember enough to give us a desire to know our stories more completely, which we can do only by listening to the narrations of others (1997: 37). She gives the example of the Greek hero Odysseus who only learns the complete story of his travels when he overhears it sung by the poet Tiresias. This overwhelms Odysseus with emotion because it satisfies his desire to know his story more fully.

This disagreement that Cavarero has with Arendt – over whether we are wholly unaware (Arendt) or partially aware (Cavarero) of our own life-stories – is linked to a second disagreement, about mortality. Cavarero believes that Arendt's account of narrative uncritically reflects the influence of the death-centred symbolic order. Arendt thinks that we each have a desire to overcome our mortality, and that we come closest to fulfilling this desire when we act. This is because, when we act, we make it possible for others to tell narratives about us which continue to circulate after our deaths and through which we attain a kind of immortality (Arendt 1958: 19). For instance, Achilles has lived on through Homer's *Iliad* which tells of Achilles's deeds in the Trojan War. Cavarero denies that there is this universal human desire for immortality, which, she thinks, only exists in a culture pre-occupied with death. Our deeper desire, Cavarero says, is to hear our stories narrated by others *during* our lifetimes (Cavarero 1997: 33).

Thirdly, Cavarero rejects Arendt's belief that actions can only take place in public space. She rejects this belief because, like many feminist political thinkers, she criticizes the traditional opposition between 'public' and 'private' spheres (see Cavarero 1992). Traditionally, political thinkers saw the state as something that is opposed to the family or household. (Political thinkers sometimes counted 'society' and the world of work as 'public' compared to the family and sometimes as 'private' compared to the state.)

Both ancient philosophers such as Aristotle and modern philosophers such as Locke held that, within the family, wives and children are naturally subordinate to male heads of household. In contrast, they thought that all those who participate in the public sphere are free and equal – i.e. all the *men* who enter the public sphere, since women, as natural domestic subordinates, are unsuited to public life.[7] Hence Aristotle, Locke and others took it that the family is women's domain while the public sphere is men's domain (Cavarero 1992: 33).

Arendt accepts this public/private opposition. She thinks that people can only act freely within public space, whereas families are where people labour under the compulsion of their biological needs. Nor does Arendt challenge the idea that the family is women's domain. On the contrary, she takes childbearing to be one of the main forms of the labour done in the family (Arendt 1958: 30).

Feminist political thinkers object that if husbands have ruled over their wives in the family, this state of affairs has not been natural. Rather it has come to pass because *political* institutions and laws have regulated the family into male-dominant forms, through 'laws about rape and abortion . . . policies on child-care and the allocation of welfare benefits' (Pateman 1983: 131). But if the family is in fact regulated by the state, then family and state are interrelated, rather than being opposed spheres which spontaneously run on different principles (Pateman 1983: 121–2). Still, as Pateman says, from the fact that family and state are interrelated rather than opposed feminists need not conclude that no valid public/private distinction exists at all.[8] Some feminists, including Cavarero, continue to distinguish between the political sphere understood as the site where citizens 'negotiate rules and objectives of common living' (Cavarero 1990: 84) and the private sphere understood to consist of people's various personal and intimate relationships.

But although Cavarero retains this minimal public/private distinction, she rejects Arendt's opposition between free public life and biology-bound private life.[9] For Cavarero, our personal interactions and deeds can be just as free as any 'heroic' deeds we may perform in public. Cavarero denies that there is a difference in kind between public deeds and the 'small gestures and doings that [occur] everyday . . .' (Benhabib 1996: 130) within people's personal relationships. All these doings – one's way of styling one's hair or interacting with one's children as much as one's speech-making at a party-political meeting – are actions by which we show ourselves to others. Thus for Cavarero the 'space of appearance' – the space in which we exhibit ourselves to one another – consists of all social relationships, not only the public sphere as Arendt thought (1958: 208).

So while Arendt and Cavarero agree that it is through action that we build up the life-stories that make us each unique, they conceive action very differently – as heroic political deeds for Arendt, and for Cavarero as any deeds through which we disclose ourselves to others. We can now return to the question of how action, under both conceptions, relates to natality, the fact that each of us is born.

7. Natality, power and sex

Arendt argues that our natality is what makes it possible for each of us to act (as long as public spaces are also available in our society). She explains:

> men are equipped for . . . making a new beginning because they themselves are new beginnings and hence beginners . . . the very capacity for beginning is rooted in natality, in the fact that human beings appear in the world by virtue of birth. (1963: 211)

Whenever individuals act, they can be said to 'begin' something, because they are initiating something freely, without being caused to do so by any sequences of prior events (Arendt 1958: 177). What enables individuals to 'begin' things in this way, for Arendt, is the fact that each human being is a 'beginning' because of being born.

But if being born is something that each of us undergoes passively, rather than something that we actively initiate, then how can the capacity to initiate actions derive from the fact of being born? Arendt explains that although children cannot act freely as soon as they are born, each child is a new and unprecedented individual with respect to all the causes that have brought it into being. '[W]ith each birth something uniquely new comes into the world. With respect to this somebody who is unique it can be truly said that nobody was there before' (1958: 178). As such the child symbolizes the capacity to initiate actions that have no prior causes. The child's parents acquire the responsibility to educate the child so that it realizes this capacity for free action which, at birth, it merely symbolizes.

Arendt's account of how natality enables action may seem straightforward, but on closer inspection it contains tensions. These tensions arise because Arendt accepts the opposition between the public and private spheres – or so Seyla Benhabib (1996: 129–30, 135–7) argues.

1a On the one hand, Arendt holds that we are each 'exposed' to others from our birth onwards. From birth, Arendt says, others see one's physical shape and gestures, hear one's cries and voice. These claims of Arendt's imply that as soon as we become exposed – at birth – others begin to build up a web of narratives about us, long before we are fit to enter the public sphere or to embark on any heroic deeds (Benhabib 1996: 112).

1b Arendt also says that learning to act means learning to 'take upon [oneself] the naked fact of [one's] original physical appearance' and learning to expose oneself actively and deliberately rather than non-voluntarily (1958: 176–7). Thus, it seems that for Arendt individuals only become capable of public action because they begin life within webs of personal interactions and narrations. Only because individuals are already exposed to these narrations in the family can they learn to actively assume this already-existing condition.

2   Yet, on the other hand, Arendt's stated view is that narratives only concern public actions, so that narratives can only form about a person once he or she enters public space. If so, then individuals cannot be caught up in webs of narratives ever since birth. But, according to 1b, individuals can only ever learn *to* act if they are caught up in these webs from birth. Thus, Arendt's account of how natality enables action strains beyond the public/private opposition which she accepts.

Having rejected Arendt's public/private opposition, Cavarero can develop Arendt's account of natality in a way that makes it consistent. Hence Cavarero takes it that a web of narratives begins to surround each of us from birth, narratives that concern deeds that may range from infantile gestures and sounds through personal interactions with others to political acts. These deeds make up my unique story which unfolds from my birth onwards, starting at the unique time, place and circumstances of my birth.

So far, Cavarero has criticized Arendt for: (1) claiming that we depend wholly on others for awareness of our narratives; (2) claiming that we each desire immortality; (3) opposing the public and private spheres – which introduces tensions into her concept of natality. Cavarero also (4) objects that the death-centred symbolic order leads Arendt to 'accept the Greek meaning of birth as a coming from nothing' instead of seeing birth as 'a coming from the mother's womb' (Cavarero 1990: 6). Cavarero instead claims that each of us is born of a particular woman, herself born of a particular woman, and so on (1990: 60). Who one's mother is or was forms part of the unique set of circumstances from which one's life-story begins. In turn, who one's mother is or was depends on her life-story, which unfolded beginning from her birth from *her* unique mother, and so on.

As Cavarero sees it, then, crucial to a birth-centred symbolic would be not only the idea that each of us is born, but also the idea that each of us is born of a woman and only ever of a woman. But these ideas entail that women uniquely have the one power – birth-giving – which is central to the existence of human beings as natals. This means that there is a problem with the kind of birth-centred symbolic order which Cavarero imagines. Although Cavarero does not say so herself, this kind of symbolic order would see men as less important than women. This would be undesirable in itself, and it would also make any birth-centred culture unstable, by motivating men to restore a death-centred culture.

The problem is that it seems impossible to recognize women's 'power-to' give birth without also giving women 'power-over' men. Plausibly, this problem arises for Cavarero because she too quickly accepts Rich's distinction between female 'power-to' and male 'power-over'.[10] And arguably this acceptance is part of a more general failure on Cavarero's part to think closely about power. Butler (2001, 2005) has argued that Cavarero's lack of attention to power shows up when Cavarero distinguishes between the 'who' and the 'what'. This distinction is crucial to Cavarero's account of narrative, but it is problematic.

Cavarero claims that, as well as having a unique life-story from birth, I have various properties in common with others – e.g. I am a philosopher, I am fair-haired. For Cavarero (following Arendt), these properties that I share with others define *what* I am, whereas my unique story makes me *who* I am (Cavarero 1997: 39; Arendt 1958: 181). The properties that I share with others define what general categories I fall under, whereas my unique story makes me the unique individual that I am. This uniqueness cannot be captured by general categories, Cavarero holds, but only by the narrative of my life-story.

How viable is this who/what distinction? It is not clear how my story can be narrated without the narrator(s) invoking general categories to classify my actions and the character-traits that my actions, over time, display: 'she acted in a *heroic/foolish* way in jumping in to save him'; 'she always does things like that: she is a *heroic/foolish* person'. But then Cavarero's who/what distinction collapses. 'Whom' others can recognize me to be depends on 'what' categories they have available from which to create the narratives through which they recognize me (Butler 2005: 34–5).

Moreover, these general categories are usually if not always normative, embodying judgements about whether or not the actions or character-traits in question are desirable. (Heroism potentially is, but foolishness is probably not.) Thus, as Butler says, what narratives individuals can construct about one another depends on what norms exist in their societies (2005: 36). These norms pre-exist people's one-to-one interactions and govern what they can say about one another. Yet, Butler believes, these norms also reflect and maintain various forms of power relation amongst people. Since our narratives have to draw on these norms, these narratives too will end up maintaining the power relations that already exist in society.

Cavarero's conception of sex brings out this problem with the who/what distinction. Cavarero insists that just because we are each born, we are each sexed as well (1997: 38). However, she denies that being born male or female is the same thing as being born with particular physical properties. For Cavarero, being sexed is part of 'who' one is, not a matter of 'what' one is. That is, being sexed is not a matter of having certain biological properties in virtue of which one falls under either the general category 'male' or the general category 'female'. So what *does* being sexed consist in, for Cavarero? Presumably, she thinks that my being sexed is a matter of other people structuring their narratives concerning my life-story around their perception that I am either female or male. Other people might do this by taking my being female or male to be part of the unique set of circumstances from which my life-story begins, or by understanding the meanings of my actions differently depending on whether they see me as male or female.

Yet in structuring their narratives concerning my life-story in this way, other people *are* still drawing on available general categories – 'male'/'female' – and are classifying me as falling under one or the other category. Presumably others are so classifying me – contrary to what Cavarero claims – on the basis of my observed or presumed physical properties. Again, then, the who/what distinction breaks down. My sex may be a crucial thread in my life-story, but it is also a property that I share with all the other members of my sex.

Moreover, sex categories, insofar as they feature in our narratives about one another's lives, carry normative implications. My act of getting my hair cut very short may be seen as appropriately practical if I am taken to be male or as aggressively unfeminine if I am taken to be female. And, as we saw in earlier chapters, gender norms like these support power relations which, generally, subordinate women to men.

In sum: Cavarero thinks that narratives permit us to recognize one another in our uniqueness and that seeing someone as female or male is part of recognizing their uniqueness. This overlooks how narratives are structured by social norms, norms that help to hold men and women in their expected places within power relations.

8. Conclusion

Birth might initially have seemed to be a somewhat narrow topic, but it has turned out to raise and to intersect with many problems in both feminist and non-feminist philosophy.

1   The question of what birth has proved to be is closely connected to the question of what power is. Can we recognize women's 'power-to' give birth without giving women 'power-over' men? How deep is the distinction between 'power-to' and 'power-over'? (On feminist conceptions of power, see Allen 1999: ch. 1, Allen 2005.)
2   Thinking about birth leads us to revisit philosophical discussions of death. Would death seem less daunting if birth were seen as the more central feature of human existence? If death were understood with reference to birth rather than vice versa, then would this affect what we take death to consist in?
3   The question of 'personal identity' embraces a number of questions in philosophy. One of these is what makes each of us a unique, distinctive person. As we have seen, one feminist view – Cavarero's – is that my unique life-story makes me a unique individual, and that this story begins at my birth, which is an event that always occurs in a specific time, place and milieu and which always throws me into a particular web of relationships. On this view, being born is a necessary condition of being a unique individual.

As well as adjoining these existing areas of philosophy, feminist inquiries into birth raise new philosophical questions. How do women experience pregnancy, and what can these experiences tell us about the nature of embodied experience generally? Assuming that we can speak of such a thing as 'western culture', to what extent does it privilege death over birth? Would a birth-centred symbolic order be more desirable? And how must human selfhood be understood given that human selves enter the world via birth?

Notes

1   Two major feminist writers on birth whom this chapter omits are Christine Battersby (1998) and Julia Kristeva (1977). Jantzen (1998: 200–3) introduces Kristeva's work on birth.

2 Young admits (1984: 161) that women who have not chosen to be pregnant will not be able to aesthetically enjoy their state. But Mullin thinks
   that women's experiences of pregnancy are affected by other social
   factors besides just voluntariness or involuntariness.

3 Because Beauvoir distinguishes being *féminin* (or *masculin*) from being
   femelle (or *mâle*) I think it is still correct to translate her word *féminin* as
   'feminine'.

4 Contrary to Butler (1986: 35), who falsely runs the two distinctions
   together.

5 Young (2002) argues on similar grounds that feminists must use the
   concept of gender as well as that of the lived body.

6 Other Italian feminists also combine ideas from radical feminism –
   especially from Rich – with ideas from Irigaray; see Bono and Kemp
   1991: 12–14.

7 However, Aristotle also excludes male slaves from the political sphere
   and he qualifies how far male citizens are equal to one another. See
   Cavarero 1992: 33.

8 However, some feminists do conclude that there is no valid
   public/private distinction as power pervades all areas of social life
   equally.

9 So do many other feminists, e.g. Rich 1979: 203–14.

10 Arendt also understands power as 'power-to', but as the power-to not of
   individual women but of collectives of people who, when gathered in
   public space, can agree to act together in pursuit of shared goals (Arendt
   1958: 200).

Further Reading

Radical feminism   Tong 1989 ch. 3 clearly explains radical feminist debates
   about birth; Rich 1976: 11–14 introduces her own position.
Pregnancy and its phenomenology   See Mullin 2005 on pregnancy in general.
   For phenomenological studies see Young 1984; Weiss 1999: ch. 2.
The lived body   Moi 1999: 59–83; Young 2002.
Symbolic birth and death   Cavarero 1990: ch. 3; Jantzen 1998: ch. 6.
Feminism and Arendt   Honig 1995 is a good anthology.

7 Feminism

1. Philosophy and the diversity of feminism

In this book we have repeatedly seen that there is a huge diversity of feminist views. This diversity makes it hard to see what all feminist views have in common that makes them feminist. In the Introduction I argued that, given this diversity, we may only say that all feminists believe that women are subordinated and that this can and should be changed. But different feminists believe this under different interpretations.

This diversity of interpretations of women's subordination is not confined to that of the liberal, radical, socialist and black forms of feminism which we met in the Introduction. As feminist philosophers have criticized male biases and rethought concepts such as sex, gender or essentialism, they have produced new philosophical forms of feminism, expanding the range of feminist positions. For instance, Gilligan's criticisms of male bias in ethics led her to rethink the nature of women's subordination. For Gilligan, women are subordinated in that their distinctive values and virtues are neither recognized nor respected. On this basis she redefines the aim of feminism: for her, feminists should aim to win recognition of and respect for women's distinctive values and virtues.

In particular, feminist philosophers and theorists have become motivated to devise new forms of feminism by:

1   their criticisms of male-biased concepts and traditions (e.g. Gilligan's criticisms of male-biased moral theory).
2   their criticisms of pre-existing feminist positions. (For instance, French and Italian difference feminists criticized the project of gaining women equal access to existing social institutions. They

objected that this project ignored how all these institutions are shaped by a male-defined symbolic order.)

3   their thinking about core feminist concepts such as gender and essentialism. (For instance, Butler's account of gender norms leads her to redefine the aim of feminism as being to subvert the 'heterosexual matrix').

So, few feminist philosophers adhere simply to liberal, radical or socialist schools of feminism. Most feminist philosophers either support philosophically refined versions of those forms of feminism, or they support new forms of feminism (difference feminism, sexual difference feminism, gender-subversive feminism) to which their philosophical thinking has led them. This confirms that feminist philosophers are *philosophers*: they rethink the political positions that have inspired or influenced them instead of accepting those positions uncritically.

But we still have not considered one of the most original of these forms of feminism born out of philosophical considerations: the feminism of Simone de Beauvoir. Chapter 6 looked at Beauvoir's idea of the lived body, but now we must look at her existentialist feminism as a whole. Sections 3 and 4 will consider again whether my earlier definition that feminists oppose women's subordination can really hold up faced with the range of philosophical forms of feminism.

2. Beauvoir's existentialist feminism

Beauvoir's *The Second Sex* has been described as the twentieth century's most influential feminist work. Yet, published in 1949, it predates the emergence both of feminist philosophy and of the mass feminist activism of the 1960s and 1970s (in which Beauvoir later became involved). Unconstrained by any prior commitment to a particular form of feminist politics, Beauvoir worked out an original form of feminism based on the existentialist philosophy that she and Sartre had developed.

Beauvoir's key claim is that women have always been viewed as the Other of men. That is, women have always been thought to exist only in relation to men and to be inferior versions of men. Why has this view prevailed? Beauvoir's explanation is complex and relies on Sartre's account of what he calls the 'look' (Sartre 1943:

252–303. Catalano 1980: 159–68 clearly explains Sartre's account of the look).

As we saw in chapter 6, section 4, Sartre and Beauvoir believe that each conscious individual is free to choose his or her own projects and values. We each perceive the objects around us in relation to our projects and as a result those objects take on particular meanings for us. For example, a mountain might take on the meaning of being beautiful or ugly to a tourist, while to a climber it takes on the meaning of being easy, hard or impossible to climb (Sartre 1943: 488).

Now, Sartre holds that I am fundamentally aware of other people as beings who are free, or who are *subjects* – who are not inert objects but are the authors of their lives. I become aware of others as free beings whenever I experience myself being looked at by them. Sartre's famous example is of a man who, 'moved by jealousy, curiosity or vice', is spying through a keyhole when he becomes aware that someone else sees him doing this (Sartre 1943: 259). Formerly this man was wholly absorbed in his chosen project of spying, but now he becomes aware that he has a physical body that others can see – that he has an aspect of being a physical object as well as an aspect of being a subject. The man also becomes aware that in the eyes of the other subject he is merely 'a nosey parker' or 'a jealous type'. He appears to the other to have a fixed set of properties which are compelling him to act.

These experiences of being 'looked-at' occur to us constantly, surrounded by others as we are. But every experience of being looked-at threatens one's freedom. We each reassert our freedom by determining to view any other person whose look threatens us as a mere object, defined by their body and by fixed properties, and so not really qualified to threaten our own freedom. As Beauvoir sums up, any subject when objectified by others 'sets up a reciprocal claim' (1949: 17) – a claim that he or she is a subject while the other is a mere object.

But, Beauvoir says, throughout history women have failed to make these reciprocal claims (1949: 17–18). Men have followed their inevitable human tendency to objectify women, but women have not objectified men in turn. Instead women have accepted and internalized men's view that they are defined by their bodies and by fixed characteristics such as frailty, inconstancy, vanity, hysteria, etc.

Women have let men define them as beings with an essence – 'woman's nature' – rather than as subjects who *exist*, that is, who are responsible for choosing the course of their own lives.[1] Why have women done this?

Beauvoir's explanation has three parts. (1) She refers to the time when humans lived in nomadic tribes (Beauvoir 1949: 93–7). Without birth control, women had to spend all their time on childbirth and childcare, while men hunted. By risking their lives in hunting, men proved that they were free to create values. Specifically men proved that they were free to overcome (or 'transcend') the previously unquestioned value of individual self-preservation in favour of new self-created values – the values of conquering nature and serving the whole tribe (1949: 95; Heinämaa 2003: 108). Meanwhile, instead of creating their own values, women were absorbed in pursuing goals (gestation, childcare) that their pregnant bodies forced on them. In Beauvoir's terms, women were confined to a state of **immanence** – having their goals given to them by their bodies – rather than achieving **transcendence** – creating their own goals. So when men inevitably began to objectify women, women could not convincingly make a counter-claim to be free subjects.

However, Beauvoir thinks, the twentieth-century development of contraceptive techniques and of technology and industry mean that women need no longer be confined in immanence (1949: 152). These developments now make it possible for women to live freely and so to make reciprocal claims against men. Yet, Beauvoir believes, most women still accept men's objectifying view of them. Why? Here Beauvoir explains that (2) women tend to accept men's objectifying view of them just because that view has, over the centuries, come to pervade western culture and has built up into a web of 'myths of woman'. When women accept these myths that they are ruled by their bodies and cannot make free choices, they become deceived into not exercising the freedom that they actually have (Bergoffen 1997: 106–7, 149–51). This in turn reinforces the myths of woman.

(3) Furthermore, it benefits women to collude with men's view of them (Beauvoir 1949: 21). For if women exercise their freedom and so deviate from what men expect, they will probably be judged to be acting contrary to 'woman's nature', which will arouse many men's hostility. For example, Sartre's fictional character Ivich is accused by her brother of being troublesome and unnaturally masculine when

she chooses to reject her marriage and to act in a tough, aggressive way (Collins and Pierce 1976: 122).

Sartre thought that people who deceive themselves that they are not free commit the moral fault of being in 'bad faith'. Beauvoir thinks, however, that women are deceived, and seduced into self-deception, by men. So rather than being at moral fault, women are *oppressed* (Beauvoir 1949: 29). Here Beauvoir defines oppression as being deceived or tempted into not exercising one's freedom.

Beauvoir's account of history seems to imply that female bodies are an inherent obstacle to transcendence because they are prone to get pregnant. Genevieve Lloyd (1984: 86–102) suggests that Beauvoir views the female body in this negative way because immanence had all along been symbolized *as* female by Sartre. Sartre indeed speaks of the 'moist and feminine sucking' exerted by the 'slimy', by which he means anything that threatens to pull people down into immanence (Sartre 1943: 776). So it would be no surprise if being female seemed to Beauvoir to conflict with transcendence. But if transcendence is indeed symbolically male, then in taking it – as Beauvoir appears to (e.g. 1949: 726) – that a life of transcendence is the best human life, she assumes that what is symbolically male is superior to what is symbolically female. And she seems to assume that women should take on symbolically male traits.

However, some recent scholars (Bergoffen 1997; Heinämaa 2003) have argued that Beauvoir, unlike Sartre, does not actually favour a life of sheer transcendence. According to Beauvoir's version of existentialism in her *Ethics of Ambiguity* (1947), all human lives are lives partly of transcendence and partly of immanence. As such the human condition is *ambiguous* and we should each acknowledge and embrace this ambiguity, Beauvoir thinks. Women's biology makes it harder for them to recognize one side of their ambiguity – their freedom (Heinämaa 2003: 72). This difficulty has been reinforced by a lack of contraceptive and other technologies (until recently), and by men's myths of woman. The same myths have led men to see immanence as an exclusively female trait. Hence men have had difficulty recognizing their immanent side – recognizing, for instance, that they are just as affected by their hormones as women are.

Still, for Beauvoir both sexes should learn to recognize their ambiguity. Beauvoir thinks that sexual relationships show the way forward here, revealing that:

[M]an, like woman, is flesh, therefore passive, the plaything of his hormones and of the species . . . And she, like him, in the midst of the carnal fever, is a consenting, a voluntary gift, an activity; they live out in their several fashions the strange ambiguity of existence made body. (1949: 737)

Rather than valuing transcendence as opposed to immanence, then, Beauvoir considers both to be valuable. Her complaint is that these modes of existence have been unevenly distributed across the sexes rather than being shared equally between them (1949: 737). Rather than wanting women to become symbolically male, Beauvoir wants *both* men and women to take on symbolically male (transcendence) *and* female (immanence) traits.

Beauvoir's existentialism has led her to create a distinctive form of feminism. According to this, women have been subordinated in that they have been confined to immanence, but this can and should be changed. Beauvoir's proposed solution is for all human beings to embrace their ambiguous condition. Beauvoir's work confirms how philosophical thinking – existentialist thinking in her case – can lead to new versions of feminist politics.

3. Subordination, equality and difference

The diversity of philosophical forms of feminism creates some puzzles for my definition of feminists as those who oppose women's subordination. Recall that being subordinated means being treated as inferior, secondary or subservient to another group. Plausibly, then, to oppose women's subordination is to insist that women are of equal worth to men and should be treated as such. Yet whereas this implies that all feminists support equality for women, earlier (chapter 4, section 7) I argued that equality feminism is just one form of feminism, which other types of feminist – notably difference feminists – reject. Difference feminists think that demanding equality for women *perpetuates* women's subordination by assuming the superior worth of the (traditionally) masculine pursuits and institutions to which equal access for women is demanded. Truly to end women's subordination, difference feminists think, we need instead to recognize the worth of women's own distinctive, family-focused values. Given that difference feminists are opposing women's subordination here, it seems that opposing subordination cannot mean demanding equality after all. But then it becomes unclear what subordination is.

We can solve these puzzles by disentangling two kinds of equality to which feminists may be committed:

1   Equality in the broad sense (or **moral equality**): women are not second-rate beings but are equal to men in moral worth and should be treated as such.

2   Equality in a narrow sense (or '**access equality**'): women should have equal access either to (i) the full range of existing social institutions or to (ii) a full range of social institutions which have been reformed or transformed so that women can access these institutions on equal terms. (Liberal feminists are perhaps more likely to pursue access to (i), while socialist feminists and those radical feminists who are pro-equality are more likely to pursue access to (ii). But we should remember that there are no clear-cut divisions here, since some liberal feminists do advocate quite far-reaching social reforms.)

Now, I suggest that all feminists, by virtue of opposing women's subordination, endorse the principle that women and men are morally equal. However, not all feminists support access equality. But the most prominent group of feminists who do not – difference feminists – reject access equality because they think that it devalues women's perspective and hence treats women as subordinate. So these feminists reject access equality in the name of women's moral equality. Consider Irigaray too. She thinks that if we pursue equal access then we fail to question the male-centred *symbolic* order. In that case we leave in place the symbolic degrading of the female which ultimately causes women's subordination. Thus, she also opposes access equality in the name of women's moral equality.

To be sure, Irigaray (1991: ch. 1) and other sexual difference and difference feminists may *say* that they oppose equality just as such. But in saying this they falsely conflate the strategy of pursuing equal access with equality as a whole. They do so even though their own resistance to women's subordination rests on a commitment to the principle of women's moral equality.

Irigaray might object that, as I stated it above, the principle of women's moral equality falls into the tradition of thinking about women only with reference to men. But we can reformulate the principle to avoid this:

1a Equality in the broad sense (or **moral equality**): all human indi-
    viduals are equal in moral worth and deserve to be treated as such;
    women are no exception to this.

We may conclude, then, that those whom I have called (and will
continue to call) 'equality feminists' actually support equality in two
ways. Firstly, like all feminists, they support the principle of women's
moral equality. Secondly, *un*like some other feminists, their interpretation of what it would be for women to be treated as moral equals is
for women to achieve equal access to the full range of social institutions (or to the 'public' sphere, taking the public sphere to mean not
only the state but all areas of life outside the family).

However, there is at least one further objection that might be made
to my distinction between the two kinds of equality to which feminists
may be committed. This objection is that the principle of the moral
equality of all human beings is a liberal principle. So, if (as I claim) all
feminists endorse this principle, then all feminists must be liberal
feminists. But this is false: as we have seen, liberal feminism is only
one form of feminism.

To get round this objection, we must recall that 'liberal feminism'
generally refers to the form of feminism which pursues equal access to
existing social institutions or to reformed versions of these. But since
feminists can support the principle of moral equality without thereby
becoming supporters of equal access in any form, feminists can also
support moral equality without thereby becoming 'liberal feminists' as
'liberal feminism' is generally understood. The fact that not all feminists are liberal feminists in this generally accepted sense is consistent
with all forms of feminism (radical, socialist, liberal, difference, and
others) resting on a moral principle to which liberals are also committed: the principle that all human individuals deserve equal treatment.

Nothing that I have said about the definition of equality feminism
so far resolves its conflict with difference feminism. Difference feminists object that equality feminists fail to respect women's distinctive
voice and want women to embrace masculine values and activities,
and so to become the same as men.[2] But equality feminists reply that
we cannot respect women's distinctive 'voice' without also reinforcing
the marginalized, family-focused role which produces that voice.

Complicating this debate, feminist critics of essentialism object that
there *is* no one voice with which all women speak and that there *is* no

single caring role that all women share. However, I argued in chapter 5 that although there are no universal values/roles/experiences which all women share, we may still make statistical generalizations such as 'British full-time women workers earn 82 per cent of what their male counterparts earn' or 'in Britain women do between 66 and 80 per cent of all housework and childcare'. To be sure, not all women are focused mainly or exclusively on their families. And women from different races and classes might well tend to adopt different approaches to house- and childcaring work. Working-class and non-white women are relatively likely to do paid house- and childcaring work for other (white, middle-class) women on top of attending to their own families. Nevertheless, the 66–80 per cent statistic above suggests that women (of diverse kinds) will *tend* to espouse the values of care more than men do. So difference feminists can still recommend recognition of the distinctive caring voice which many women will tend to have to some extent and in some form. And so the conflict between equality and difference feminism remains real.

Several feminist philosophers (e.g. Cornell 1993; Minow 1990) have looked for ways beyond this conflict. I will now argue that one way beyond the conflict is to recognize that women will be unable to achieve genuinely equal access to the public world unless that public world is 'feminized'. That is, the public world needs to come to embrace (what tend currently to be) feminine values.

How would society have to change for women to be able to participate in it on a genuinely equal footing? Plausibly, there would have to be a total restructuring of the work/family division which has, for a long time, assigned men to work and women to family.[3] The Victorian poet Alfred Tennyson immortalized this division with his line 'Man for the field and woman for the hearth, man for the sword and for the needle she'. This gender division has shaped how most jobs have developed and become defined. It has meant that most jobs have come to involve long hours of work away from home, so that they cannot easily be combined with extensive childcare responsibilities. But since women – due to gender norms – tend to do most of the childcare within families, they are left in no position to participate equally in the worlds of work or politics.

One might infer that the way to enable equal access to work and politics for women is for childcare to be shared equally between men and women. But as work is currently organized – on the assumption that workers do not have extensive childcare responsibilities – shared parenting would only make it relatively hard for either men or women to take full part in work. Thus, the current organization of work creates a pressure (upon heterosexual couples) for the man to focus on work and the woman on the home.

The way to enable equal access for women, then, is to restructure work around an assumption that all workers do (or at least may) have significant childcare responsibilities. Amongst other things, this means that all work schedules must be flexible, that free or subsidized childcare must be available at or near all workplaces, and that all workers should be entitled to parental leave (Saul 2003: 36). These arrangements would enable women to participate in work on equal terms and would enable men and women to distribute work and childcare responsibilities evenly between them.

However, Tina Chanter (2006: 20–2) has recently argued that this whole way of thinking about women's inequality – as largely caused by the work/home division – is inadequate to the experience of many immigrant and non-white women whose work *is* childcare for other more privileged women, work that may involve living in those women's homes. According to Chanter, then, the home/work distinction reflects the experience only of relatively privileged white women. I am not convinced that this fact that some women's work is done in the homes of others invalidates my argument for restructuring how work is organized. Rather, I think that it is important that childcaring work should *also* be organized on the assumption that the women (and sometimes men) doing it may well also have significant childcare responsibilities of their own.

To return to the equality/difference debate, the strategy of restructuring work is still 'equality feminist'. It aims to transform social institutions so that women can participate equally in, gain equal access to, or benefit equally from social life in its full range. Yet it may well be that work could only successfully be restructured in the way I have suggested if social institutions came to embrace the distinctive values and perspectives that women presently tend to have. Workplaces could not genuinely accept that all workers have or may well have extensive childcaring duties unless those workplaces came to embody a belief that childcaring has value in itself, because of the distinctive virtues and ethical perspectives that it embodies. Otherwise, the allowance that workplaces made for childcare duties would always be grudging. Employers would always be prone to revert to making as little provision for childcare duties as possible and to favouring job candidates who lack such duties.

Arguably, then, securing genuinely equal access for women requires social institutions to recognize the distinctive family-focused values which women tend to hold given existing gender norms. (This is not to say that these institutions could or should recognize *only* caring values. Any large-scale institution requires general rules that distribute rights and obligations fairly amongst all its members. So large-scale institutions would have to recognize the value of justice as well as that of care.) Moreover, if care duties were redistributed between men and women then men would come to recognize and adopt caring values as well. So gaining genuinely equal access to society for women turns out to require just that recognition of women's caring values – by men and within social institutions at large – which difference feminists advocate. However, this requirement can be interpreted in two ways.

1   Some feminists might say that women's difference must be recognized only as a *means to* obtaining equal access to social life and not as an end in itself. If so, then difference feminists might still object to these feminists that they see getting women into the whole public world as the only ultimate goal, and hence that they fail to see that women's family-focused voice has value for its own sake.

2   Other feminists might say that recognizing women's difference is one of the key *elements of* genuinely equal access to society. On this view, the recognition of (what currently tend to be) women's different values partly constitutes what truly equal access is. So if gaining equal access to society is an end in itself, and if recognizing women's difference is a major part of what it *is* to gain equal access, then recognizing that difference must also be an end in itself.

Feminists who take this latter view endorse the goals *both* of equality feminism *and* of difference feminism. So this latter feminist position can be recommended as providing a way beyond the equality/ difference conflict. Moreover, this latter position also offers a prospect of reconciling both equality and difference with the goal of abolishing gender. For if both men and women were expected to embrace public *and* family-based activities and values, rather than men being expected to be public-focused and women to be family-focused, then one major area in which males and females are now expected to act in systematically different ways would have disappeared.

4. Feminism and 'women'

The fact that difference feminists reject 'equality' does not damage my definition of feminism because difference feminists actually accept the general principle of women's moral equality. A second family of objections to my definition of feminism concerns whether it can rightly be said that all feminists oppose the subordination of *women* in particular. Many contemporary feminists argue that, instead of focusing solely on women, feminists should – or already do – 'resist . . . oppression and discrimination in its various forms – whether based on gender, race, class, religion, or geographical location' (Schott 1998: 41). Others argue that feminists should question rather than rely on the category 'women'. Let us take these two arguments in turn.

One route to the conclusion that feminists should oppose the whole range of forms of oppression is as follows. Let us start with the idea that feminists oppose the subordination of women. Presumably they do so because this subordination harms women. But if harm to women is what feminists really oppose, then feminists should oppose all the oppressive social divisions, including race and class, which harm many women by forcing them to wrestle with racism and/or poverty. (Of course, class and race harm many men in the same way. But, on the view we are considering, what feminists object to *as feminists* is harm to women. Feminists might also object to oppressive systems because they harm men, but these objections are not specifically feminist.)

A more fine-grained view is that feminists oppose not simply harms to women but the distinctive kind of oppression that women suffer *as* women, in virtue of being women or females. In this vein, bell hooks defines feminism as a 'movement to end sexist oppression' (hooks 1984: 31) as distinct from a movement to end race or class oppression. 'Sexist oppression' can be defined, following Haslanger and Tuana (2006), as oppression that is imposed on people because they are perceived or imagined to be female. Hence 'sexist oppression' is, precisely, oppression that women suffer *as* females.

However, hooks argues that opposing sexist oppression need not conflict with, but may well require, opposing the full range of forms of oppression. She argues that if feminists take themselves to oppose sexist oppression (rather than, say, inequality), then their attention will be directed (1) to 'the inter-relatedness of sex, race and class oppression' and (2) to 'systems of domination' (hooks 1984: 31). Her arguments are these:

1   As we saw in chapter 5, sexist (or gender) oppression only ever exists in class- and race-specific forms. Thus, feminists cannot oppose sexist oppression without also criticizing race and class insofar as they shape the forms that sexist oppression takes. But in criticizing race and class on these grounds, feminists are criticizing race and class *as* feminists. They are criticizing these systems for shaping particular, race- and class-specific, sets of gender norms which oppress women as race- and class-specific kinds of women.
2   If defined as a struggle against sexist oppression, feminism becomes part of a broader struggle against all 'systems of domi-nation' – including, therefore, systems that affect men. That is, because feminists oppose (sexist) *oppression* they must not only be feminists but must also oppose oppression in general.

We can make a similar argument to hooks's second argument if we define feminism in terms of opposition to women's subordination. As we have seen, opposition to women's subordination rests on a general commitment to the principle that all human beings are morally equal. So consistently with their own normative commitment to humanity's moral equality, feminists should also object to class and race inequali-ties. However, they will be doing so not *as* feminists – since feminism opposes women's subordination in particular – but as egalitarians more broadly.[4]

I conclude that we can consistently say both (1) that feminists are defined by their opposition to women's subordination and (2) that feminists also should (and often do) oppose all forms of oppression – both (i) as feminists (because women's subordination always exists in specific forms that are shaped by these various oppressive systems) and (ii) as egalitarians (because feminism presupposes a broader com-mitment to egalitarianism).

Let us turn to the argument that feminists should not oppose women's subordination because in doing so they undesirably rely on the category 'women'. There are at least two sets of reasons why relying on this category might be undesirable. The French-based (but Bulgarian-born) philosopher Julia Kristeva expresses the first set of reasons in a famous passage:[5]

> [W]e must use 'we are women' as an advertisement or slogan for our demands. On a deeper level, however, a woman cannot 'be'; it is something which does not even belong in the order of *being*. It follows that a feminist practice can only be negative, at odds with what already exists so that we may say 'that's not it' and 'that's still not it'. In 'woman' I see something that cannot be represented, something that is not said. (Kristeva 1974b: 137)

Kristeva accepts that at an everyday level feminists must rely on the category 'women' so as to demand abortion rights, day-care centres and other improvements on 'women's' behalf. But feminists should not rely on the category 'women' in the further sense of thinking that women 'are' at a deep level. Following Lacan, Kristeva sees 'man' and 'woman' as positions or identities that are defined by the symbolic order (i.e. by language), and so defined that 'woman' is merely the opposite of 'man' and is not a positive identity. Thus at a deep level women 'are not' women (1) because no individual ever perfectly conforms to the symbolic position or identity (as a man or a woman) that they have taken up and (2) because the symbolic identity of being a woman is not a positive identity anyway.

But Kristeva does not wholly accept Lacan's view of language. Unlike him, she holds (Kristeva 1974a) that all language has a **semiotic** aspect. Words and sentences are not only meaningful but also have non-meaningful rhythmic and melodic aspects. These rhythmic and melodic aspects express the drives (the biological impulses) which pulsate through the bodies of all individuals and which have been patterned in specific ways in each individual by their early relationship to their mother. Thus the semiotic aspect of language keeps alive our early state of symbiotic unity with our mothers.

Ordinarily, Kristeva thinks, the symbolic side of language dominates its semiotic side. But modernist, avant-garde writing lets the semiotic side of a piece of writing – its rhythmic and melodic aspects – compete with and 'transgress' (i.e. temporarily suspend) its symbolic, meaningful side (1974a: 69). Take for example this sentence, describing a woman walking across a beach, from James Joyce's novel *Ulysses*: 'She trudges, schlepps, trains, drags, trascines her load. A tide westering, moondrawn, in her wake. Tides, myriadislanded, within her, blood not mine, . . . a winedark sea' (Joyce 1922: 60). However, it is the symbolic side of language – the meanings articulated within it – which defines 'man' and 'woman' in a male-centred way. So when avant-garde writing suspends the symbolic side of language it also, temporarily, suspends the male-centredness that goes with it.

Kristeva concludes from this that modernist writing gives voice to 'the feminine' (*le féminin*) (see Kristeva 1986: 11). 'The feminine' for her does not mean a feminine gender role. Rather it means (i) just the semiotic itself, which she calls 'the feminine' because it is connected to the mother. But also (ii) 'the feminine' is the kind of writing which temporarily suspends the symbolic man/woman contrast, and which is called 'feminine' because it suspends the male privilege which that contrast embodies. (Kristeva is not suggesting that only women can produce avant-garde writing: in her view men, such as Joyce, may do so too.)

Is Kristeva's position feminist? She does not call herself a femin- ist. Yet her views might still *be* feminist. For her, the symbolic male/female contrast ultimately causes women's subordination. But does she think that women's subordination, or the symbolic contrast which produces it, can or should be changed? For her this contrast can be changed only in the very limited sense that avant-garde writing can temporarily suspend it. Still, insofar as Kristeva supports this limited form of change to what causes women's subordination, her position is feminist.

This shows that for Kristeva there actually *is* a way to oppose women's subordination without assuming that women 'are' in a deep sense. By practising feminine writing, one can (temporarily) oppose the male/female contrast and the way it subordinates those individu- als who occupy its female pole. *And*, at the same time, one acknowl- edges that those individuals 'are not' women, both because they never perfectly fit their symbolic position and because that position is defined only negatively.

Butler (1990a) gives different reasons why feminists should not rely on the category 'women'. To use this category is to strengthen its hold on our thought. But this category is one part of the heterosexual matrix of assumptions which insists that every individual must be either a man or a woman and which polices whether individuals have the 'right' gender for their sex. Because this matrix divides individuals into two genders whose members then appear to need one another as complements, the matrix oppresses those who are not heterosexual. The matrix also oppresses people whose sex/gender is ambiguous and, indeed, oppresses all of us insofar as none of us can ever perfectly conform to the gender norms imposed on us. Finally, too, the matrix oppresses women because it defines being a woman as the position of being opposed and subordinate to men. So Butler thinks that if feminists uncritically invoke the category 'women' then they strengthen the very system of thought which causes women's subordination.

It might seem that Butler cannot consistently *both* object to feminist use of the category 'women' *and* rely on that category to make the critical claim that the heterosexual matrix subordinates women. But when Butler uses the category 'women' she understands 'women' in a way that builds in her criticism of the heterosexual matrix and of the central role that the category 'women' plays in that matrix. For when she objects to the subordination of women, what she objects to is the way that the two-gender system, in classifying certain people as and obliging them to act like women, has made those people into subordinate beings.

But the fact that Butler can still criticize women's subordination in this way shows that actually it *is* possible for feminists to criticize women's subordination without reinforcing that subordination just by using the category 'women'. The solution is to find ways of using the category 'women' critically, so that it builds in recognition that this very category has oppressive effects.

Butler's claims also imply that feminists cannot consistently object only to women's subordination and not also to the oppression of 'sexual minorities' (this term comes from Rubin 1984) and of sex/gender minorities. For Butler, one cannot properly criticize women's subordination unless one sees that the heterosexual matrix is the cause of that subordination. But one cannot understand how that matrix causes women's subordination without understanding how that matrix functions in general and so how it also oppresses sexual/sex/gender minorities. Thus, feminists must criticize those other forms of oppression too. Here, though, I would again suggest that feminists will still be criticizing these oppressions both (1) *as* feminists – on account of their inseparable connection with the subordination of women – and (2) in their own right, because feminists by implication are egalitarians, who oppose (or should oppose) oppression in all forms.

I have defended my definition of feminism against two sets of objections. (1) Some feminists (hooks, Butler) seem to escape my definition because they think that feminists should be critical not only of women's oppression but equally of other – racial, class and sexual – forms of oppression. But these criticisms remain specifically *feminist* criticisms insofar as they target racial, class and sexual oppressions for their connections with or their impact on the form(s) of women's subordination. (2) Some feminists (Kristeva, Butler) seem not to fall under my definition because they think that feminists should not rely on the category 'women'. But since Kristeva and Butler continue to criticize women's subordination in ways that build in criticisms of the category 'women', they still fall under my definition of feminism. So it remains true that what unites feminists is their opposition to women's subordination.

5. 'Global' feminism?

Almost all the feminist philosophers whom this book has studied explicitly call themselves feminists. A few, such as Kristeva and Irigaray, do not. Irigaray instead voices support for 'movements of liberation of women' (Irigaray 1977b: 67). But if a philosopher does not call him- or herself a feminist, then what right have we to describe him or her as a feminist philosopher?

Consider *why* Irigaray and Kristeva avoid calling themselves feminists. Irigaray takes feminism to be a movement that pursues women's equal access to existing institutions. She is mistaken: many self-described feminists, even many equality feminists, reject this form of equality. Kristeva takes it that feminists either pursue equal access to institutions that are structured by a male-centred symbolic (1986: 193–4) or – unrealistically – reject language and social life outright (1986: 199). But again most feminists would reject both options.

So when Irigaray and Kristeva distance themselves from 'feminism', they are distancing themselves only from certain *forms* of feminism which they mistakenly equate with feminism as a whole. If we define feminists instead as those who oppose women's subordination, then Irigaray and (to a lesser extent) Kristeva fall under the heading of feminism. Likewise, the eighteenth-century author Mary Wollstonecraft may rightly be called a feminist because she opposes women's subordination – although she could not call herself a feminist because the word 'feminism' only appeared in 1882. (It first appeared in French, as the word *féminisme*; see Offen 1992: 72.)

The problem that some thinkers and activists oppose women's subordination but do not call themselves feminists becomes more complex at an international level. Some non-western women who are politically active on women's behalf refuse to call themselves feminists because they think that feminism 'has too often become a tool of cultural imperialism' (Kishwar 1990: 3). '**Imperialism**' refers to the domination of one country or group of countries by another, and specifically to the colonial rule that European countries formerly exercised over much of Africa, Asia, India and South America. The effects of this colonial system persist in the huge inequalities of power and resources which exist between most of the former colonies and most of the former colonizers, and in the power that western-owned or -based multinationals exercise in many former colonies.

The worry of some women's activists in these former colonies, then, is that western feminists often reproduce ways of thinking and acting which took hold as part of imperialism. Implicitly, western feminists often seem to assume that western countries have the most progressive attitude towards women, and that non-western countries (or Southern or Third World countries, as they may also be called) should become more like the west in this regard. These criticisms of western feminism have given rise to a vast literature debating the possibility of 'global feminism'. This literature cuts across many disciplines, including sociology, economics, politics and cultural studies, as well as philosophy. In introducing the global feminism debates, I will confine my attention to some of the more explicitly philosophical literature.

Is the criticism that western feminists often retain imperialist assumptions justified? Plausibly it is, in at least some cases. Radical feminists claim that societies the world over are patriarchal, and some, such as Robin Morgan (1984), conclude that a global feminist movement is needed to fight patriarchy. This claim that patriarchy exists everywhere implies that non-western women are oppressed in ways that are variations on the plight common to all women. On this view, all women suffer from rape, domestic violence, compulsory heterosexuality, etc., but non-western and western women suffer these problems in culturally distinct forms. For example, the radical feminist

Mary Daly criticizes (what she takes to be) the Indian tradition of *sati*, whereby widows were urged – or forced – to display their purity by throwing themselves on their husbands' funeral pyres. Daly sees *sati* as a 'variation' (1978: 111) on the 'sado-rituals' from which western women also suffer. Daly takes 'sado-rituals' to be destructive practices which men impose on women in the name of purity (Daly 1978: 130–3).

Seeing non-western and western women's oppressions as variations on the same thing can also lead to the view that the former oppression is the same as the latter but worse. If one sees foot-binding and cosmetic surgery as variations on the same thing, then one may readily come to see foot-binding as a *worse* variation – more coercive and more incapacitating. Chandra Mohanty concludes that radical feminism has a built-in tendency to portray non-western women as the ultimate victims – 'ignorant, poor, . . . tradition-bound, domestic' (1986: 56) – in contrast to western women, who (on this radical feminist picture) remain relatively free and educated despite men oppressing them. At this point, radical feminism has become complicit with the colonialist belief that non-western cultures are relatively 'backward'.

Western feminists may also become complicit with colonialism in other ways. If they speak out against the oppression of non-western women, then their speech may well trade for its moral authority on the fact that they, as westerners, are perceived to have more competence than non-westerners 'to decide the true, the just, and the culturally valuable' (Alcoff 2000: 263). This common (but usually unspoken) perception that western people have greater moral authority and competence is a legacy of the colonial attitude which saw western cultures as the most advanced. So the problem is that if western feminists speak against non-western women's oppression, their speech may reinforce their own authority and may also reinforce the oppressive view that non-western women are inarticulate victims whose cause must be championed by articulate westerners. (On this 'problem of speaking for others', see Alcoff 1991/2.)

Western feminists who want to avoid becoming complicit with colonialism in any of the above ways might conclude – as does Lorraine Code (2000: 70) – that they should avoid criticizing non-western cultures. Code suggests that western feminists should focus instead on criticizing their own cultures and societies. Tacitly, some of the feminist philosophers we have studied seem to have reached similar conclusions. For instance, Irigaray and Cavarero criticize how the female is symbolized in *western* culture.

One might object that the approach that Code recommends effectively treats non-western women as if they counted for less than western women. If one refuses to criticize non-western institutions and activities when they harm non-western women, when one would unhesitatingly criticize western institutions which – albeit in different ways – harm western women, then in effect one seems to be treating non-western women as less deserving of moral concern. To avoid these problems, Susan Okin defends the view that non-western women's oppression *is* after all 'similar [to] but worse [than]' that of western women (Okin 1994: 11).

A different, and I think more productive, objection to Code's approach is that it presumes that cultures are more self-contained and unified than they really are. As Mohanty (2003) reminds us, our social world today is increasingly 'globalized'. Multinational corporations increasingly operate across the globe, and these corporations tend to divide the jobs that they offer by gender (e.g. women are typically expected to do jobs requiring manual dexterity such as garment work). Thus these corporations export similar patterns of gender-divided labour around the world. Again, global financial institutions such as the International Monetary Fund and the World Bank constrain countries everywhere to adopt similar policies that have similar effects on women – for instance to reduce state-funded welfare provision, forcing women to take up greater burdens of caring work. So globalization tends to cause particular patterns of oppression of women to recur across different countries. Insofar as these oppressive patterns recur (albeit with variations) across western and non-western countries, western feminists cannot consistently object when these patterns occur in their own societies without also objecting when they recur elsewhere. Moreover, since it is western-based or western-owned economic institutions which are causing these patterns to recur, western feminists cannot *be* fully critical of their own societies unless they criticize the forms of oppression that these societies are exporting around the world.

Before contemporary globalization too, western and non-western cultures were already shaped by their interactions with one another, especially during colonialism. The custom of *sati*, which Mary Daly criticized, illustrates this. Uma Narayan (1997) shows that *sati*, which had only been practised by certain Hindu castes and in certain regions of India, became defined as an Indian 'tradition' as recently as the nineteenth century. This happened because British colonists, wondering whether they could outlaw *sati*, set Indian religious scholars to see what sanction *sati* had in Hindu scripture (Narayan 1997: 49, 61–2). So the idea that *sati* is an authentic Indian tradition is itself an effect of colonialism. More generally, Narayan argues, the belief in a national Indian culture only took hold in India in the nineteenth century as a reaction against colonization. This belief glossed over the fact that Indian 'culture' – like all supposed 'national cultures' – was (and is) diverse, changing and composed of many different elements, groups and claims.

Narayan's arguments imply that western feminists may criticize oppressive practices such as *sati* without becoming complicit with colonialism. Since these allegedly 'traditional' practices are not genuinely traditional at all, in criticizing them one need not be promoting western culture against Indian or other non-western 'traditions'. Such criticism *can* reinforce a belief in western superiority, though, if in criticizing practices such as *sati* western feminists *do* wrongly assume – as Mary Daly did – that these practices are part of the 'national culture' of India (or of whatever other country). In that case, these feminists will make their criticisms in ways that do imply that the non-western 'culture' in question is especially backward. To avoid this, Narayan concludes, western feminists need not only to criticize practices that oppress women (wherever they occur) but also to criticize what she calls the 'package picture' of cultures (2000: 96) – the idea that cultures are self-contained entities each defined by their own unchanging and homogeneous 'traditions'.[6]

I began this survey of debates around global feminism by noting that some non-western women activists resist the label 'feminism'. This is understandable, because these activists wish to distance themselves from forms of western feminism that have (even if inadvertently) become complicit with colonialism. The resistance of these activists to the label 'feminism' does not prevent them from fighting against women's oppression. As Jaggar says, 'Whether or not they call themselves feminist, innumerable groups outside the West are currently working to promote . . . women's "gender interests"' (2000: 12). Indeed, it is precisely because they oppose women's oppression that these groups resist forms of feminism that are complicit with colonialism, since colonialism and its after-effects are a major cause of the specific forms of oppression that non-western women experience.

6. Concluding remarks

This book has argued that feminist philosophy is a distinctive field of philosophy. What distinguishes it above all is its focus on a range of novel concepts – including sex, gender, sexuality, sexual difference, essentialism and birth – and on the problems that arise out of these concepts. Feminist philosophers also criticize male bias in traditional philosophy, and they articulate feminist political positions at a philosophical level. But feminist work in these latter two areas has spawned the new concepts – sex, gender, etc. – and problems which above all mark out feminist philosophy as an original field.

Another argument of this book has been that we should distinguish between (1) biological sex, (2) gender norms – and the gendered traits, habits and bodies of individuals living under these norms, (3) sexuality: individuals' personal patterns of erotic feeling and behaviour, and (4) sexual difference: the symbolic (or imaginary) meanings that surround being male or female, and the sexually differentiated ways in which men and women live their bodies under these meanings. I have also argued that we should distinguish (5) scientific beliefs about biological sex from sex itself and from gender norms, as well as from ideas about the symbolic meaning of sex. I think that we should retain and use all these concepts because they each pick out different phenomena. Of course, in reality, all these phenomena so influence and shape one another that they are thoroughly interwoven. Nonetheless, by distinguishing between them (and using distinct concepts to do so) we can explain and analyse, more carefully than we otherwise could, the various elements that combine to shape men's and women's lives and social relationships.

Still, none of the conclusions for which I have argued in this book are meant to be definitive, and I have left many issues unresolved: whether feminists should aim to create a genuine sexual difference or to undo gender; how feminists might understand sexuality and gender in relation to one another; whether a 'woman' is best understood as someone who has given meaning to her female body or as someone who has taken on feminine gender norms; how feminist theories of gender might fit together with theories of the lived body. These problems around the relations between gender, sexual difference, womanhood and sexuality remain, together with many other problems, for current and future feminist philosophers to unravel.

Notes

1 Thus in claiming that human beings – including women – 'exist' in this sense, Beauvoir positions herself as an 'existentialist', taking it that 'existentialism' contrasts with 'essentialism' (see chapter 5, note 1).
2 On this last criticism, see Grosz 1986: 191.
3 Caring for family members *is* work, but for simplicity I will speak as if 'work' and 'family' were contrasts.
4 I use the term 'egalitarian' broadly to mean someone who accepts the principle that all human beings are morally equal. One might object that class, race and gender divisions can be compatible with treating people as moral equals as long as people have equal opportunities to compete for the (unequal) slots within these divisions. But feminists tend to be sceptical of such arguments in relation to gender and to argue that genuine equality of opportunity requires the abolition of gendered social divisions such as the home/work division. (See Phillips 1997 and section 3 above for an argument to this effect.) So, consistently, feminists should also be – and usually are – sceptical when similar arguments are made regarding race and class.
5 I will only discuss Kristeva's early work from the 1970s. Her later thought is significantly different.
6 Similarly, Narayan suggests, Indian feminists need to fight both these oppressive practices *and* the 'package picture' of Indian culture. This picture allows Hindu nationalists to defend oppressive practices on the false grounds that they are valuable national traditions, and also to falsely accuse Indian feminists of being 'westernized' when they oppose these practices.

Further Reading

Beauvoir   The introduction to *The Second Sex* (Beauvoir 1949) sets out her key existentialist feminist claims. Lloyd 1984: 96–102 is a classic criticism of Beauvoir.

The equality/difference conflict   Jaggar 1990; Scott 1988.

Feminism and women   hooks 1984: ch. 2; Kristeva 1974b.

Global feminism   Okin 1994, Code 2000, and Narayan 2000 span a range of positions. Mohanty 1986 is a classic criticism of colonial elements in western feminism.

Bibliography

Alcoff, Linda Martín. 1991/2. 'The Problem of Speaking For Others'. *Cultural Critique* 20: 5–32. URL = <http://www.alcoff.com/content/speaothers.html>. Accessed 8 November 2006.

——. 2000. 'What Should White People Do?' In Narayan and Harding eds. 2000.

Allen, Amy. 1999. *The Power of Feminist Theory: Domination, Resistance, Solidarity.* Boulder, CO: Westview Press.

——. 2005. 'Feminist Perspectives on Power'. *Stanford Encyclopedia of Philosophy* (Winter 2005 Edition), ed. Edward N. Zalta. URL = <http://plato.stanford.edu/archives/win2005/entries/feminist-power/>. Accessed 27 April 2007.

Alsop, Rachel, Annette Fitzsimons and Kathleen Lennon. 2002. *Theorizing Gender.* Cambridge, UK: Polity Press.

Antony, Louise and Charlotte Witt, eds. 1993. *A Mind of One's Own: Feminist Essays on Reason and Objectivity.* Boulder, CO: Westview Press.

Archer, John and Barbara Lloyd. 2002. *Sex and Gender.* 2nd edn. Cambridge, UK: Cambridge University Press.

Arendt, Hannah. 1958. *The Human Condition.* Chicago, IL: University of Chicago Press.

——. 1963. *On Revolution.* Harmondsworth: Penguin.

Bar On, Bat-Ami. 1992. 'The Feminist Sexuality Debates and the Transformation of the Political'. *Hypatia* 7 (2): 45–58.

Barrett, Michèle. 1988. *Women's Oppression Today: The Marxist/Feminist Encounter.* 2nd, rev., edn. London: Verso.

Bartky, Sandra. 1990. *Femininity and Domination: Studies in the Phenomenology of Oppression.* London and New York: Routledge.

Bartlett, Katharine T. and Rosanne Kennedy, eds. *Feminist Legal Theory: Readings in Law and Gender.* Boulder, CO: Westview Press, 1991.

Battersby, Christine. 1989. *Gender and Genius: Towards a Feminist Aesthetics*. London: The Women's Press.

——. 1998. *The Phenomenal Woman: Feminist Metaphysics and the Patterns of Identity*. Cambridge, UK: Polity Press.

Beauvoir, Simone de. 1947. *The Ethics of Ambiguity*. Trans. (1964) Bernard Frechtman. New York: Citadel Press.

——. 1949. *The Second Sex*. Trans. (1972) H. M. Parshley. Harmondsworth: Penguin.

Benhabib, Seyla. 1996. *The Reluctant Modernism of Hannah Arendt*. London: Sage.

Bergoffen, Debra. 1997. *The Philosophy of Simone de Beauvoir: Gendered Phenomenologies, Erotic Generosities*. Albany: SUNY Press.

Bigwood, Carol. 1991. 'Renaturalizing the Body (With the Help of Merleau-Ponty)'. *Hypatia* 6 (3): 54–72.

Biology and Gender Study Group. 1988. 'The Importance of Feminist Critique for Contemporary Cell Biology'. *Hypatia* 3 (1): 61–76.

Bleier, Ruth. 1984. *Science and Gender: A Critique of Biology and its Theories on Women*. New York: Pergamon Press.

Bock, Gisela and Susan James, eds. 1992. *Beyond Equality and Difference: Citizenship, Feminist Politics and Female Subjectivity*. London and New York: Routledge

Bono, Paola and Sandra Kemp, eds. 1991. *Italian Feminist Thought: A Reader*. Oxford: Blackwell.

Bordo, Susan. 1987. *The Flight to Objectivity: Essays on Cartesianism and Culture*. Albany, NY: SUNY Press.

——. 1993. *Unbearable Weight: Feminism, Western Culture, and the Body*. Berkeley, CA: University of California Press.

Bornstein, Kate. 1994. *Gender Outlaw: On Men, Women, and the Rest of Us*. London and New York: Routledge.

Boyd, Richard. 1988. 'How to Be a Moral Realist'. In *Essays on Moral Realism*, ed. Geoffrey Sayre-McCord. Ithaca, NY: Cornell University Press.

Braidotti, Rosi. 1998. 'Sexual Difference Theory'. In Jaggar and Young eds. 1998.

Brennan, Teresa. 1991. 'An Impasse in Psychoanalysis and Feminism'. In Gunew ed. 1991.

Brison, Susan. 1997. 'Outlining Oneself: Trauma, Memory, and Personal Identity'. In *Feminists Rethink the Self*, ed. Diana Meyers. Boulder, CO: Westview Press.

Bryson, Valerie. 1992. *Feminist Political Theory: An Introduction*. Basingstoke: Macmillan.

Bryson, Valerie. 1993. 'Feminism'. In *Contemporary Political Ideologies*, ed. Roger Eatwell and Anthony Wright. London: Pinter Publishers.

Bubeck, Diemut. 1995. *Care, Gender, and Justice*. Oxford: Clarendon Press.

Bunch, Charlotte. 1972. 'Lesbians in Revolt'. *The Furies: Lesbian/Feminist Monthly* 1: 8–9. URL = <http://scriptorium.lib.duke.edu/wlm/furies/>. Accessed 27 April 2007.

Butler, Judith. 1986. 'Sex and Gender in Simone de Beauvoir's *Second Sex*'. *Yale French Studies* 72: 35–49.

——. 1987. 'Variations on Sex and Gender: Beauvoir, Wittig and Foucault'. In *Feminism as Critique*, ed. Drucilla Cornell and Seyla Benhabib. Minneapolis, MN: University of Minnesota Press.

——. 1990a. *Gender Trouble*. London and New York: Routledge.

——. 1990b. 'Performative Acts and Gender Constitution: An Essay on Phenomenology and Feminist Theory'. In *Writing on the Body*, ed. Katie Conboy, Nadia Medina and Sarah Stanbury. New York: Columbia University Press, 1997.

——. 1991. 'Imitation and Gender Subordination'. In Nicholson ed. 1997.

——. 1993. *Bodies That Matter: On the Discursive Limits of 'Sex'*. London and New York: Routledge.

——. 2001. 'Giving an Account of Oneself'. *Diacritics* 31 (4): 22–40.

——. 2004. *Undoing Gender*. London and New York: Routledge.

——. 2005. *Giving an Account of Oneself*. New York: Fordham University Press.

Carter, Angela. 1982. *The Passion of New Eve*. London: Virago.

Catalano, Joseph S. 1980. *A Commentary on Jean-Paul Sartre's* Being and Nothingness. Chicago, IL: University of Chicago Press.

Cavarero, Adriana. 1990. *In Spite of Plato: A Feminist Rewriting of Ancient Philosophy*. Trans. (1995) Serena Anderlini-d'Onofrio and Áine O'Healy. Cambridge, UK: Polity Press.

——. 1992. 'Equality and Sexual Difference: Amnesia in Political Thought'. In Bock and James eds. 1992.

——. 1993. 'Towards a Theory of Sexual Difference'. In *The Lonely Mirror: Italian Perspectives on Feminist Theory*, ed. Sandra Kemp and Paola Bono. London: Routledge.

——. 1997. *Relating Narratives*. Trans. (2000) Paul A. Kottman. London and New York: Routledge.

Chanter, Tina. 2006. *Gender: Key Concepts in Philosophy*. London and New York: Continuum.

Chodorow, Nancy. 1978. *The Reproduction of Mothering: Psychoanalysis and the Sociology of Gender*. Berkeley, CA: University of California Press.

Cixous, Hélène. 1975. 'Sorties'. In *The Newly Born Woman*, Hélène Cixous and Catherine Clément. Trans. (1986) Betsy Wing. Manchester: Manchester University Press.

Clark, Wendy. 1987. 'The Dyke, the Feminist and the Devil'. In Feminist Review, ed. 1987.

Code, Lorraine. 2000. 'How to Think Globally: Stretching the Limits of Imagination'. In Narayan and Harding eds. 2000.

Collins, Margery L. and Christine Pierce. 1976. 'Holes and Slime: Sexism in Sartre's Psychoanalysis'. In *Women and Philosophy: Toward a Theory of Liberation*, ed. Carol C. Gould and Marx W. Wartofsky. New York: Putnam's Sons.

Combahee River Collective. 1979. 'A Black Feminist Statement'. In Nicholson ed. 1997.

Cornell, Drucilla. 1993. *Transformations: Recollective Imagination and Sexual Difference*. London and New York: Routledge.

Crenshaw, Kimberlé. 1989. 'Demarginalizing the Intersection of Race and Sex: A Black Feminist Critique of Antidiscrimination Doctrine, Feminist Theory and Antiracist Politics'. In Bartlett and Kennedy eds. 1991.

Daly, Mary. 1978. *Gyn/Ecology: The Metaethics of Radical Feminism*. London: The Women's Press.

Delmar, Rosalind. 1986. 'What Is Feminism?' In *What Is Feminism?*, ed. Juliet Mitchell and Ann Oakley. Oxford: Blackwell.

Delphy, Christine. 1984. *Close to Home: A Materialist Analysis of Women's Oppression*. Trans. Diana Leonard. London: Hutchinson.

——. 1993. 'Rethinking Sex and Gender'. *Women's Studies International Forum* 16 (1): 1–9.

Diamond, Irene and Lee Quinby, eds. 1988. *Feminism and Foucault: Reflections on Resistance*. Boston, MA: Northeastern University Press.

Dreger, Alice. 1998. *Hermaphrodites and the Medical Invention of Sex*. Cambridge, MA: Harvard University Press.

Dupré, John. 1993. *The Disorder of Things: Metaphysical Foundations of the Disunity of Science*. Cambridge, MA: Harvard University Press.

Eisenstein, Hester. 1980. Introduction to *The Future of Difference*, ed. Hester Eisenstein and Alice Jardine. Boston, MA: G. K. Hall & Co.

English, Amber Hollibaugh and Gayle Rubin. 1987. 'Talking Sex: A Conversation on Sexuality and Feminism'. In Feminist Review, ed. 1987.

Fausto-Sterling, Anne. 2000. *Sexing the Body: Gender Politics and the Construction of Sexuality*. New York: Basic Books.

Feinberg, Leslie. 1993. *Stone Butch Blues: A Novel*. Ithaca, NY: Firebrand Books.

Feminist Review, ed. 1987. *Sexuality: A Reader*. London: Virago.

Ferguson, Ann. 1984. 'Sex War: The Debate Between Radical and Libertarian Feminists'. *Signs* 19 (1): 106–112.

Firestone, Shulamith. 1970. *The Dialectic of Sex: The Case for Feminist Revolution*. New York: Morrow.

Flax, Jane. 1984. 'Political Philosophy and the Patriarchal Unconscious: A Psychoanalytic Perspective on Epistemology and Metaphysics'. In Harding and Hintikka eds. 1984.

Foucault, Michel. 1966. *The Order of Things: An Archaeology of the Human Sciences*. Trans. (1970) Alan Sheridan. London and New York: Routledge.

——. 1975. *Discipline and Punish: The Birth of the Prison*. Trans. (1977) Alan Sheridan. London: Allen Lane.

——. 1976a. *The History of Sexuality Volume I: An Introduction*. Trans. (1979) Robert Hurley. London: Allen Lane.

——. 1976b. 'Disciplinary Power and Subjection'. In *Power*, ed. Stephen Lukes. Oxford: Blackwell, 1986.

Fraser, Nancy. 1997. 'From Redistribution to Recognition? Dilemmas of Justice in a "Postsocialist" Age'. In *Justice Interruptus: Critical Reflections on the 'Postsocialist' Condition*. London and New York: Routledge.

Freud, Sigmund. 1905. 'Three Essays on the Theory of Sexuality'. In Freud 1977.

——. 1924. 'The Dissolution of the Oedipus Complex'. In Freud 1977.

——. 1925. 'Some Psychical Consequences of the Anatomical Distinction Between the Sexes'. In Freud 1977.

——. 1926. 'The Question of Lay Analysis'. In *Historical and Expository Works on Psychoanalysis*. Trans. James Strachey. Ed. Albert Dickson. Harmondsworth: Penguin, 1986.

——. 1931. 'Female Sexuality'. In Freud 1977.

——. 1933. 'Femininity'. In *New Introductory Lectures on Psychoanalysis*. Trans. (1973) James Strachey. Harmondsworth: Penguin.

——. 1977. *On Sexuality*. Trans. James Strachey. Ed. Angela Richards. Harmondsworth: Penguin.

Fricker, Miranda and Jennifer Hornsby, eds. 2000. *The Cambridge Companion to Feminism in Philosophy*. Cambridge, UK: Cambridge University Press.

Frye, Marilyn. 1983. *The Politics of Reality: Essays in Feminist Theory*. Freedom, CA: The Crossing Press.

——. 1990. 'Lesbian "Sex"'. In *Lesbian Philosophies and Cultures*, ed. Jeffner Allen. Albany, NY: SUNY Press.

——. 1996. 'The Necessity of Differences: Constructing a Positive Category of Women'. *Signs* 21 (4): 991–1010.

Garry, Ann and Marilyn Pearsall, eds. 1996. *Women, Knowledge and Reality*. Second edition. London and New York: Routledge.

Gatens, Moira. 1983. 'A Critique of the Sex/Gender Distinction'. In Gatens 1996b.

——. 1992. 'Power, Bodies and Difference'. In Gatens 1996b.

——. 1996a. 'Through a Spinozist Lens: Ethology, Difference, Power'. In *Deleuze: A Critical Reader*, ed. Paul Patton. Oxford: Blackwell.

——. 1996b. *Imaginary Bodies*. London and New York: Routledge.

—— and Genevieve Lloyd. 1998. *Collective Imaginings: Spinoza, Past and Present*. London and New York: Routledge.

Gilligan, Carol. 1982. *In a Different Voice: Psychological Theory and Women's Development*. Cambridge, MA: Harvard University Press.

Gordon, Linda and Ellen duBois. 1984. 'Seeking Ecstasy on the Battlefield: Danger and Pleasure in Nineteenth-Century Feminist Sexual Thought'. In Vance ed. 1984.

Griffin, Susan. 1984. *Woman and Nature: The Roaring Inside Her*. London: The Women's Press.

Grimshaw, Jean. 1986. *Feminist Philosophers: Women's Perspectives on Philosophical Traditions*. Hemel Hempstead: Harvester Wheatsheaf.

Grosz, Elizabeth. 1986. 'What Is Feminist Theory?' In *Feminist Challenges: Social and Political Theory*, ed. Carole Pateman and Elizabeth Grosz. London: Allen & Unwin.

——. 1989. *Sexual Subversions: Three French Feminists*. London: Allen & Unwin.

——. 1990a. *Jacques Lacan: A Feminist Introduction*. London and New York: Routledge.

——. 1990b. 'A Note on Essentialism and Difference.' In Gunew ed. 1990.

——. 1994. *Volatile Bodies: Toward a Corporeal Feminism*. Bloomington, IN: Indiana University Press.

Gunew, Sneja, ed. 1990. *Feminist Knowledge: Critique and Construct*. London and New York: Routledge.

——, ed. 1991. *A Reader in Feminist Knowledge*. London and New York: Routledge.

Halberstam, Judith. 1998. *Female Masculinity*. Durham, NC: Duke University Press.

Haraway, Donna. 1991. 'Situated Knowledges: The Science Question in Feminism and the Privilege of Partial Perspective'. In Donna Haraway, *Simians, Cyborgs and Women*. London: Free Association Books.

Harding, Sandra. 1986. *The Science Question in Feminism.* Ithaca, NY: Cornell University Press.

—— and Merrill B. Hintikka, eds. 1984. *Discovering Reality: Feminist Perspectives on Epistemology, Metaphysics, Methodology, and Philosophy of Science.* Dordrecht: David Reidel.

Harris, Angela. 1990. 'Race and Essentialism in Feminist Legal Theory'. In Bartlett and Kennedy eds. 1991.

Hartmann, Heidi. 1979. 'The Unhappy Marriage of Marxism and Feminism'. In Nicholson ed. 1997.

Hartsock, Nancy. 1983. *Money, Sex and Power: Toward a Feminist Historical Materialism.* Boston, MA: Northeastern University Press.

——. 1990. 'Foucault on Power: A Theory for Women?' In *Feminism/Postmodernism*, ed. Linda Nicholson. London and New York: Routledge.

Haslanger, Sally. 2000. 'Gender, Race: (What) Are They? (What) Do We Want Them To Be?' *Noûs* 34 (1): 31–55.

—— and Nancy Tuana. 2006. 'Topics in Feminism'. The Stanford Encyclopedia of Philosophy (Summer 2006 Edition), Edward N. Zalta (ed.), URL = <http://plato.stanford.edu/archives/sum2006/entries/feminism-topics/>. Accessed 27 April 2007.

Hegel, G. W. F. 1807. *Phenomenology of Spirit.* Trans. (1977) A. V. Miller. Oxford: Oxford University Press.

Heinämaa, Sara. 1997. 'What Is a Woman? Butler and Beauvoir on the Foundations of the Sexual Difference'. *Hypatia* 12 (1): 20–39.

——. 2003. *Toward a Phenomenology of Sexual Difference: Husserl, Merleau-Ponty, Beauvoir.* Lanham, MD: Rowman & Littlefield.

Held, Virginia. 1993. *Feminist Morality: Transforming Culture, Society, and Politics.* Chicago: University of Chicago Press.

Herman, Barbara. 1993. 'Could It Be Worth Thinking About Kant on Sex and Marriage?' In Antony and Witt eds. 1993.

Heyes, Cressida. 2000. *Line Drawings: Defining Women Through Feminist Practice.* Ithaca, NY: Cornell University Press.

Hill Collins, Patricia. 1990. *Black Feminist Thought: Knowledge, Consciousness, and the Politics of Empowerment.* Boston, MA: Unwin Hyman.

Hoagland, Sarah. 1988. *Lesbian Ethics: Toward New Value.* Palo Alto, CA: Institute of Lesbian Studies.

Hobbes, Thomas. 1647. *De Cive (On the Citizen).* Ed. and trans. (1998) Richard Tuck and Michael Silverthorne. Cambridge: Cambridge University Press.

Honig, Bonnie, ed. 1995. *Feminist Interpretations of Hannah Arendt.* University Park, PA: Penn State Press.

hooks, bell. 1984. *Feminist Theory: From Margin to Center*. Boston, MA: South End Press.

Hull, Carrie. 2005. *The Ontology of Sex: A Critical Inquiry into the Deconstruction and Reconstruction of Categories*. London: Routledge.

Irigaray, Luce. 1974. *Speculum of the Other Woman*. Trans. (1985) Gillian C. Gill. Ithaca. NY: Cornell University Press.

——. 1977a. *This Sex Which Is Not One*. Trans. (1985) Catherine Porter with Carolyn Burke. Ithaca, NY: Cornell University Press.

——. 1977b. 'Women's Exile'. Trans. Couze Venn. *Ideology and Consciousness* 1: 62–76.

——. 1979. 'And the One Doesn't Stir Without the Other'. Trans. (1981) Helene Vivienne Wenzel. *Signs* 7 (1): 60–67.

——. 1989. *Thinking the Difference: For a Peaceful Revolution*. Trans. (1994) Karin Montin. London: Athlone.

——. 1991. *The Irigaray Reader*. Ed. Margaret Whitford. Oxford: Blackwell.

——. 1995. 'The Question of the Other'. Trans. Noah Guynn. *Yale French Studies* 87: 7–19.

Jackman, Mary R. 1999. 'Gender, Violence, and Harassment'. In *Handbook of the Sociology of Gender*, ed. Janet Saltzman Chafetz. Dordrecht: Kluwer.

Jaggar, Alison. 1983a. *Feminist Politics and Human Nature*. Totowa, NJ: Rowman & Littlefield.

——. 1983b. 'Human Biology in Feminist Theory'. In *Knowing Women: Feminism and Knowledge*, ed. Helen Crowley and Susan Himmelweit. Cambridge, UK: Polity Press.

——. 1990. 'Sexual Difference and Sexual Equality'. In Rhode ed. 1990b.

——. 2000. 'Globalizing Feminist Ethics'. In Narayan and Harding eds. 2000.

—— and Iris Marion Young, ed. 1998. *A Companion to Feminist Philosophy*. Oxford: Blackwell.

Jantzen, Grace. 1998. *Becoming Divine: Towards a Feminist Philosophy of Religion*. Manchester: Manchester University Press.

——. 2005. *Foundations of Violence: Death and the Displacement of Beauty*. London and New York: Routledge.

Joyce, James. 1922. *Ulysses*. Reprint edition, 1960. London: Bodley Head.

Kanneh, Katiadu. 1998. 'Black Feminisms'. In *Contemporary Feminist Theories*, ed. Stevi Jackson and Jackie Jones. Edinburgh: Edinburgh University Press.

Kant, Immanuel. 1798. *Anthropology from a Pragmatic Point of View*. Trans. (1974) Mary J. Gregor. The Hague: Nijhoff.

——. 1997. *Lectures on Ethics*. Trans. Peter Heath. Cambridge: Cambridge University Press.

Kaplan, Gisela and Lesley Rogers. 1990. 'The Definition of Male and Female: Biological Reductionism and the Sanctions of Normality'. In Gunew ed. 1990.

Kessler, Suzanne. 1998. *Lessons from the Intersexed*. New Brunswick, NJ: Rutgers University Press.

Kishwar, Madhu. 1990. 'Why I do not Call Myself a Feminist'. *Manushi: A Journal about Women and Society* 61: 2–8.

Kristeva, Julia. 1974a. *Revolution in Poetic Language*. Trans. (1984) Margaret Waller. New York: Columbia University Press.

——. 1974b. 'Woman Can Never Be Defined'. Trans. (1981) Marilyn A. August. In *New French Feminisms: An Anthology*, ed. Elaine Marks and Isabelle de Courtivron. London: Harvester Wheatsheaf.

——. 1977. 'Stabat Mater'. In Kristeva 1986.

——. 1986. *The Kristeva Reader*. Ed. Toril Moi. Oxford: Blackwell.

Lacan, Jacques. 1966. *Écrits: A Selection*. Trans. (1977) Alan Sheridan. London: Tavistock.

——. 1982. *Feminine Sexuality: Jacques Lacan and the École Freudienne*. Ed. Juliet Mitchell and Jacqueline Rose. London: MacMillan.

Langton, Rae. 1993. 'Speech Acts and Unspeakable Acts'. *Philosophy & Public Affairs* 22 (4): 293–330.

Laqueur, Thomas. 1990. *Making Sex: Body and Gender from the Greeks to Freud*. Cambridge, MA: Harvard University Press.

Leeds Revolutionary Feminist Group. 1981. 'Political Lesbianism: The Case Against Heterosexuality'. In *The Woman Question: Readings on the Subordination of Women*, ed. Mary Evans. London: Fontana, 1982.

Lloyd, Genevieve. 1984. *The Man of Reason: 'Male' and 'Female' in Western Philosophy*. London and New York: Routledge.

——. 1993. 'Maleness, Masculinity and the "Crisis" of Reason'. In Antony and Witt eds. 1993.

——. 2000. 'Feminism in History of Philosophy: Appropriating the Past'. In Fricker and Hornsby eds. 2000.

Locke, John. 1698. *Two Treatises of Government*. Ed. Peter Laslett. Student edition, 1988. Cambridge: Cambridge University Press.

Longino, Helen. 1990. *Science as Social Knowledge: Values and Objectivity in Scientific Inquiry*. Princeton: Princeton University Press.

Lugones, Maria and Elizabeth Spelman. 1983. 'Have We Got a Theory for You! Feminist Theory, Cultural Imperialism, and the Demand for 'The Woman's Voice''. *Women's Studies International Forum* 6 (6): 573–81.

MacCannell, Juliet Flower. 1992. 'The Unconscious'. In *Feminism and Psychoanalysis: A Critical Dictionary*, ed. Elizabeth Wright. Oxford: Blackwell.

Mackenzie, Catriona. 1998. Review of *Feminists Rethink the Self* (ed. Meyers). *APA Newsletters* 97 (2). <http://www.apa.udel.edu/apa/archive/newsletters/v97n2/feminism/mackenzie.asp> Accessed 22 September 2006.

MacKinnon, Catherine. 1982. 'Feminism, Marxism, Method and the State: An Agenda for Theory'. *Signs* 7 (3): 515–44.

——. 1983. 'Feminism, Marxism, Method and the State: Toward Feminist Jurisprudence'. *Signs* 8 (4): 635–58.

——. 1987. *Feminism Unmodified: Discourses on Life and Law*. Cambridge, MA: Harvard University Press.

——. 1989. *Toward a Feminist Theory of the State*. Cambridge, MA: Harvard University Press.

Martin, Emily. 1987. *The Woman in the Body: A Cultural Analysis of Reproduction*. Milton Keynes: Open University Press.

Merleau-Ponty, Maurice. 1945. *Phenomenology of Perception*. Trans. (1962) Colin Smith. London and New York: Routledge.

Meyers, Diana, ed. 1997. *Feminist Social Thought: A Reader*. London and New York: Routledge.

Mikkola, Mari. 2005. *Classifying Women: A Solution to the Feminist Problem of Universals*. Unpublished PhD thesis. University of Sheffield (UK).

Millett, Kate. 1971. *Sexual Politics*. London: Virago.

Minow, Martha. 1990. *Making All the Difference: Inclusion, Exclusion and American Law*. Ithaca, NY: Cornell University Press.

Minsky, Rosalind, ed. 1996. *Psychoanalysis and Gender: An Introductory Reader*. London and New York: Routledge.

Mirza, Heidi Safia, ed. 1997. *Black British Feminism: A Reader*. London and New York: Routledge.

Mitchell, Juliet. 1974. *Psychoanalysis and Feminism*. Harmondsworth: Penguin.

Mohanty, Chandra Talpade. 1986. 'Under Western Eyes: Feminist Scholarship and Colonial Discourses'. In Mohanty 2003.

——. 2003. *Feminism Without Borders: Decolonizing Theory, Practicing Solidarity*. Durham. NC: Duke University Press.

Moi, Toril. 1985. *Sexual/Textual Politics: Feminist Literary Theory*. London and New York: Routledge.

——. 1999. *What is a Woman?* Oxford: Oxford University Press.

Morgan, Robin, ed. 1970. *Sisterhood is Powerful: An Anthology of Writings from the Women's Liberation Movement*. New York: Random House.

——. 1984. 'Planetary Feminism: The Politics of the 21st Century'. In *Sisterhood is Global: The International Women's Movement Anthology*, ed. Robin Morgan. New York: Doubleday.

Moulton, Janice. 1983. 'A Paradigm of Philosophy: The Adversary Method'. In Harding and Hintikka eds. 1984.

Mullin, Amy. 2005. *Reconceiving Pregnancy and Childcare*. Cambridge: Cambridge University Press.

Nagl-Docekal, Herta. 2004. *Feminist Philosophy*. Trans. Katharina Vester. Cambridge, MA: Westview Press.

Narayan, Uma. 1997. *Dislocating Cultures: Identities, Traditions, and Third World Feminism*. London and New York: Routledge.

——. 'Essence of Culture and a Sense of History: A Feminist Critique of Cultural Essentialism'. In Narayan and Harding eds. 2000.

—— and Sandra Harding, ed. 2000. *Decentering the Center: Philosophy for a Multicultural, Postcolonial, and Feminist World*. Bloomington, IN: Indiana University Press.

Nicholson, Linda, ed. 1997. *The Second Wave: A Reader in Feminist Theory*. London and New York: Routledge.

Nussbaum, Martha. 1995. 'Objectification'. *Philosophy & Public Affairs* 24 (4): 249–91.

Nye, Andrea. 2003. *Feminism and Modern Philosophy*. London and New York: Routledge.

Oakley, Ann. 1972. *Sex, Gender and Society*. London: Maurice Temple Smith.

Offen, Karen. 1992. 'Defining Feminism: A Comparative Historical Approach'. In Bock and James eds. 1992.

Okin, Susan Moller. 1994. 'Gender Inequality and Cultural Differences'. *Political Theory* 22 (1): 5–24.

——. 2000. 'Feminism, Women's Human Rights, and Cultural Differences'. In Narayan and Harding eds. 2000.

Pateman, Carole. 1983. 'Feminist Critiques of the Public/Private Dichotomy'. In *The Subjection of Women*. Cambridge, UK: Polity, 1989.

——. 1988. *The Sexual Contract*. Cambridge, UK: Polity Press.

Phillips, Anne. 1997. 'What has Socialism to do with Sexual Equality?' in *Equality*, ed. Jane Franklin. London: Institute for Public Policy Research.

Piercy, Marge. 1978. *Woman on the Edge of Time*. London: The Women's Press.

Plumwood, Val. 1989. 'Do We Need a Sex/Gender Distinction?' *Radical Philosophy* 51: 2–11.

Prosser, Jay. 1998. *Second Skins: The Body Narratives of Transsexuality*. New York: Columbia University Press.

Proudfoot, Michael, ed. 2003. *The Philosophy of Body*. Oxford: Blackwell.

Radicalesbians. 1970. 'The Woman-Identified Woman'. In Nicholson ed. 1997.

Ragland-Sullivan, Ellie. 1986. *Jacques Lacan and the Philosophy of Psychoanalysis*. Illinois: University of Illinois Press.

Rhode, Deborah L. 1990a. 'Theoretical Perspectives on Sexual Difference'. In Rhode ed. 1990b.

——, ed. 1990b. *Theoretical Perspectives on Sexual Difference*. New Haven, CT: Yale University Press.

Rich, Adrienne. 1976. *Of Woman Born: Motherhood as Experience and Institution*. London: Virago.

——. 1979. *On Lies, Secrets and Silence: Selected Prose, 1966–1978*. London: Virago.

——. 1980. 'Compulsory Heterosexuality and Lesbian Existence'. *Signs* 5 (4): 631–60.

Riley, Denise. 1989. *'Am I That Name?': Feminism and the Category of 'Women' in History*. Basingstoke: Macmillan.

Rose, Jacqueline. 1982. 'Introduction – II'. In Lacan 1982.

Rouse, Joseph. 1987. *Knowledge and Power: Toward a Political Philosophy of Science*. Ithaca, NY: Cornell University Press.

Rubin, Gayle. 1975. 'The Traffic in Women: Notes on the "Political Economy" of Sex'. In *Toward an Anthropology of Women*, ed. Rayna Reiter. New York: Monthly Review Press.

——. 1984. 'Thinking Sex: Notes for a Radical Theory of the Politics of Sexuality'. In Vance ed. 1984 .

Ruddick, Sara. 1980. 'Maternal Thinking'. In Meyers ed. 1997.

——. 1989. *Maternal Thinking: Towards a Politics of Peace*. London: The Women's Press.

Russ, Joanna. 1975. *The Female Man*. New York: Bantam.

Sartre, Jean-Paul. 1943. *Being and Nothingness: An Essay on Phenomenological Ontology*. Trans. (1958) Hazel E. Barnes. London: Methuen.

——. 1960. *Critique of Dialectical Reason. Volume I: Theory of Practical Ensembles*. Trans. (1976) Alan Sheridan-Smith. London: New Left Books.

Saul, Jennifer Mather. 2003. *Feminism: Issues & Arguments*. Oxford: Oxford University Press.

——. 2005. 'Feminist Philosophy of Language'. *The Stanford Encyclopedia of Philosophy* (Fall 2005 Edition), ed. Edward N. Zalta. URL = <http://plato.

stanford.edu/archives/fall2005/entries/feminism-language/>. Accessed 27 April 2007.

Saussure, Ferdinand de. 1916. *Course in General Linguistics*. Trans. (1974) Wade Baskin. Revised edition. London: Peter Owen.

Sawicki, Jana. 1991. *Disciplining Foucault: Feminism, Power, and the Body*. London and New York: Routledge.

Schiebinger, Londa. 1989. *The Mind Has No Sex?: Women in the Origins of Modern Science*. Cambridge, MA: Harvard University Press.

——, ed. 2000. *Feminism and the Body*. Oxford: Oxford University Press.

Schott, Robin May. 1998. 'Kant'. In Jaggar and Young eds. 1998.

Scott, Joan W. 1988. 'Deconstructing Equality-Versus-Difference'. In Meyers ed. 1997.

Segal, Lynne. 1988. *Is the Future Female? Troubled Thoughts on Contemporary Feminism*. London: Virago.

Smith, Barbara, ed. 1983. *Home Girls: A Black Feminist Anthology*. Kitchen Table: Women of Color Press.

Soble, Alan. 1998. 'Philosophy of Sexuality'. In *The Routledge Encyclopaedia of Philosophy*, ed. Edward Craig. London and New York: Routledge.

Spelman, Elizabeth. 1988. *Inessential Woman: Problems of Exclusion in Feminist Theory*. London: The Women's Press.

Steedman, Carolyn. 1986. *Landscape for a Good Woman*. London: Virago.

Spender, Dale. 1980. *Man Made Language*. London and New York: Routledge.

Spivak, Gayatri Chakravorty. 1984–85. 'Feminism, Criticism and the Institution'. *Thesis Eleven* 10/11: 175–87.

Stoljar, Natalie. 1995. 'Essence, Identity, and the Concept of Woman'. *Philosophical Topics* 23 (2): 261–293.

Stoller, Robert. 1968. *Sex and Gender: On the Development of Masculinity and Femininity*. London: Hogarth Press.

Stone, Sandy. 1991. 'The Empire Strikes Back: A Post-Transsexual Manifesto'. In *Body Guards: The Cultural Politics of Gender Ambiguity*, ed. Julia Epstein and Kristina Straub. London and New York: Routledge.

Sullivan, Shannon. 2001. *Living Across and Through Skins: Transactional Bodies, Pragmatism, and Feminism*. Bloomington, IN: Indiana University Press.

Tanesini, Alessandra. 1999. *An Introduction to Feminist Epistemologies*. Oxford: Blackwell.

Taylor, Charles. 1979. 'The Validity of Transcendental Arguments'. *Proceedings of the Aristotelian Society* 79: 151–165.

Taylor, Diane. 2006. 'The Pregnancy Police are Watching You'. *The Guardian* (London, UK). 4 September.

Taylor, Paul. 2004. *Race: A Philosophical Introduction*. Cambridge, UK: Polity Press.

Tong, Rosemarie. 1989. *Feminist Thought: A Comprehensive Introduction*. London and New York: Routledge.

——. 2003. 'Feminist Ethics'. *The Stanford Encyclopedia of Philosophy* (Winter 2003 Edition), ed. Edward N. Zalta. URL = <http://plato.stanford.edu/archives/win2003/entries/feminism-ethics/>. Accessed 27 April 2007.

Vance, Carole S., ed. 1984. *Pleasure and Danger: Exploring Female Sexuality*. London and New York: Routledge.

Warnke, Georgia. 2001. 'Intersexuality and the Categories of Sex'. *Hypatia* 16 (3): 126–37.

Weiss, Gail. 1999. *Body Images: Embodiment as Intercorporeality*. London and New York: Routledge.

Wikipedia. 2006a. Entry on 'Gender'. URL = <http://en.wikipedia.org/wiki/Gender>. Consulted 3 September 2006.

——. 2006b. Entry on 'Vorname'. URL = <http://de.wikipedia.org/wiki/Vorname>. Consulted 28 November 2006.

Witt, Charlotte. 1995. 'Anti-Essentialism in Feminist Theory'. *Philosophical Topics* 23 (2): 321–44.

Wittgenstein, Ludwig. 1969. *The Blue and Brown Books*. Second edition. Oxford: Blackwell.

Wittig, Monique. 1973. *The Lesbian Body*. Trans. (1976) David leVay. New York: Avon Books.

——. 1981. 'One is Not Born a Woman'. In Wittig 1992.

——. 1992. *The Straight Mind and Other Essays*. Boston, MA: Beacon Press.

Wollstonecraft, Mary. 1792. *A Vindication of the Rights of Woman*. Ed. (1992) Miriam Brody. Harmondsworth: Penguin.

Woolf, Virginia. 1927. *To the Lighthouse*. Reprint edition, 1977. London: Grafton.

Young, Iris Marion. 1980. 'Throwing Like a Girl: A Phenomenology of Feminine Body Comportment, Motility and Spatiality'. In Young 1990.

——. 1981. 'Beyond the Unhappy Marriage: A Critique of the Dual Systems Theory'. In *Women and Revolution: A Discussion of the Unhappy Marriage of Marxism and Feminism*, ed. Lydia Sargent. London: Pluto Press.

——. 1984. 'Pregnant Embodiment: Subjectivity and Alienation'. In Young 1990.

——. 1990. *Throwing Like a Girl and Other Essays in Feminist Philosophy and Social Theory*. Bloomington. IN: Indiana University Press.

——. 1994. 'Gender as Seriality: Thinking about Women as a Social Collective'. *Signs* 19 (3): 713–38.

Young, Iris Marion. 2002. 'Lived Body vs. Gender: Reflections on Social Structure and Subjectivity'. In Young 2005.

——. 2005. *On Female Body Experience: "Throwing Like a Girl" and Other Essays*. Oxford: Oxford University Press.

Zack, Naomi. 2005. *Inclusive Feminism: A Third Wave Theory of Women's Commonality*. Lanham, MD: Rowman & Littlefield.

Zita, Jacquelyn. 1998a. 'Male Lesbians and the Postmodernist Body'. In Jacquelyn Zita, *Body Talk: Philosophical Reflections on Sex and Gender*. New York: Columbia University Press.

——. 1998b. 'Sexuality'. In Jaggar and Young eds. 1998.

Index

Breinigsville, PA USA
01 February 2011
254522BV00005B/18/P

9 780745 638836